W9-AOT-600

Susan L. Scheiberg
Shelley Neville
Editors

Transforming Serials: The Revolution Continues

Transforming Serials: The Revolution Continues has been co-published simultaneously as *The Serials Librarian*, Volume 44, Numbers 1/2 and 3/4 2003.

Pre-publication
REVIEWS,
COMMENTARIES,
EVALUATIONS . . .

TRANSFORMING SERIALS: THE REVOLUTION CONTINUES

Proceedings of the NORTH AMERICAN SERIALS INTEREST GROUP, Inc.

**17th Annual Conference
June 20-23, 2002
The College of William and Mary
Williamsburg, Virginia**

Transforming Serials: The Revolution Continues has been co-published simultaneously as *The Serials Librarian*, Volume 44, Numbers 1/2 and 3/4 2003.

The Serials Librarian Monographic "Separates"

Below is a list of "separates," which in serials librarianship means a special issue simultaneously published as a special journal issue or double-issue *and* as a "separate" hardbound monograph. (This is a format which we also call a "DocuSerial.")

"Separates" are published because specialized libraries or professionals may wish to purchase a specific thematic issue by itself in a format which can be separately cataloged and shelved, as opposed to purchasing the journal on an on-going basis. Faculty members may also more easily consider a "separate" for classroom adoption.

"Separates" are carefully classified separately with the major book jobbers so that the journal tie-in can be noted on new book order slips to avoid duplicate purchasing.

You may wish to visit Haworth's website at . . .

http://www.HaworthPress.com

. . . to search our online catalog for complete tables of contents of these separates and related publications.

You may also call 1-800-HAWORTH (outside US/Canada: 607-722-5857), or Fax 1-800-895-0582 (outside US/Canada: 607-771-0012), or e-mail at:

docdelivery@haworthpress.com

E-Serials Cataloging: Access to Continuing and Integrating Resources via the Catalog and the Web, edited by Jim Cole, MA, and Wayne Jones, MA, MLS (Vol. 41, No. 3/4, 2002). *"A VERY TIMELY AND USEFUL REFERENCE TOOL FOR LIBRARIANS. THE BEST . . . on various aspects of e-serials: from standards to education and training, from policies and procedures to national and local projects and future trends. As a technical services librarian, I found the sections on policies and procedures and national projects and local applications very valuable and informative." (Vinh-The Lam, MLS, Head, Cataloging Department, University of Saskatchewan Library, Canada)*

Women's Studies Serials: A Quarter-Century of Development, edited by Kristin H. Gerhard, MLS (Vol. 35, No. 1/2, 1998). *"Candidly explores and analyzes issues which must be addressed to ensure the continued growth and vitality of women's studies. . . . It commands the attention of librarians, scholars, and publishers." (Joan Ariel, MLS, MA, Women's Studies Librarian and Lecturer, University of California at Irvine)*

E-Serials: Publishers, Libraries, Users, and Standards, edited by Wayne Jones, MA, MLS (Vol. 33, No. 1/2/3/4, 1998). *"Libraries and publishers will find this book helpful in developing strategies, policies, and procedures." (Nancy Brodie, National Library of Canada, Ottawa, Ontario)*

Serials Cataloging at the Turn of the Century, edited by Jeanne M. K. Boydston, MSLIS, James W. Williams, MSLS, and Jim Cole, MLS (Vol. 32, No. 1/2, 1997). *Focuses on the currently evolving trends in serials cataloging in order to predict and explore the possibilities for the field in the new millennium.*

Serials Management in the Electronic Era: Papers in Honor of Peter Gellatly, Founding Editor of The Serials Librarian, edited by Jim Cole, MA, and James W. Williams, MLS (Vol. 29, No. 3/4, 1996). *Assesses progress and technical changes in the field of serials management and anticipates future directions and challenges for librarians.*

Special Format Serials and Issues: Annual Review of . . . , Advances in . . . , Symposia on . . . , Methods in . . . , by Tony Stankus, MLS (Vol. 27, No. 2/3, 1996). *A thorough and lively introduction to the nature of these publications' types.*

Serials Canada: Aspects of Serials Work in Canadian Libraries, edited by Wayne Jones, MLS (Vol. 26, No. 3/4, 1996). *"An excellent addition to the library literature and is recommended for all library school libraries, scholars, and students of comparative/international librarianship." (Library Times International)*

Serials Cataloging: Modern Perspectives and International Developments, edited by Jim E. Cole, MA, and James W. Williams, MSLS (Vol. 22, No. 1/2/3/4, 1993). *"A significant contribution to understanding the 'big picture' of serials control. . . . A solid presentation of serious issues in a crucial area on librarianship." (Bimonthly Review of Law Books)*

Making Sense of Journals in the Life Sciences: From Specialty Origins to Contemporary Assortment, by Tony Stankus (Supp. #08, 1992, 1996). *"An excellent introduction to scientific periodical literature and the disciplines it serves." (College & Research Libraries News)*

Making Sense of Journals in the Physical Sciences: From Specialty Origins to Contemporary Assortment, by Tony Stankus, MLS (Supp. #07, 1992, 1996). *"A TOUR DE FORCE . . . It will immeasurably help science serials librarians to select journal titles on a rational and defensible basis, and the methodology used can be extended over time and to other fields and other journals." (International Journal of Information and Library Research)*

The Good Serials Department, edited by Peter Gellatly (Vol. 19, No. 1/2, 1991). *"This is recommended for library educators, students, and serials specialists. It should be useful both to novices and veterans." (Journal of Academic Librarianship)*

Scientific Journals: Improving Library Collections Through Analysis of Publishing Trends, by Tony Stankus, MLS (Supp. #6, 1990). *"Will be of great value to science librarians in academic, industrial, and governmental libraries as well as to scientists and professors facing problems in choosing the most economical and useful journals for library collections." (American Scientist)*

Implementing Online Union Lists of Serials: The Pennsylvania Union List of Serials Experience, edited by Ruth C. Carter, MA, MS, PhD, and James D. Hooks, PhD, MLS (Supp. #05, 1989). *"This practical and very readable book provides not only a useful guide to the development and use of online union lists, but also a fine example of library co-operation and hard work." (Library Association Record)*

Newspapers in the Library: New Approaches to Management and Reference Work, edited by Lois Upham, PhD, MSLS (Supp. #04, 1988). *"Lively, varied and written with good sense and enthusiasm. Recommended for those working in or administering newspaper collections for the first time, and also those who, immersed in the problems of this seemingly intractable material, need the inspiration of solutions devised by others." (Riverina Library Review)*

Scientific Journals: Issues in Library Selection and Management, by Tony Stankus, MLS (Supp. #3, 1988). *"This book has significance for those for those who select scientific journals for library collections and for the primary users and producers of the literature as well. More works of this type are needed." (American Reference Books Annual)*

Libraries and Subscription Agencies: Interactions and Innovations, edited by Peter Gellatly (Vol. 14, No. 3/4, 1988). *"Put[s] developments in context and provide[s] useful background information and advice for those contemplating implementation of automation in this area." (Library Association Record)*

Serials Cataloging: The State of the Art, edited by Jim E. Cole, MA, and Jackie Zajanc (Vol. 12, No. 1/2, 1987). *"Really does cover an amazingly broad span of serials cataloging topics . . . Well worth its purchase price." (Lois N. Upham, PhD, Assistant Professor, College of Library and Information Science, University of South Carolina)*

Serial Connections: People, Information, and Communication, edited by Leigh Chatterton, MLS, and Mary Elizabeth Clack, MS (Vol. 11, No. 3/4, 1987). *"The essays are uniformly lively and provide excellent overviews of the aspects of serials control, from acquisition to automation." (Academic Library Book Review)*

Serials Librarianship in Transition: Issues and Development, edited by Peter Gellatly (Vol. 10, No. 1/2, 1986). *"Well-written and tightly edited . . . Specialists in the 'serials chain' and students interested in serials librarianship should give this book top priority in their professional reading lists." (Library and Information Science Annual)*

The Management of Serials Automation: Current Technology and Strategies for Future Planning, edited by Peter Gellatly (Supp. #2, 1984). *"A thoroughly documented review of the progress and problems in serials automation strategy and technology." (Information Retrieval & Library Automation)*

Union Catalogues of Serials: Guidelines for Creation and Maintenance, with Recommended Standards for Bibliographic and Holdings Control, by Jean Whiffin, BA, BLS (Vol. 8, No. 1, 1983). *"A clearly written and easily read set of guidelines . . . Recommended for library science collections. Essential where union catalogs are contemplated." (Public Libraries)*

Serials Librarianship as an Art: Essays in Honor of Andrew D. Osborn, edited by Peter Gellatly (Vol. 6, No. 2/3, 1982). *An exploration of the advantages and excellences of the manual check-in operation versus automation.*

Sex Magazines in the Library Collection: A Scholarly Study of Sex in Serials and Periodicals, edited by Peter Gellatly (Supp. #01, 1981). *"Recommended for librarians with collections that include sex periodicals, as well as for those librarians who haven't quite made up their minds and are looking for more background information." (Technicalities)*

The North American Serials Interest Group (NASIG) Series

Transforming Serials: The Revolution Continues, edited by Susan L. Scheiberg and Shelley Neville (Vol. 44, No. 1/2/3/4, 2003). *"A valuable and thought-provoking resource for all library workers involved with serials." (Mary Curran, MLS, MA, Head of Cataloguing Services, University of Ottawa, Ontario, Canada)*

NASIG 2001: A Serials Odyssey, edited by Susan L. Scheiberg and Shelley Neville (Vol. 42, No. 1/2/3/4, 2002). *From XML to ONIX and UCITA, here's cutting-edge information from leading serials librarians from the 16th NASIG conference.*

Making Waves: New Serials Landscapes in a Sea of Change, edited by Joseph C. Harmon and P. Michelle Fiander (Vol. 40, No. 1/2/3/4, 2001). *These proceedings include discussions of the Digital Millennium Copyright Act, and reports on specific test projects such as BioOne, the Open Archives Project, and PubMed Central.*

From Carnegie to Internet 2: Forging the Serials Future, edited by P. Michelle Fiander, Joseph C. Harmon, and Jonathan David Makepeace (Vol. 38, No. 1/2/3/4, 2000). *Current information and practical insight to help you improve your technical skills and prepare you and your library for the 21st century.*

Head in the Clouds, Feet on the Ground: Serials Vision and Common Sense, edited by Jeffrey S. Bullington, Beatrice L. Caraway, and Beverley Geer (Vol. 36, No. 1/2/3/4, 1999). *"Practical, common sense advice, and visionary solutions to serials issues afoot in every library department and in every type of library today. . . . An essential reference guide for libraries embracing electronic resource access." (Mary Curran, MA, MLS, Coordinator, Bibliographic Standards, Morisset Library, University of Ottawa, Ontario, Canada)*

Experimentation and Collaboration: Creating Serials for a New Millennium, Charlene N. Simser and Michael A. Somers (Vol. 34, No. 1/2/3/4, 1998). *Gives valuable ideas and practical advice that you can apply or incorporate into your own area of expertise.*

Pioneering New Serials Frontiers: From Petroglyphs to Cyberserials, edited by Christine Christiansen and Cecilia Leathem (Vol. 30, No. 3/4, and Vol. 31, No. 1/2, 1997). *Gives you insight, ideas, and practical skills for dealing with the changing world of serials management.*

Serials to the Tenth Power: Traditions, Technology, and Transformation, edited by Mary Ann Sheble, MLS, and Beth Holley, MLS (Vol. 28, No. 1/2/3/4, 1996). *Provides readers with practical ideas on managing the challenges of the electronic information environment.*

A Kaleidoscope of Choices: Reshaping Roles and Opportunities for Serialists, edited by Beth Holley, MLS, and Mary Ann Sheble, MLS (Vol. 25, No. 3/4, 1995). *"Highly recommended as an excellent source material for all librarians interested in learning more about the Internet, technology and its effect on library organization and operations, and the virtual library." (Library Acquisitions: Practice & Theory)*

New Scholarship: New Serials: Proceedings of the North American Serials Interest Group, Inc., edited by Gail McMillan and Marilyn Norstedt (Vol. 24, No. 3/4, 1994). *"An excellent representation of the ever-changing, complicated, and exciting world of serials." (Library Acquisitions Practice & Theory)*

If We Build It: Scholarly Communications and Networking Technologies: Proceedings of the North American Serials Interest Group, Inc., edited by Suzanne McMahon, MLS, Miriam Palm, MLS, and Pamela Dunn, BA (Vol. 23, No. 3/4, 1993). *"Highly recommended to anyone interested in the academic serials environment as a means of keeping track of the electronic revolution and the new possibilities emerging." (ASL (Australian Special Libraries))*

A Changing World: Proceedings of the North American Serials Interest Group, Inc., edited by Suzanne McMahon, MLS, Miriam Palm, MLS, and Pamela Dunn, BA (Vol. 21, No. 2/3, 1992). *"A worthy publication for anyone interested in the current and future trends of serials control and electronic publishing." (Library Resources & Technical Services)*

The Future of Serials: Proceedings of the North American Serials Interest Group, Inc., edited by Patricia Ohl Rice, PHD, MLS and Jane A. Robillard, MLS (Vol. 19, No. 3/4, 1991). *"A worthwhile addition to any library studies collection, or a serials librarian's working library . . . I would recommend separate purchase of the monograph. NASIG plays too important a role in the serials universe to ignore any of its published proceedings." (Library Acquisitions: Practice & Theory)*

The Serials Partnership: Teamwork, Technology, and Trends, edited by Patricia Ohl Rice, PhD, MLS, and Joyce L. Ogburn, MSLS, MA (Vol. 17, No. 3/4, 1990). *In this forum, scholars, publishers, vendors, and librarians share in discussing issues of common concern.*

Serials Information from Publisher to User: Practice, Programs, and Progress, edited by Leigh A. Chatterton, MLS, and Mary Elizabeth Clack, MLS (Vol. 15, No. 3/4, 1988). *"[E]xcellent reference tools for years to come." (Gail McMillan, MLS, MA, Serials Team Leader, University Libraries, Virginia Polytechnic Institute and State University)*

The Serials Information Chain: Discussion, Debate, and Dialog, edited by Leigh Chatterton, MLS, and Mary Elizabeth Clack, MLS (Vol. 13, No. 2/3, 1988). *"It contains enlightening information for libraries or businesses in which serials are a major concern." (Library Resources & Technical Services)*

Transforming Serials: The Revolution Continues has been co-published simultaneously as *The Serials Librarian*, Volume 44, Numbers 1/2 and 3/4 2003.

The development, preparation, and publication of this work has been undertaken with great care. However, the publisher, employees, editors, and agents of The Haworth Press and all imprints of The Haworth Press, Inc., including The Haworth Medical Press® and Pharmaceutical Products Press®, are not responsible for any errors contained herein or for consequences that may ensue from use of materials or information contained in this work. Opinions expressed by the author(s) are not necessarily those of The Haworth Press, Inc.

Cover design by Thomas J. Mayshock Jr.

Library of Congress Cataloging-in-Publication Data

North American Serials Interest Group. Conference (17th : 2002 : College of William and Mary)
　　　Transforming serials : the revolution continues : proceedings of the North American Serials Interest Group, Inc. 17th Annual Conference, June 20-23, 2002, the College of William and Mary, Williamsburg, Virginia / Susan L. Scheiberg, Shelley Neville, editors.
　　　　　p. cm.
　　　"Co-published simultaneously as The serials librarian, v. 44, nos. 1/2 and 3/4 2003."
　　　Includes bibliographical references and index.
　　　　　ISBN 0-7890-2281-8 (alk. paper) – ISBN 0-7890-2282-6 (pbk : alk. paper)
　　　1. Serials librarianship–Congresses. 2. Libraries–Special collections–Electronic journals–Congresses. 3. Electronic journals–Congresses. I. Scheiberg, Susan L. II. Neville, Shelley. III. Serials librarian. IV. Title.
　　　　　Z692.S5N67 2002
　　　　　025.17′32–dc21
　　　　　　　　　　　　　　　　　　　　　　　　　　　　　　　　　　　2003005542

TRANSFORMING SERIALS:
THE REVOLUTION CONTINUES

Proceedings of the
NORTH AMERICAN SERIALS
INTEREST GROUP, Inc.

17th Annual Conference
June 20-23, 2002
The College of William and Mary
Williamsburg, Virginia

Susan L. Scheiberg
Shelley Neville
Editors

The Haworth Information Press
An Imprint of
The Haworth Press, Inc.
New York • London • Oxford

Indexing, Abstracting & Website/Internet Coverage

This section provides you with a list of major indexing & abstracting services. That is to say, each service began covering this periodical during the year noted in the right column. Most Websites which are listed below have indicated that they will either post, disseminate, compile, archive, cite or alert their own Website users with research-based content from this work. (This list is as current as the copyright date of this publication.)

Abstracting, Website/Indexing Coverage . . . . Year When Coverage Began

- *Academic Abstracts/CD-ROM* **1993**

- *Academic Search: Database of 2,000 selected academic serials, updated monthly: EBSCO Publishing* **1993**

- *Academic Search Elite (EBSCO)* **1993**

- *caredata CD: the social & community care database <www.scie.org.uk>* **2003**

- *Chemical Abstracts Services <www.cas.org>* **1982**

- *CINAHL (Cumulative Index to Nursing & Allied Health Literature), in print, EBSCO, and SilverPlatter, Data-Star, and PaperChase. (Support materials include Subject Heading List, Database Search Guide, and instructional video.) <www.cinahl.com>* **1991**

- *CNPIEC Reference Guide: Chinese National Directory of Foreign Periodicals* **1995**

(continued)

(continued)

Special Bibliographic Notes related to special journal issues (separates) and indexing/abstracting:

- indexing/abstracting services in this list will also cover material in any "separate" that is co-published simultaneously with Haworth's special thematic journal issue or DocuSerial. Indexing/abstracting usually covers material at the article/chapter level.
- monographic co-editions are intended for either non-subscribers or libraries which intend to purchase a second copy for their circulating collections.
- monographic co-editions are reported to all jobbers/wholesalers/approval plans. The source journal is listed as the "series" to assist the prevention of duplicate purchasing in the same manner utilized for books-in-series.
- to facilitate user/access services all indexing/abstracting services are encouraged to utilize the co-indexing entry note indicated at the bottom of the first page of each article/chapter/contribution.
- this is intended to assist a library user of any reference tool (whether print, electronic, online, or CD-ROM) to locate the monographic version if the library has purchased this version but not a subscription to the source journal.
- individual articles/chapters in any Haworth publication are also available through the Haworth Document Delivery Service (HDDS).

NASIG Officers and Executive Board

2001/2002

Officers:

Margaret Rioux, President, Woods Hole Oceanographic Institution
Eleanor Cook, Vice-President/President Elect, Appalachian State University
Margaret Mering, Secretary, University of Nebraska-Lincoln
Denise Novak, Treasurer, Carnegie Mellon University
Connie Foster, President, Western Kentucky University

Executive Board:

Donnice Cochenour, Colorado State University
Christa Easton, Stanford University
Marilyn Geller, Information Management Consultant
Ann McKee, Big 12 Plus Libraries Consortium
Mary Page, Rutgers University
Kevin Randall, Northwestern University

2002 Program Planning Committee

Co-Chairs:

Stephen Clark, College of William and Mary
Joyce Tenney, University of Maryland, Baltimore County

Committee Members:

Ladd Brown, Virginia Polytechnic Institute
Lauren Corbett, Emory University
Rachel Frick, Virginia Commonwealth University
Sharon Gasser, James Madison University
Diane Hollyfield, Virginia Commonwealth University
JoAnn Keys, George Mason University
Merle Kimball, College of William and Mary
Steve Murden, Freelance Librarian and Consultant
Allison Sleeman, University of Virginia
Beth Weston, National Library of Medicine

Fritz Schwartz Serials Education Scholarship

Angela Riggio, University of California, Los Angeles

NASIG Conference Student Grant Award Recipients

Denise M. Branch, Catholic University of America

Meg Manahan, Queen's College, City University of New York

Vanessa Mitchell, Catholic University of America

Yolande R. Shelton, University of Maryland

John W. Wiggins, Drexel University

Horizon Award Winner

Pauline La Rooy, Victoria University of Wellington

Mexico Student Conference Grant

Paula de la Mora Lugo, Universidad Nacional Autonoma de Mexico

ABOUT THE EDITORS

Susan L. Scheiberg, MSLIS, MA, is Assistant Director of the RAND Library in Santa Monica, California. Previously she was Team Leader for Serials Acquisitions at the University of Southern California. Her publications include "Acquiring Minds: Acquisitions in Two Contexts" (*Library Collections, Acquisitions, and Technical Services*), "Emotions on Display: Personal Decoration of Work Space" (*American Behavioral Scientist*), and "A Folklorist in the Family: On the Process of Fieldwork Among Intimates" (*Western Folklore*). She was a contributor to the 1999 NASIG proceedings and was co-editor of *NASIG 2001: A Serials Odyssey* (The Haworth Press, Inc.), which documented the 2001 Proceedings.

Shelley Neville, MSLIS, is Library Systems Analyst in Product Engineering at epixtech, inc., where she has worked since 1988, starting as an intern while attending library school. She is also Education Chair for BASIC (Books and Serials Industry Communications). She has been active in NASIG for several years, serving as the SISAC (Serials Industry Standards Advisory Committee) representative from 1998-2000. She was co-editor of *NASIG 2001: A Serials Odyssey* (The Haworth Press, Inc.), which documented the 2001 Proceedings.

Transforming Serials:
The Revolution Continues

CONTENTS

CONCURRENT SESSIONS

Introduction

The participants in the 17th Annual Conference of the North American Serials Interest Group (NASIG) on the campus of The College of William and Mary in Williamsburg, Virginia proved once again that NASIG members are leading the revolution in serials management. With the cry of "onward and upward," participants went to battle to provide insights, new techniques and tools, and solutions to problems that vex serialists everywhere.

Two pre-conference workshops began the onslaught of information, both of which addressed the changing landscape in serials. The first presented the new standards for holdings statements and provided a detailed, in-depth look at this "usable revolution." The second covered electronic journals from a front-line librarian's point of view; she shared her experiences on the field of e-journal management. The three plenary sessions were future oriented, focusing on information access in all formats. Howard Strauss provided insights into the often-misunderstood concept of information portals, while Emily Mobley attempted to corral the crisis of sci-tech journals. Finally, David Seaman discussed the worldwide demand for digitized resources.

The eight concurrent sessions ranged far and wide, from the good, bad, and ugly to the future of multimedia cataloging and journal linking; from current to future scholarly publishing models; and from the risks of canceling our old warhorses, print journals, in favor of the ubiquitous access that e-journals may provide. There was much to consider.

A total of twenty-six workshops provided a huge and diverse theater of operations, although consistent themes emerged. We learned management

[Haworth co-indexing entry note]: "Introduction." Scheiberg, Susan L., and Shelley Neville. Co-published simultaneously in *The Serials Librarian* (The Haworth Information Press, an imprint of The Haworth Press, Inc.) Vol. 44, No. 1/2, 2003, pp. 1-2; and: *Transforming Serials: The Revolution Continues* (ed: Susan L. Scheiberg, and Shelley Neville) The Haworth Information Press, an imprint of The Haworth Press, Inc., 2003, pp. 1-2. Single or multiple copies of this article are available for a fee from The Haworth Document Delivery Service [1-800-HAWORTH, 9:00 a.m. - 5:00 p.m. (EST). E-mail address: docdelivery@haworthpress.com].

http://www.haworthpress.com/store/product.asp?sku=J123
10.1300/J123v44n12_01

techniques to guide staff through a "minefield of change," and the "art" of supervising student assistants. We learned how to recover when disaster strikes our library, and how to "push the (strategic) envelope" "out of the box."

Serials cataloging is facing a major revolution with the revisions to AACR2. Refusing to surrender to the sometimes-confusing changes, several workshops addressed these amendments for a variety of formats. Serials acquisitions did not emerge unscathed either, as new cooperative efforts and technologies such as the CONSER initiatives on cooperative prediction pattern databases were discussed at length. Perhaps the most revolutionary speaker of all was Rick Anderson, who suggested that serials check-in be discontinued–a surgical strike, indeed!

Perhaps suffering from battle fatigue, Kathleen Bauer and Kimberly Parker asked, "Is it all worth it?" It seems that the answer is a resounding yes–the challenges, opportunities, quirks, and puzzles that serials present to those of us who work with them on a daily basis seem to provide an unending source of inspiration. How lucky are we that we have this conference to share all that we learn!

Once again, we are in awe of our colleagues who volunteer to come together every year to put on a conference of this caliber. We wish to thank all the presenters and recorders–their hard work and unflagging spirit has made our jobs that much easier. We wish to thank Mary Page, our NASIG Board liaison, who not only was the essence of efficiency, but who laughed with us when we needed it, and who endured our whining and complaining with the utmost good will. The Program Planning Committee and the Conference Committee have also been invaluable in their willingness to supply lists (and lists and lists) so that we could put this volume together. A most heartfelt thanks is due to Nancy Deisroth of Haworth Press–her patience in seeing this project through despite all the unforeseen problems has been a comfort; her faith in the completion a wonder. We also wish to thank Melissa Devendorf and Zella Ondrey for seeing us through the very early process. We'd like to thank our colleagues at epixtech, inc. and RAND for their support (and chocolate!), and to our colleagues in NASIG. Vive la revolution!

Susan L. Scheiberg
Shelley Neville
Editors

PRECONFERENCE PROGRAMS

Implementing MARC 21 for Holdings

Diane Hillmann
Ruth Hass
Rachel Hollis
Stephanie Schmitt

Presenters

Pat Loghry

Recorder

SUMMARY. Implementing MARC 21 for holdings was a comprehensive line-by-line, field-by-field explanation of the coding and tagging for MARC 21. Participants were given a history of the standards. The pairing relationship of the 853/4/5 and 863/4/5 was explained and the session concluded with hands-on exercises. *[Article copies available for a fee from The Haworth Document Delivery Service: 1-800-HAWORTH. E-mail address: <docdelivery@haworthpress.com> Website: <http://www.HaworthPress.com>]*

Hillmann began the program by saying that we are again moving into a shared environment for holdings records, similar to the shared environment created with bibliographic data. A shared environment creates a more global view of the holdings process and changes the way we

[Haworth co-indexing entry note]: "Implementing MARC 21 for Holdings." Loghry, Pat. Co-published simultaneously in *The Serials Librarian* (The Haworth Information Press, an imprint of The Haworth Press, Inc.) Vol. 44, No. 1/2, 2003, pp. 5-9; and: *Transforming Serials: The Revolution Continues* (ed: Susan L. Scheiberg, and Shelley Neville) The Haworth Information Press, an imprint of The Haworth Press, Inc., 2003, pp. 5-9. Single or multiple copies of this article are available for a fee from The Haworth Document Delivery Service [1-800-HAWORTH, 9:00 a.m. - 5:00 p.m. (EST). E-mail address: docdelivery@haworthpress.com].

look at local practices regarding check-in, reporting serials, and creating holdings records.

Why should we implement MARC 21? A standard format allows sharing between individual institutions via bibliographic utilities. Shareable data promote higher quality records and create a larger investment in content. MARC 21 holdings support both predictive and non-predictive check-in for both serials and non-serials. MARC 21 allows applications to support more standard manipulation of data and easier maintenance routines. Use of the standard allows data to be migrated with little or no loss. MARC holdings can be used for regular or irregular serials and monographic series. It can be used for sets as well as supplements, indexes, and accompanying materials of all kinds, whether or not they are in the same format.

Some of the previous standards included Z39.42 (summary holdings for serials), Z39.44 (serials holdings) and Z39.57 (non-serial holdings). The current standard is Z39.71, which is, essentially, the harmonization of the previous standards. Standard Z39.71 includes serials and non-serials, and defines how to *record* holdings as opposed to how to *communicate* holdings. Holdings can be recorded at various levels (for example, summary vs. detailed, open vs. closed) and provides the standards for recording captions.

Standard Z39.71 specifies four levels with mandatory or optional data elements. Level 1 identifies the item and holdings institution; level 2 provides for additional general information and data; level 3 is a summary statement only; and level four is the detailed holdings statement, which may be either itemized or compressed, open or closed. Levels may be mixed–mostly in the case of retrospective holdings where there may be missing information. For example, level three may be used for retrospective and level four detailed for projective holdings. However, Z39.71 does not have anything to do with prediction. There have been efforts to keep Z39.71 synchronous with MARC 21, although MARC changes are updated every six months and standards updated every five years. What is the relationship of Z39.71 to MARC? Standard Z39.71 is what the data should include and what the display of data should look like. MARC enables machine transmission and manipulation and provides labels for the data.

Textual holdings conventions can be formatted in one of two ways: "enumeration-enumeration (chronology-chronology)" or "enumeration (chronology) enumeration (chronology)." This allows for compression across publication pattern changes. Both textual holding conventions have summary holdings statements and occasionally have separate statements for incomplete holdings.

Bibliographic MARC requires leader and variable control fields in the 008 and 007, and link and sequence numbers. Notes are provided for in the 5XX for the entire holdings record and in the 8XX for the parts/groups. The physical location is noted in the 852 and remote access information is notes in the 856, which is at the version, not the title, level.

Leader 17 encoding levels are: 17(1) item, library; 17(2) item, library, report date, optional polices; 17(3) item, library, policies, summary holdings; 17(4) item, library policies, detailed holdings; 17(5) item, library policies, detailed holdings, piece designations.

There is support for interlibrary loan and other functions in the 008: 008(06) is receipt or acquisitions status; 008(07) is the method of acquisition; 008(08-11) is the intent to cancel date; 008(12-15) specifies general and specific retention policies like "retain latest only"; 008(16) completeness; and 008(20-21) specifies the lending and reproduction policies.

MARC 21 tags indicate whether the item in question is a basic bibliographic unit, a supplement, or an index. All the pieces are put together with the link and sequence numbers (see Figure 1).

Captions indicate to what the patterns apply. In the 853-855 sub-fields, a-f allow for six different caption levels for enumeration; g-h provide two caption levels for alternative enumeration; i-m allow for five regular caption levels and one alternative caption level; o-t are sub-fields for type and copies; and in u-z are the publication pattern specifics.

Sub-fields that relate to prediction are as follows: u is the bibliographic unit per next highest level; v is the numbering continuity; w is the frequency; x indicates when the calendar restarts for the volume; y is the regularity pattern; and z is the numbering scheme.

FIGURE 1. Tag structure of MFHD 8XX

	BASIC	SUPPLS.	INDEX
Captions/Patterns	853	854	855
Paired Holdings associated with Caption/Pattern	863	864	865
Textual Holdings	866	867	868
Item Information	876	877	878

Enumeration and chronology data fields that go along with the caption and patterns information are in the 863-865 sub-fields: a-f are the six levels of enumeration; g-h are two levels of alternative enumeration; i-m are five regular levels and one alternative level of chronology; and p-z have the piece and copy information as well as the notes.

Important definitions to understand are as follows: in the 853-855 fields, itemized holdings list items one at a time (e.g., v. 1,, v. 2, v. 3 . . .) versus compressed holdings, which collapse the items (e.g., v. 1-3). In the 863-865 fields, itemized information is in the form of a list, as demonstrated above. Summarized holdings (e.g., volume/year) comprise the first and highest level of enumeration-chronology, as opposed to detailed holdings (e.g., vol, no. pt. and yr, month, day) which define the most specific level of information apart from the bibliographic unit. Composite holdings provide information about two or more copies in their entirety rather than presenting part of holdings in one statement and the rest in another. Copy-specific holdings are detailed so that one can ascertain which volumes are located in what building. Much complexity is supported as one can have multiple holdings records for one bibliographic entity, multiple records for multiple versions and multiple locations reported in one institution.

Ruth Haas began her part of the presentation by outlining the uses of holdings records. Benefits of holdings records are that they supply such information as copy specific holdings, location information, information specific to the holding organization, information needed for local processing, maintenance, or preservation of an item, and version information.

She also discussed the record structure, which repeated some of the information in the first presentation. Continuing on from that information, she detailed the variable data fields as follows: the 010-845 includes control numbers, codes, notes and holdings data; location and access are noted in 852-856; captions and patterns in the 853-855, enumeration and chronology in the 863-865; textual holdings in the 866-868; and the item information in the 876-878. She also discussed the 852 fields and the indicators. Much of the leader information is supplied by the system, but the operator supplies the type code in the 006 with x for a single-part item, v for multi-part item and y for serials.

Haas spent the remaining time giving a line-by-line, sub-field by sub-field view of the 853-55, the 863 sub-field, and the 863-864 first and second indicators.

After the detailed record analysis Rachel Hollis and Stephanie Schmitt helped the audience code holdings records for examples that were provided to them. The detailed presentations given by the first two speakers were excellent but were duplicative, leaving little time for participants to work on the actual examples. Participants ended up somewhat frustrated that they were unable to complete the hands-on exercises.

CONTRIBUTORS' NOTES

Diane Hillmann is in Database Quality and Enrichment at Cornell University; Ruth Haas is Serials Cataloging Team Leader and Head, HUL CONSER Office, Harvard University; Rachel Hollis is Bibliographic Services Manager, California State University, Monterey Bay; and Stephanie Schmitt is Manager, Serials Services, Yale University Law School. Pat Loghry is Head, Serials Acquisitions, University of Notre Dame.

Everything You Always Wanted to Know About Electronic Journals But Were Afraid to Ask

Stefanie Wittenbach

Presenter

John Hughes

Recorder

SUMMARY. As is implied in the title, this workshop covered the different issues involved with electronic journals (e-journals). Wittenbach, the head of acquisitions for the University of California, Riverside (UCR) Library, discussed these issues based on her four years of dealing with e-journals. She covered e-journals and how they are handled in three main areas of librarianship: acquisitions/vendors, processing/online integration, and public services/collection development. *[Article copies available for a fee from The Haworth Document Delivery Service: 1-800-HAWORTH. E-mail address: <docdelivery@haworthpress.com> Website: <http://www.HaworthPress.com>]*

[Haworth co-indexing entry note]: "Everything You Always Wanted to Know About Electronic Journals But Were Afraid to Ask." Hughes, John. Co-published simultaneously in *The Serials Librarian* (The Haworth Information Press, an imprint of The Haworth Press, Inc.) Vol. 44, No. 1/2, 2003, pp. 11-24; and: *Transforming Serials: The Revolution Continues* (ed: Susan L. Scheiberg, and Shelley Neville) The Haworth Information Press, an imprint of The Haworth Press, Inc., 2003, pp. 11-24. Single or multiple copies of this article are available for a fee from The Haworth Document Delivery Service [1-800-HAWORTH, 9:00 a.m. - 5:00 p.m. (EST). E-mail address: docdelivery@haworthpress.com].

http://www.haworthpress.com/store/product.asp?sku=J123
10.1300/J123v44n12_03

INTRODUCTION

Wittenbach began the session by explaining that this workshop was designed as an introduction for librarians who are new to e-journals. She has been in her current position at UCR for four years. Upon beginning in that position, she was given the task of dealing with e-journals, and has worked in this area since. Over the past four years, she has come to realize that "there is a need for a new breed of librarian, who understands the entire electronic information scenario: procurement, organization, access, and public services." This need prompted her to create this workshop–to provide some insight into this area of librarianship. The information provided included the basics of e-journals and her personal experiences at UCR.

ACQUISITION/VENDOR ISSUES

Publisher Packages

In nearly all cases, license agreements are required for publisher packages. For any agreement, unacceptable terms or language need to be negotiated directly with the publisher. Due to the many opportunities covering licensing, Wittenbach did not go into much detail concerning licenses in this workshop, she just pointed out different possible licensing issues that apply to the different areas that she covered. She also provided further information for an online training opportunity in licensing,[1] and an additional Website for licensing information.[2]

Currently publishers offer most of their journals in online format, either as individual titles or in a package. Options for purchasing journal subscriptions include e-journals bundled with the print journal, print only, or online only access. Some publishers, however, are doing away with the print only option, requiring subscribers to purchase to the online version.

Pricing Models

In pricing, libraries are faced with a number of different models that vary as much as the different providers. Wittenbach explained the different models that libraries can face.

The first model is print plus online subscriptions, the cost of which is usually five to ten percent more than for a print only subscription. In this case, the cost for an online only subscription is generally the same as the price for a print only subscription. Another pricing model is one that is based on the number of simultaneous users, like the model used for databases. However it is not used as commonly with e-journals. Often, pricing is based on population. For a public library, this would be based on the population of the public community served; in an academic setting it would be based on the number of FTE students or the number of graduate students and faculty in the particular discipline that is served by the e-journal. Pricing can also be based on location. The price will differ based on whether the resource is accessed only in the library, campus-wide, at other branches and facilities, or even via proxy access. In this model, the key is whether each location falls under the same administrative agency. Related to the location model is the pricing model that is based on IP address. To expand on this, Wittenbach provided an explanation of IP addresses, and explained that certain publishers may have price differences based on the IP level, for instance whether the IP level is class B or class C.

In consortial purchasing, there are additional complications in pricing and in policies and procedures for individual libraries pay for the online content. In the case of the California Digital Library (CDL) consortium, the member libraries pay for online content through the consortium, while they continue to pay for their print subscriptions as individual libraries. Depending on the publisher, content fees may vary for journal subscriptions. For example, the subscription may be broken down into a percentage that is applied to the print while the rest is applied towards the online access. As the member libraries pay their subscription agents, they pay close attention to their invoicing to ensure that they are receiving the discounted price for the print. Wittenbach provided a citation in her bibliography for an article that deals with bundled content.[3]

In 2001, the International Coalition of Library Consortia (ICOLC)[4] updated their statement on *Current Perspective and Preferred Practices for the Selection and Purchase of Electronic Information*. In this document, ICOLC made several recommendations to publishers regarding the pricing structures. This was an effort by ICOLC to help guide pricing structures.

Aggregator Databases

Aggregators collect online journal content from publishers and bring that content together, making it available in a common interface and often with a common search engine. Some aggregators charge an extra fee for accessing full-text content, while most offer free abstracts. Publishers will generally offer their content to several aggregators, resulting in overlap between different aggregators. Examples of these aggregators include: SpringerLink, Project Muse, Catchword/Ingenta, JSTOR, EBSCOHost, and Swetsnet Navigator.

There are several advantages to using an aggregator. These include the use of persistent uniform resource locators (PURLs), a common search interface, links to full-text content from abstracting and indexing (A&I) databases, and usage statistics.

Access Issues

Concerning access, there are numerous issues that need to be considered by librarians. One of the most evident is whether to purchase an e-journal that requires a username and password, as opposed to one that provides access via IP address. At UCR Wittenbach makes a conscious effort not to choose e-journals that require a username and password.

Proxy access is probably one of the biggest issues involved in providing access to e-journals. A proxy sever allows users to log in to the campus server, temporarily assigning their home computers an IP address within the campus range. In doing this, the e-journals will recognize the IP address, allowing users access to the electronic journal from workstations that are off campus. To do this, the user must be authenticated with a user name and a password in order to log in to the proxy server. This will allow a user to be traced, so it is important to ensure that a user privacy agreement is written into the license agreement to protect the individual rights.

Concerning licensing and access, the main point that Wittenbach made was that libraries are responsible for communicating with patrons and what their responsibilities are in the use of these electronic resources. One solution is to provide a "click-through" page that the user must pass through before using online resources. This page reminds the user of their responsibilities, and in doing so satisfies the library's responsibility for notifying their patrons of the restrictions.

Content/Usability/Linking

For e-journals, there are many factors in making subscription decisions that do not come into play with print subscriptions. Many of these factors are related to content. These include whether or not the online version mirrors the print journal, whether only current content is available, if archives are priced separately, and if there are embargoes on the content. Other important factors deal with usability; these include search features, display format, and the ability to download, print, or e-mail the content. Finally, linking is also important in making purchase decisions. Questions in this area relate to whether the e-journals provide linking from A&I databases or direct linking from the library's online catalog. To address this issue, enhanced full text linking of electronic resources is currently made available through technology, such as SFX (by Ex Libris)[5] and Linkfinder Plus (by Endeavor).

PROCESSING/ONLINE CATALOG INTEGRATION

Libraries are finding that the acquisitions and processing of e-journals involve more staff and time, and a higher staff skill level than that of their print counterparts. An MIT study in this area also found that rather than being predictable, e-journals tend to be cyclical and varied. In addition, this study also reported that e-journals required more coordination of technical services, public services, and collection development than the handling of print journals required.

Who Does What?

In an ideal situation, there would be an electronic resources coordinator to oversee all of the aspects of e-journals, a position that would include many aspects that are not traditional technical services responsibilities. This, however, is not always possible, so libraries need to be creative in how they assign tasks relating to e-journals.

Potential Electronic Journal Subscriptions

With potential electronic journal purchases, collection development needs to work very closely with acquisitions to address many issues, particularly concerning content and availability. It will fall to collection development to make purchase decisions based on these issues, and it is important to address them prior to the purchase decision. One way to assess e-journals is through trials. At Wittenbach's institution, they provide a trial page on the Web that is available to all library staff. Free e-journals need to be evaluated based on the same criteria as those that are purchased.

To provide direction, Wittenbach has created a Web page that serves as a checklist for handling e-journals. The checklist begins with collection development and goes through acquisitions and cataloging; the checklist allows the library staff to track the electronic resource as it is processed.

New Acquisitions

Once collection development makes the decision to purchase the subscription to a new e-journal, the very first step takes place in acquisitions, who review the license and finalize it with the publisher or vendor. In addition, to set up access to the electronic journal, acquisitions also needs to work with the subscription agent, if they have a print subscription to the journal, and/or the aggregator, if that is how the e-journal will be accessed. Often the subscription agent will handle the process with the aggregator. If the library is part of a consortium, they may be required to notify them of the new subscriptions.

When access is gained, acquisitions needs to communicate with public services the many aspects of accessing the e-journal, so that they can then communicate this information to the patrons. These include how and from where the e-journal can be accessed. Other license agreement clauses can affect public services as well, such as interlibrary loan restrictions or availability of using content in course packs. Rather than having public services and interlibrary loan staff call technical services for license agreement details, it is preferable to have this information already available. To address this, Wittenbach places this information in the order record, which is available to all the library staff.

Once the license agreement is signed and the e-journal is activated, acquisitions needs to document all of the steps that are involved with the e-journal. One mechanism for communicating all of these important elements of new e-journals to the library staff is to use the order record, as mentioned above. Because of space restrictions in the order record, however, this information is limited and can be inadequate. Another possibility is to provide this information in a separate database that resides outside of the online catalog, allowing for more information. Many libraries are creating these databases and are using them to provide fuller information about their electronic resources. For instance, they will often scan in the license agreement for all of the library staff to view. Among the examples that she provided for this type of database, Wittenbach mentioned the Penn State ERLIC database.[6] A citation to an article that provides information about other e-journal management projects was also provided.[7]

There are currently some not-for-profit organizations like Jake[8] and some for-profit organizations like Serials Solutions[9] and TDNet[10] that are providing databases for e-journal management. Some of them are offering subscription management services, which will indicate in which databases and services certain e-journals are available. This information goes beyond the information that is provided in the order record at UCR, and creates a situation where the library will need two databases–one for the library staff which shows the license details and the relationship between the online subscription and the print, and the other database for information about access and coverage. If the library has a very large e-journal collection, it is critical that it provide both types of information.

Currently, there are no vendors providing databases with the technical services type of information on e-journals, so libraries need to provide this themselves. However, Wittenbach suspects that a vendor will produce this type of product in the near future, because of the need. Many libraries may be willing to pay for such a database because of the lack of personnel to produce one in-house. The International Organization for Standardization (ISO) and the Digital Library Federation are working on standards to facilitate the creation of these e-journal management databases.

Ongoing Maintenance and Troubleshooting

In Wittenbach's words, this is probably the most time consuming aspect of e-journal management. Two major aspects relating to this are access and content.

Librarians will find that access to e-journals will often be lost, quite often pointed out by patrons at the reference desk. There are many reasons why access to a certain e-journal might be compromised. For example, access may change from free online with print to paid access, and the library either did not receive notice or did not see the notice on the invoice. At this point, the decision needs to be made, in collaboration with the bibliographers, whether to pay for and reinstate online access, go with print only access, or even choose online only access, if it is available. Another reason for lost access is when the publisher changes the uniform resource locator (URL), which is an issue if a library is not accessing the titles through an aggregator that provides stable URLs. Sometimes publishers will move their titles from one aggregator to another, which can also result in lost access. Because of the many ways that access can be lost it is imperative for the librarians to keep better track of their e-journals.

Training Staff

Training staff on the variety of issues relating to e-journals is also very important. It is, however, difficult to train staff on this, because each e-journal or package can be so different in the requirements for setting up access. Staff need to know how the e-journals are being acquired, understanding the relationship between the subscription agent, publisher, aggregator, and the consortium, if one is involved. In addition, they also need to know the relationship between the print and online subscriptions. Technical services staff also need to be able to troubleshoot subscription problems.

Bibliographic and Holdings Records

One major issue is the question of whether to use single or dual records for journal titles that are held in print and online. In the University of California (UC) system they are currently using a single bibliographic record for the print and online versions of the same title. In this case they are using the print record as the primary record. Even if they have online only access, they are still using the print record as the primary one, so that all of their bibliographic records merge into one record in the union catalog. This is important because some schools may have print only, others may have electronic only, and yet others may maintain both print and online access.

Other libraries are opting to use dual records for print and online versions of the same title. One of the advantages of this is that they can easily do a batch migration of records into their OPAC and update their online holdings by deleting out the old records and replacing them with new ones.

Another issue is making a detailed holdings statement for the e-journal available to the patrons. The solution used at UCR is to include the holdings in the check-in record and also to put them into the 856 field of the MARC record.

In addition to providing an example of a bibliographic record from UCR, Wittenbach also provided a URL for the catalog at UNC Wilmington, where one bibliographic record is being used.[11] She also provided a citation for an article that discusses this issue in more detail.[12]

URL Maintenance

Another major issue is maintenance of the e-journal's URL. After defining the URL, Wittenbach went on to explain the importance of a URL checker. This tests all of the URLs in the 856 fields in a library's online catalog and reports back any dead links.

One of the advantages of using an aggregator for access to e-journals is that most of them offer stable URLs to be used in the 856 field of the MARC record. To accomplish this, the aggregator creates a PURL, which provides the library with a linking point for the e-journal. While the e-journal's URL may change, the PURL will remain the same.

Government Publications

The proliferation of government information is an issue that librarians deal with on a regular basis, as more and more government information is moving to online only access. These government Web sites often have both a URL and a PURL. Wittenbach pointed out that libraries might want to address this by going with the PURL only in their OPAC. At UCR they purchase GPO records and then do a small amount of manipulation to the 856 field of the records. They then put in a generic statement for the patron to "check Website for coverage." This helps with holdings of government publications.

Statistics

For standard national statistical gathering purposes libraries need to be able to report both the number of subscriptions and the number of titles they have. For instance, when the library has print and online access to a given title they may have one title and two subscriptions. The statistics that we report have not quite caught up with the e-journals world as far as clearly specifying how we are to report the relationship between print and online. The questions are whether we should count a journal as one title when we have both a print subscription and an online subscription, or whether we count it as two separate subscriptions.

At UCR they are working on methods to count the e-journals separately from the print. They are also working on adding separate order records for the e-journals. This is becoming more and more important as they cancel print subscriptions and keep the online version. Also, more and more academic programs are asking to see what and how many titles the library provides access to for specific disciplines. When they purchase a package of e-journals, it also provides them with the means to divide the number of titles by the cost, so they will have some rough estimate of what they pay per title.

PUBLIC SERVICES/COLLECTION DEVELOPMENT ISSUES

Training Staff and Patrons

Staff in public services and collection development need to know as much information about e-journals as technical services staff. You need to find ways to explain to them the relationships involved in e-journals. One effective tool is the use of an e-journal management database, such as the one that was mentioned above. Information that the staff requires includes how to access the e-journal, whether it is part of a consortial purchase, and if proxy access is permitted. They will need this information on a regular basis, and it is beneficial for the information to be readily available in a readily-accessible database. Another effective strategy is to use training sessions to explain all that is involved in gaining access to e-journals. These strategies should help them in their work in troubleshooting access problems, answering patrons' questions, providing interlibrary loan, and providing course packs or e-reserves.

Patrons are often overwhelmed by all that we offer electronically. Therefore, it is imperative that librarians teach patrons some core competencies in using these resources. Since we cannot teach them about all of the intricacies of each database and e-journal, we can teach them about what they may find. For example, we can teach them about content issues, such as archives and backfiles. We can also teach them about what they will find on an e-journal page, such as abstracts, links to full text, how to e-mail the content or download or print it out.

Promotion

Because of the additional cost of e-journals and the additional labor involved in processing them, we need to promote their use. There are several ways to accomplish this, such as featuring the e-journals on the library homepage, providing a proxy server help page, special training sessions just on the virtual library, and labels in the stacks with the print version that say "now online." These methods, as well as others, will help in this area.

Impact on Print Journals

As more e-journals are added to the library and as the budget remains flat or decreases, the library needs to look at the possibility of canceling print subscriptions when there is online availability. However, there are many questions that need to be answered when considering canceling print subscriptions, including whether to keep core titles in both formats.

Librarians at the UC campuses are involved in an evaluation to look at the use of print versus online versions of journals. This is called the Collection Management Initiative.[13] In addition, Wittenbach provided a citation of an article describing a similar project that was conducted at Old Dominion.[14]

Evaluation and Usage Statistics

In making collections decisions about print and e-journals, usage statistics are crucial. Unfortunately, usage statistics are not readily available for all e-journals. Even if the publisher does provide usage statistics, some will only provide overall usage statistics, but will not break them down title-by-title. This can hinder the library in making collections decisions about e-journals.

One issue when trying to compare online usage versus print usage is that when a survey is conducted of print journals, the statistics are usually only gathered for volume level access, because the issues are bound together into one volume. This can not be correlated with online usage, because online statistics usually report usage at the article level.

ICOLC has recently updated its guidelines for statistical measures of usage of Web-based information resources. There is also a new project coming out called Counting Online Usage of Networked Electronic Resources (COUNTER).[15] The goal of this project is to produce a single code or standard for measuring online usage.

BREAK-OUT SESSION

In the break-out session, the participants broke up into three main groups: technical services staff, collection development staff, and public services staff. Each individual group discussed a given question, and then reported back to the entire group.

The technical services group discussed the question "Given your current staffing, where would you/have you assigned the various parts of the electronic journal processing that we've talked about today?" The collection development group had the question "What factors should be considered in determining whether or not e-journals should replace print subscriptions?" The public services group had the question "Besides traditional bibliographic instruction and Web links, what other ways do you/could you promote electronic journal use?"

Many important issues came out of the discussions. The collection development group agreed that one of the main points to consider in making the decision to cancel print and choose online only access was whether there would be perpetual access to the content that had been purchased online if the library decided to cancel the e-journal. The public services group came up with several ideas for promoting e-journals use, such as visiting academic departments to provide the information, distributing brochures and pamphlets on e-journals at the university's academic fair, and writing articles for the student newspaper. From the technical services groups came many examples of current staff assignments and suggestions for changes. These included a central staff person to serve as coordinator for all aspects of e-journals, a committee to handle the coordination, and in the case of a small library, a Web page librarian handles e-journals while a different model is being developed.

FUTURE/WRAP-UP

Wittenbach pointed out that some say that the print journal will cease to exist altogether, but at the very least we do know that e-journals will continue to proliferate, possibly affecting journals published by small societies. The future has many things in store for libraries, relating to e-journals. These include less availability of print, more hypertext and video content, and more linking technology. There will also be more movement of content from aggregator to aggregator, which will cause further difficulties for librarians in the areas of licensing and bibliographic records maintenance.

Other issues for libraries to consider include publisher's packages becoming more restrictive, archives for e-journals packaged and sold separately from the current content, e-journal packages containing titles that are irrelevant to the library's needs, and issues relating to the publishers holding the archives versus the print model of the libraries maintaining them.

Patron usage behavior is changing in a variety of ways as libraries provide more and more e-journals for their use. One issue of note is how associations, such as the Association of Research Libraries (ARL), will take this into consideration and whether they will be willing to change the current measure of standards for libraries.

Finally, e-journals require much more management, communication, and instruction than print titles do, affecting all areas of library service. In making the transition to a larger online collection, there will be a decrease in staffing required to manage print collections and therefore a decrease in operational costs in this area. In the same respect, staffing costs will increase in the areas of selection, acquisitions, database and Web page maintenance, instructional programs and reference, and systems. All of these are higher-level positions.

Because of this, the new costs associated with e-journals are greater than the cost savings in cutting staff associated with managing print collections. Libraries are not transferring their collections wholesale from print to electronic; therefore staff will need to be maintained to work with the print journals. At the same time new high-level positions will need to be created to coordinate the electronic collections, resulting in even greater costs in staffing for libraries. As e-journals continue to evolve, libraries will continue to struggle to adjust to the new information world.

CONCLUSION

Because of the timeliness of the information provided, this workshop was well received and there was much interest and discussion from the participants, concerning many issues. It was obvious that many libraries are wrestling with e-journals and how to gain control of them and provide them to their patrons. Some questions and discussions from the participants included who signs license agreements for the institution, issues relating to IP addresses, proxy access, aggregators' details, notification of new e-journals, single versus dual records, e-journal management databases, issues relating to commercial database providers, Open URL technology, embargoes, bibliographic control, URL checker software, etc. The breakout sessions were very beneficial as well, because they facilitated more discussion in the different areas of e-journals than possibly would have occurred otherwise.

NOTES

1. "Signing on the Dotted Line: Licensing Essentials for Library Professionals," sponsored by ALA's Office for Information Technology Policy. Contact OITP at 800/941-8478 or cbrown@alawash.org.

2. Liblicense model license agreement information, http://www.library.yale.edu/~llicense.modlicintro.html

3. *Implications of Aggregate Subscriptions to Electronic Journals.* Birmingham, AL: EBSCO Subscription Services, 2001.

4. International Coalition of Library Consortia (ICOLC), http://www.library.yale.edu/consortia

5. SFX (Exlibris), http://www.sfxit.com

6. Penn State's Electronic Resources Licensing and Information Center (ERLIC) database, http://www.libraries.psu.edu/iasWeb/fiscal_data/ERLIC_SHARE

7. Schulz, Nathalie. "E-journal Databases: a Long-term Solution?" *Library Collections, Acquisitions, & Technical Services,* 25 (2001): 449-459.

8. JAKE (Jointly Administered Knowledge Environment), http://jake.med.yale.edu

9. Serials Solutions, http://www.serialssolutions.com/Home.asp

10. TDNet, http://www.tdnet.com/

11. University of North Carolina, Wilmington Library (records for Lexis-Nexis, Proquest, etc.), http://library.uncwil.edu

12. Sanders, Thomas R., Helen Goldman, and Jack Fitzpatrick. "Title-level Analytics for Journal Aggregators," *Serials Review,* 26 (2000): 18-29.

13. University of California Collection Management Initiative, http://www.ucop.edu/cmi

14. Frazer, Stuart L. and Pamela D. Morgan. "Electronic-for-print Journal Substitutions: a Case Study," *Serials Review,* 25 (1999): 1-7.

15. COUNTER (Counting Online Usage of Networked Electronic Resources), http://projectCounter.org

CONTRIBUTORS' NOTES

Stefanie Wittenbach is Head of Acquisitions, University of California, Riverside Library. John Hughes is Director of Libraries, Psychological Studies Institute.

PLENARY SESSIONS

Web Portals:
The Future of Information Access
and Distribution

Howard Strauss

Presenter

INTRODUCTION

The enterprise Web portals that are appearing on campuses and in corporations are changing the way people use the Web and the way in which Web pages are built. Today, users of the Web as an information delivery system are faced with over 3 billion Web pages and millions of services. Of this expanding universe of data, most people commonly use only a few dozen Web pages and services, but of course everyone uses a different subset. Enterprise Web portals allow users of the Web to gain quick access to just the Web pages and services they commonly use as well as other electronic information, such as word processors and services on local area networks that they use.

This sharply contrasts with the use of ubiquitous home pages on the Web that deliver the same general information to all who look. Home pages are *institution-centric*. They give every user who keys in their URL (Web address) exactly the same general information. They proclaim the wonders of the institution and allow a user to navigate the maze of institutional Web pages and billions of Web pages beyond.

[Haworth co-indexing entry note]: "Web Portals: The Future of Information Access and Distribution." Strauss. Howard. Co-published simultaneously in *The Serials Librarian* (The Haworth Information Press, an imprint of The Haworth Press, Inc.) Vol. 44. No. 1/2, 2003, pp. 27-35; and: *Transforming Serials: The Revolution Continues* (ed: Susan L. Scheiberg, and Shelley Neville) The Haworth Information Press, an imprint of The Haworth Press, Inc., 2003, pp. 27-35. Single or multiple copies of this article are available for a fee from The Haworth Document Delivery Service [1-800-HAWORTH, 9:00 a.m. - 5:00 p.m. (EST). E-mail address: docdelivery@haworthpress.com].

http://www.haworthpress.com/store/product.asp?sku=J123
10.1300/J123v44n12_04

Enterprise Web portals are *user-centric*. Each page that such a portal displays is tailored to just one and only one user. All the information and services in a portal attempts to be exactly the subset of information that a user would choose if he or she had the time and expertise to build their perfect set of Web pages. Of course a user can easily access the rest of the Web and beyond, but if the portal is properly built such excursions will be rare.

Building traditional Web pages in an institution is typically done by a Web creation group that is part of a central IT (information technology) organization. To build home pages and the like, this group needs to know only about very general institutional data. Building a portal requires that all data and electronic services across the institution be shared and that rules for data ownership and integrity be resolved. Because of this, the normal Web creation group cannot build the portal without the assistance and cooperation of many institutional information stakeholders. Creating the structure and culture to build enterprise Web portals is a task much more formidable than any of the many very challenging technical hurdles that must be passed.

WHAT IS A PORTAL?

There are many different kinds of portals and many differing ideas as to what constitutes one. Some people claim that a portal is nothing more than a new name for a home page and have simply called their home pages portals and declared portal victory. Nothing is an enterprise portal unless it is user-centric. If large groups of users see the same Web page it is not a true portal.

Companies such as Netscape, Yahoo, and Excite claim to have Web sites that are portals. Although they do not meet the test for user-centricity at first, it is possible for users to *personalize* them to make them user-centric. These portals are called horizontal portals. All potential portal users and builders should try one to gain experience with portal personalization, an important feature found in horizontal portals and in all enterprise portals.

Some people claim that a portal is nothing more than a gateway to Web access, but since the Web is very interconnected, nearly any Web page would meet that criterion. Others have said that a Web page is a hub from which users can locate all the Web content they commonly use. That is necessary, though not sufficient. Extremely important is the caveat that the portal gives quick access, not to all the data that one might *ever* use, but just to those resources that one commonly uses.

Perhaps the best portal definition is that a portal is a user-centric customized, personalized, adaptive desktop (CPAD). The very best enterprise portals will exhibit all CPAD features.

CPAD

Customization

A user of an enterprise portal must authenticate to it by providing some proof of identity, typically an ID and password. Once the portal system knows who a user is, it can gather all the information the institution has about the user to attempt to build the best possible, most user-centric set of Web pages. These pages will necessarily be different for each person. Information such as a person's job function, employment status, manager, subordinates, benefit plans, years of service, vacation schedule, and much more are used to build a set of Web pages that will give each user access to an optimum collection of information and services. The creation of user-centric Web pages *by the portal system* is called *customization*. Customization also includes reformatting Web pages and other information to fit the particular device from which the portal is accessed. A user would want quite a different format on a three-inch PDA screen than on a twenty-one-inch desk top computer monitor.

Personalization

Even the best customization cannot decide how every person works best. One user might prefer benefit information on a portal page to be at the top left, another might prefer it at the bottom right, and another might only want to see it once a year. Many users have their own favorite Web search engine. Customization will not be able to decide how to give everyone access to only the one search engine they'd prefer. Even for the ideal customized portal page, there are dozens of changes that could be made to optimize its use for each user. An enterprise portal allows a user to make those changes. The changes that *a user makes* to tailor a customized portal page are called *personalization*.

Adaptation

Since the portal knows each user's schedule, workflow, and all of the information that an institution knows about a user, it changes to adapt to changes in a user's status. If someone gets promoted, goes from being a junior to a senior, changes departments, gets married, or changes in any of the thousands of ways someone does everyday, the portal presents a customized, personalized face that matches a user's current status.

The portal also *watches* how each user works and attempts to adapt. A simple example of this kind of thing is our use of spell checkers. When one first enters a word such as *deconstructionism*, most spell checkers will mark it as misspelled. Yet if one commonly writes about literary criticism it might be a fine word that one might add to a personal dictionary and have it not reported as misspelled. After a time, as users add terms to their own spell checking dictionaries, each user's spell checker becomes personalized to each user's use of language. Effectively, the spell checker adapts to each user.

Portal software will also help each user discover shortcuts and opportunities for working more effectively. One needs only to look at Amazon.com's "readers of this book also bought" to imagine a portal suggesting "other office managers who used this link found the Library Reference channel useful to subscribe to."

Desktop

Once every user has a customized, personalized, adaptive portal available via any Web browser on every computer, it will replace the *desktop* that is displayed on today's computers. The desktop paradigm that one sees on Linux, Windows, and Mac computers (and many others) is a convenient way for a user to navigate to all the information they commonly use. Since that function will be taken over by a portal, when a user turns on his or her computer or other information access device, the first thing they will see is their Web portal. For many users, that's all they will ever need to see. For most others, seeing anything else will be very rare. Since the portal can be accessed by any Web browser, the particular hardware and operating system (e.g., Windows, MacOS, Linux) that one uses will become much less important.

Enterprise Portals

Universities and corporations will get the most benefit from building *enterprise* portals. These portals are able to do customization because they have access to institutional information about each user. Horizontal portals such as myExcite and myYahoo do not have such access though they have many features that should be included in any enterprise portal, such as their excellent personalization and the many general interest channels they make available.

An important feature of enterprise portals is that they support *single sign on* or at least *simple sign on*. Single sign on is the ability of users to identify themselves (usually called authentication) to a portal and then have the portal authenticate to all of the applications that a user is allowed to use. For a user, instead of authenticating to the many systems within a portal, there is a need to authenticate or sign on only once.

Simple sign on is what is done when single sign on cannot be done. It attempts to reduce the number of times a user has to sign on and to attempt to synchronize password usage. Single sign on is much preferred over simple sign on.

PORTALS: WHY ONE AND ONLY ONE?

By providing a single place where each user can access *all* of the information and services she or he commonly uses, a portal greatly increases the efficiency and effectiveness of all users. It will be tempting to have a student portal, a faculty portal, an alumni portal, and possibly a library portal. However, none of these will become the single place for information access for all but a few people. Many students are also employees. They work in the library, in dining services, and elsewhere on campus. Graduate students often serve as junior faculty, and everyone uses the library. No separate portal will be able to cover all the needs of the entire university community. Only a single portal will be able to do that. To get the most benefit from a portal, there should be one and only one.

If a university wants to start slowly with portals they should build a portal for some small constituency area and then slowly grow the portal into other areas using a single portal. What they must not do is start several different portal projects using different software and hope that they can grow all those efforts together. Doing so is very difficult, very expensive and has a very low probability of success.

A PORTAL OVERVIEW

A portal is one or more customized, personalized, adaptive Web pages that become each user's computer desktop. The portal gives each user access to all of the digital information and services he or she uses. Because most users have access to more information than will conveniently fit on a single Web page, most portals consist of multiple pages. Some method to move from page to page is necessary. The most common way to achieve that is with a descriptive tab on each page. A portal may also have an area at the top of all pages for portal-level *alerts*. Alerts are context-sensitive messages that may appear at any level in the portal and may be directed at any subset of users.

A portal page consists of columns of information. Three columns is normal usage, but the number of columns may be personalized by each user. Each column consists of one or more channels. A channel is a window-like area containing related information. Information in a channel may be updated on request by a user (pulled) or updated automatically in response to external events (pushed). A channel can contain channel level alerts, text, multi-media of every stripe, links to information and applications, navigation, search, help, and cameos.

Two kinds of cameos, data cameos and application cameos are commonly used in portal channels. Data cameos are small amounts of data from a Web page, database, or other information source. Instead of having a link to an entire Web page, database report, or other information source, a cameo allows a portal to continuously display just a small amount of information, for example one's current budget balance. An application cameo is a text area which is attached to a small part of a large application or to a special use of an application. Instead of linking to an application, a user can just enter data into a text area within a channel and have those data passed to a specific application.

A simple use of this would be to implement access to a Web search engine within a portal channel. Since users will have different preferences for search engines, one might just allow users to personalize a portal channel with a link to their favorite search engine. However, that would require a user to click on the link, wait for the search engine Web page to load, enter their search, set their favorite search parameters, and then start the search. With an application cameo, a small text box would appear in a portal channel. It would be linked to the user's favorite search engine with his or her search parameters already set. A user would just enter a search request into the box and the search would begin. This is far more efficient than using a link. In general, a cameo is always preferred to a link when possible.

WHY IS THE WEB SO HARD TO SEARCH?

Since for many users, if information is not on the Web it does not exist, if users were just able to find information effectively on the Web much of their information retrieval problem would be solved. But the Web is very difficult to search and nothing short of changing the way Web pages are built will change that. The existing three billion or so Web pages that have been written in HTML (HyperText Markup Language) cannot be effectively searched with any current or future technology *if the Web pages themselves* don't change. In addition to that nearly insurmountable difficulty, an increasing number of Web pages are inaccessible to any Web search engine because they are built on the fly and do not exist until someone asks for one. The only way to search those is to be able to search their underlying databases.

HTML cannot be effectively searched because it is a formatting language not a document description language. One could search HTML for the word "yellow" in bold type, but could not effectively find all of the yellow cars for sale on the Web.

One solution is to add key words to HTML so that they could be searched. For limited applications that is fairly effective, but standards are difficult to enforce and search engines would need to be modified to have this work. Another solution is to use XML (Extensible Markup Language). XML is a true document description language and would be very searchable with the right search tools. To make XML effective, a standard vocabulary called a *schema* is required. Many schemas exist, such as one for the hotel business and another for K-12 schools. XML, however, cannot be used to display Web pages directly since it does not encode any formatting information. Some scheme for transforming XML into the HTML required by the Web is needed. Typically XSL or XSLT (extensible style language translator) is used to render XML as HTML. The effect of this is to make Web sites built with XML almost as unsearchable as those built with HTML.

A LIBRARY PORTAL?

Should universities and organizations build a library portal? If they were to do so, the portal would have to be a vertical niche portal (similar to http://www.millstones.com), a university's only portal, or if a university were misguided enough, one of several portals at a university. None of these implementations would provide a university with the great advantages of a portal that allows each person to use a portal to access all of the digital information and services they commonly use from a small set of customized, personalized, adaptive Web pages. Yet, the information that libraries provide is vital for people who use portals. While libraries should not build their own portals, their information and services need to appear within all portals on campus.

The simplest way to be part of other portals is for libraries to build library portal pages. A portal page is a regular Web page built in a conventional way that is associated with a tab in a portal. Universities might have a *library* tab that brings up the library portal page. While most portal pages consist of columns and channels, that format is not required. To make a library's portal pages better fit the spirit of a portal, it would be helpful for a library to design a series of portal pages aimed at different constituencies. For example, a library could design one portal page for students, another for faculty, and another for staff. During customization of the portal, the appropriate page could be selected.

A better, though more difficult, choice is to design many library portal channels. These could be made available to portals internationally for free or for a fee. Library portal channels would also make library portal pages much more versatile.

Lastly, libraries should build library data and application cameos. These would allow builders of other channels to include library content within them in the most effective way.

PORTAL WISDOM

Here are a few ideas to keep in mind during a portal project. These principles apply to most endeavors in information technology.

- You can't just build a portal; you'll have to market it. The best time to start marketing is *before* you start building.
- Keep the design very simple for users. Give users the power to control the portal.
- Don't build for high-tech users. They will be able to use the portal if you design it for technology disadvantaged users, but the converse is not true.
- Accept information any way you can get it. A long time ago even data on stone tablets proved useful.
- Do lots of planning, but avoid paralysis by analysis. Eventually the planning must end and the building must begin.
- Ignore the naysayers. Anyone can find reasons not to do something. You need to find a way to build a great portal in spite of the obstacles.

- An information system, which is what a portal is, is 90% information and 10% system. The information a portal delivers is much more important than the details of the system that delivers that information.
- It is far more important to offer cutting-edge service than to offer cutting-edge technology.
- A portal is just a tool to help people get their work done more efficiently and effectively. The same tools can be used to make a Mona Lisa or a monstrosity. It depends on who uses them and how they are used.

CONTRIBUTOR'S NOTES

Howard Strauss is Manager of Technology Strategy and Outreach at Princeton University.

Serials Challenges and Solutions:
The View from the Director's Chair

Emily R. Mobley

Presenter

SUMMARY. Serials challenges, particularly the pricing of sci-tech serials have been with us for more than 20 years. These challenges continue to consume inordinate amounts of time of many persons in the academy. Are there solutions or are we destined to stay on the merry-go-round? Who are the players and what are their roles? *[Article copies available for a fee from The Haworth Document Delivery Service: 1-800-HAWORTH. E-mail address: <docdelivery@haworthpress.com> Website: <http://www.HaworthPress.com>]*

Serials challenges have been with me for most of my career. Attempts to solve these challenges continue to consume inordinate amounts of time of many persons in the academy, particularly mine. Many of these challenges have focused on pricing issues, particularly the escalation of prices for scientific journals. You frequently hear the word crisis used in referring to escalating prices. We no longer have a crisis, but a constant state of affairs. While the annual double digit inflation has ceased, the annual increases still average more than twice the rate of general inflation in the U.S. The future of the journal, how schol-

[Haworth co-indexing entry note]: "Serials Challenges and Solutions: The View from the Director's Chair." Mobley, Emily R. Co-published simultaneously in *The Serials Librarian* (The Haworth Information Press, an imprint of The Haworth Press, Inc.) Vol. 44, No. 1/2, 2003, pp. 37-44; and: *Transforming Serials: The Revolution Continues* (ed: Susan L. Scheiberg, and Shelley Neville) The Haworth Information Press, an imprint of The Haworth Press, Inc., 2003, pp. 37-44. Single or multiple copies of this article are available for a fee from The Haworth Document Delivery Service [1-800-HAWORTH, 9:00 a.m. - 5:00 p.m. (EST). E-mail address: docdelivery@haworthpress.com].

arly communication will look in the future, and how your jobs as serials librarians will look in the future consume more and more of a director's time.

Let's look at a little historical perspective. The average prices of scientific journals have always been higher than other disciplines. In 1963, the average price of chemistry and physics journals was $16.07, about 2.5 times that of all disciplines combined. In 1996, the average price of these journals was $867.00, slightly over 5 times the average price of all disciplines combined. By last year, only five years later, the average price was $1407.00, around 6 times the average price of all disciplines combined. Actually, zoological journal prices had the highest overall rates of inflation. As the average prices of these journals are less than half of those for chemistry and physics, it may not have seemed as egregious.

What was happening in these disciplines to cause such substantial price increases? Was it purely greed? Many of the most prestigious journals in these disciplines are controlled by a handful of very powerful scientific societies, thus how could prices rise so dramatically? A complex series of events moved us to the serials environment of today. I've identified six major groups of players who have or have had a role in creating today's environment. The actions of these groups, coupled with the research, business and economic climate, and technology, have brought us to today.

The scientific journal crisis had its roots in the era of "big science," the years following the Sputnik Era of the late fifties when the U.S. government supported scientific endeavors with "deep pockets." America wished to be the world's preeminent scientific power. Science faculties in universities grew along with the output of graduate students. New research fronts were developing at a rapid pace, followed quickly by new journals covering the new research. Research staffs in business and industry also grew rapidly, particularly in those industries connected with the space program, even those connected tangentially. The number of graduate programs grew as many colleges expanded their programs and changed into full-blown universities to take advantage of the profusion of funds available. Traditional scientific societies could not keep up with the demand for new publication outlets. All of these new faculties, with the demands for research and publication in order to obtain tenure, placed great demands on scientific publishing. More scientific societies arose, faculties were editing and publishing new journals under the aegis of their universities, and commercial publishers started seeing opportunities for scientific publishing. A connection with "big science" was glamorous.

The downturns in industry and the recessions of the 80s started the erosion of public support for the academy. The hallowed halls of academe began to feel the same "pain" as industry. University administrators, now facing rising costs due to all the programs, faculty, and staff added during the "gravy" days, were now faced with how to pay for these sins of the past in a future with shrinking dollars. So they looked around their institutions to find places where resources could be easily reduced without making the hard decisions such as "Do we really need all of these academic programs?" Thus, one of the first things to go was support for publications which faculty had been producing in-house with the use of "supplemental" resources. By the 90s, university administrators had to deal with a number of rising costs other than serials. Utility costs, infrastructure costs resulting from years of deferred building maintenance, health care for employees, and the costs of keeping technology updated were some of the most expensive items with which university administrators had to and still continue to grapple. These needs exist at a time when public universities continue to receive a smaller and smaller portion of their operating expenditures from public funds. Even though more costs have been passed on to students through higher tuition and fees and more and larger fund-raising programs are announced and successfully carried out, the need to find additional funds continues unabated. The HEPI (higher education price index) has exceeded general inflation for many years.

Earlier I stated that there are six major groups of players who have roles in how we have arrived at the serials situation of today. These groups are: faculty; university administrators; government; non-profit publishers, including university presses; commercial publishers; and librarians.

The faculty have the most to gain or lose from what happens in the future with scholarly communications, particularly the scientific disciplines. Yet too many of them continue to be oblivious to the situation. The faculty have a unique role in that they are both creators and consumers of the contents of serials. They edit the journals, referee the papers which are selected for publication, and sit on editorial boards–what a powerful position. They knowingly give away copyright or accept very limited rights (although thankfully, there have been some changes here). As editorial board members they either by commission or omission approve price increases or policies and/or operating agreements which lead to increases. Editorial boards continually increase the number of published pages because "the number of submissions require increasing the number of articles published." When quality control is suggested as an approach, the immediate comment is that more outlets for publication are needed due to the demands of promotion and tenure. These editors and board members are usually the same senior faculty who sit on tenure and promotion committees and make the rules. Thus, it is also within their power to change requirements to accommodate more limited publication outlets. The results of citation analysis studies indicate that we could do with a lot less publication and still have what is deemed important available.

University administrators as a group have done little to lead change to solve the serials challenges although admittedly, more are getting involved with some of the initiatives to find solutions. Some provosts have even posed solutions but the faculty in their own institutions have not bothered to follow. At the same time that we talk about looking within the institution to help effect change such as using university presses, the withdrawal of subsidies from presses by these same administrators continues unabated. Library directors, however, continue to receive pressure from these same administrators to do something such as develop more cooperative agreements so that we can share. When we tactfully tell our administrations that the need for duplication among consortium members is a direct result of the duplication and research among the universities and, hence, sharing can only go so far, the silence is deafening.

The government has now become a large player with electronic publishing due to the rules and regulations surrounding intellectual property rights, including copyright, in the digital era. Frankly, the jury is still out on whether or not libraries will end up with laws and regulations favoring our values. Some of the laws and legal rulings have certainly not been in our favor. The need to stay abreast of what is happening on the legal front with intellectual property rights is another of those items that have landed on my desk, giving me another set of players both on and off-campus with whom to work.

As librarians, most of us are quite cognizant of our roles. I'm very happy to see that we are no longer accepting the idea that the serials problem is a library problem. Happily, I've noticed that now university administrators have recognized that it is a university problem. As a group we have done a good job of education these last few years. However, we will be affected by whatever solutions the future may hold. The colleagues at this conference will probably be the most affected in the library, but more about that later.

Non-profit publishers reflect the bifurcation of their roles. As publishers they must exercise prudent financial and business practices. Although profits are not the motive, if publications programs have produced a surplus, many uses can be made of that money. Many of these non-profit publishers are societies which exist for the "good" of the membership. It's no secret that in many, if not most, of the scientific societies, library subscriptions actually provide the financial supplement for producing members copies which are sold at a substantially lower rate. This was one of the points in *Tackling the Journal Crisis.*[1] In the model presented, more than 90% of the fixed costs of producing a serial was recovered by library subscriptions. By the way, I've noticed that the price increases from some large scientific society publishers have been even more egregious than some commercial publishers. The comment is that the journals cost much less to begin with, so that makes the increase percentages higher. While this is true, the increases are still quite noticeable. University presses as a group are still too often focused on the library's decreases in the purchase of monographs in order to support serials price increases as the reason university presses are in such dire straits. While there is some truth to this, too many press directors see the press's role as primarily a publisher of monographs. They are loathe to come to the table to talk about a changing role for them–changing the manner of disseminating scientific papers.

I've saved the best for last–the commercial publishers. Commercial publishing is big business. Let's briefly look at my favorite sci-tech publisher, Reed-Elsevier. It is no secret that Reed-Elsevier has a goal of being not only profitable, but also to be *the* dominant sci-tech publisher. The selling off of some units, such as its consumer magazines publishing division some years ago so it could concentrate on "higher-profit margin sci-tech journals," was a strategy. The acquisition of other publishers, such as the more recent acquisition of Academic Press titles, is a way to achieve this goal. What are we down to now? Four major commercial sci-tech publishers? Dominance in a chosen market is a key strategy for success. How a company achieves that dominance is not for the faint-hearted. Reed-Elsevier is doing exactly what it should be doing to achieve success. The fact that Reed-Elsevier's return on equity is considerably higher than that of most companies in other sectors is an indicator of great success. It should be noted that this point is also true for Kluwer and Wiley.[2] If you really wish to know the details on publicly traded companies such as Reed-Elsevier, there are a variety of ways. I know some librarians, who shall remain nameless, who own a few shares of stock in these companies–nothing like being a shareholder to get the inside information. Those of us in academe are naive to believe that these companies should be behaving differently. The company is a business and we need to recognize that they are not colleagues in the true sense of the word. Thus we must behave as customers. When was the last time you considered a car salesperson a colleague? You think it's different because with a car you have both a choice of product and a choice of company (dealership) from which to purchase. When dealing with a commercial publisher, as well as a non-profit publisher, you have choice of neither product nor company. If you think about this, publishers are quite vulnerable. If a customer withdraws his/her business, there is no other product on which to fall back. If authors no longer submit articles, there is nothing to publish, hence, nothing to sell. This sets the stage for some of the solutions for serials challenges.

SPARC, the Scholarly Publishing and Academic Resources Coalition, is probably the best known and currently the most successful of the attempts at solutions. SPARC was started to provide encouragement and support for projects which represent a direct and strong competitive alternative to existing high-priced titles in important, established STM fields. Since this beginning, SPARC has branched out into two other areas for support–the Scientific Communities Partnerships, which support the development of non-profit information aggregations or portals that serve specified scientific communities by providing high quality, reasonably priced access, peer-reviewed research, and other needed content from a variety of sources or publishers; and the Leading Edge program, which supports projects that represent a paradigm shift in technology use, introduce an innovative business model, and/or meet the scholarly and research information needs of an emerging or fast-growing STM field. The number of partners is only twenty currently, so a great impact has not yet been made. However, at least three of the titles under the Alternatives Program have successfully dislodged those comparative titles published by commercial publishers, at least in terms of reputation as measured by ISI's impact factor.[3] It is also true that one reason for recent amelioration of price increases by commercial publishers was a result of SPARC activities.

The Budapest Open Access Initiative is the most recently posed solution at the university level. Presidents and provosts seem to be lining up behind this initiative, although it does leave things flexible because an institution or group of institutions signs on to a "statement of principles." Even the CIC (the consortium of Big Ten universities plus the University of Chicago) has signed on at the consortium level. However, as the Soros Foundation is going to provide a not-insubstantial amount of funding for support, this initiative is one that bears watching. The Mellon Foundation is funding a Scholarly Communication Institute to be developed by the Council of Library and Information Resources and the Dartmouth College Library. The institute is to bring together pioneers and innovators in scholarly communication for a one-week residential experience that will allow them to discuss, plan, and organize institutional and discipline-based strategies for advancing innovation in scholarly communication.[4]

In the essence of time, I've omitted comments on a number of other initiatives. It's safe to say that many of them were ideas that did not rise far off the ground, if at all. I have also omitted the most highly successful example of high energy physics preprints and the Journal of High Energy Physics. What must be noticed is that we are starting to see a small but critical mass of initiatives. The real difference is that a combination of key role players are coming together–university administrators, faculty, and in some cases scientific societies and librarians. Add to this the availability of some funding, and environmental conditions might be ripe for a new scholarly communication paradigm, particularly in the sciences.

What does all this mean for serials librarians? I've tried to wipe away the fog from my crystal ball to peer into the future. It's still a bit cloudy, but these developments not only insure serials librarians continued employment, but a great potential to need more of them. It is possible that we will move away from the journal as we now know it. Instead the individual paper, without the journal wrapper, will become the "currency" of published scientific communication. Let's look at a scenario whereby the institution is responsible for the dissemination of papers published by its faculty and staff. Where will the papers reside? On a single university server, on school and department servers, or on the faculty or staff members' server? How will these papers be organized and by whom? How can users both internally and externally gain access and search for information? How will archiving be done, and by whom? This scenario frankly presents the most chaotic of the possibilities. I think you can see the great potential for serials librarian services in this scenario. However, I don't think this level of decentralization will occur.

What I really think is going to happen ultimately is something in between the journal as we know it today and the individual paper scenario of above. I think there will be a grouping of papers that may mimic the journals of today. The editors and referees will still have a role in insuring "quality" and will continue to be the gatekeepers. The "groupings" with the most prestige will still be the most sought-after site for submis-

sion of papers. I think scientific societies will have a role in these groupings and indicators of quality. The losers will be commercial publishers.
Your role as serials librarians will still be to acquire, maintain, possibly
archive, and provide the modes of access for users. As these groupings
will not have print counterparts, you won't be spending any more time
debating the merits, or lack thereof, of separate records for print and
electronic versions of the same title. It will, however, be more complex,
with many more sites for connections. There would be a potential for
aggregation of these groupings. I would expect that would be a common
role for scientific societies.

A few years ago I had a quite a bit of skepticism about the likeliness
of changes occurring as those posed above. I now feel that it is no longer
if, but when, and that when may actually occur more rapidly than other
revolutions. These changes are considered revolutionary. As with any
revolution, as the oft-quoted Kuhn's statements on scientific revolutions discuss, there is a period of chaos between the old and the new paradigm. Thus, we are getting ready to enter that period of chaos, so get
ready for the ride, because a new paradigm for scholarly communications in the sciences is on the way.

NOTES

1. *CPB Netherlands Bureau for Economic Policy Analysis. Working Paper no. 121. Tackling the journal crisis.* The Hague, March 2000 *http://www.cpb.nl/eng/pub/werkdoc/121*
2. Ibid.
3. Peek, Robin. "SPARC is ready to go mainstream." *Information Today,* v. 19, June 2002, p. 38.
4. Ibid.

CONTRIBUTOR'S NOTES

Emily Mobley is Dean of Libraries and the Esther Ellis Norton Distinguished Professor in Library Science at Purdue University.

The Future of Digitized Materials: Where We Have Been and Where We're Going

David Seaman

Presenter

October Ivins

Recorder

After ten years as the founding director of the E Text Center, David Seaman is leaving at the end of July to become the new director of the Digital Library Federation. At the close of the conference on Sunday morning, NASIG attendees were treated to his retrospective and prospective insights about the center's work in a delightfully witty and entertaining presentation. In his introduction, Seaman paraphrased the title of his talk, indicating that he would discuss the future of electronic publishing, or where e-publishing (including serials) is going from a full-text perspective.

The E Text Center at the University of Virginia (UVa) deals exclusively in humanities and social sciences texts and images, with a focus on owning rather than licensing content. When the center started in the early 1990s, they had no other choice than to digitize content themselves as there were few commercial sources in the humanities. Although there are many commercial sources now, in some ways their reasons for digitizing texts are valid again. Initially, they were driven by

---

[Haworth co-indexing entry note]: "The Future of Digitized Materials: Where We Have Been and Where We're Going." Ivins, October. Co-published simultaneously in *The Serials Librarian* (The Haworth Information Press, an imprint of The Haworth Press, Inc.) Vol. 44, No. 1/2, 2003, pp. 45-49; and: *Transforming Serials: The Revolution Continues* (ed: Susan L. Scheiberg, and Shelley Neville) The Haworth Information Press, an imprint of The Haworth Press, Inc., 2003, pp. 45-49. Single or multiple copies of this article are available for a fee from The Haworth Document Delivery Service [1-800-HAWORTH, 9:00 a.m. - 5:00 p.m. (EST). E-mail address: docdelivery@haworthpress.com].

"ambition, ignorance and lack of money–not by stunning insights and lots of cash." Library time is the inverse of Internet (and publisher) time. Libraries are interested in the long-term and are willing to wait several years to see a payoff on their digitizing investment.

Early on, the E Text Center made a bet that has paid off: to use SGML. It migrates and is nimble and malleable. The significance of these characteristics is coming around again. Early on, their motivator was their inability to support multiple interfaces.

UVa is a successful aggregator, and that experience has yielded two important lessons. The first key lesson is that standardized data aggregates well. It uses standard metadata and is not bound up in proprietary systems. For the time being, Web browsers provide some standardization of format and display. But the Web offers little in the way of cross-database, multi-institution access. It that regard, we are no better off than in the days of CD-ROMs, with too many isolated bits of data. This model is not sustainable: Data must interact as a library. Data must be built, not as a stand-alone product, but to work with other content. As examples, Seaman mentioned slave letters, Salem witch trial documents, and their Early American Fiction Collection. The individual documents in these collections also reside in searchable full-text databases.

Users provide other lessons. While the E Text Center has a firm service mission and is housed in an academic institution, its online users are predominantly nonscholarly. Sharing statistics about their huge usage figures, Seaman speculated that based on e-mail received, their average user is 12 years old. "Whatever you think you are, you're not if your users think you're something else." Different users have different format needs, so the E Text Center's databases contain features that can be turned on or off for different audiences. There is a huge demand for cross-database searching. Within ten years, users will be able to simultaneously search full-text collections in multiple institutions. Even in the short term, a document needs to behave differently in different applications. Consider how a Mark Twain text might differ on a special collections Web site from one created by a faculty member for her undergraduate students.

Looking back, Seaman comes to the realization that the E Text Center is much more than a file management and retrieval system for journal articles, books, etc. In a digital library, the system rarely delivers entire files. Their content is tagged so users can get just pieces–a chapter, or references. The Center is becoming increasingly familiar with providing "gobbets of information." The 70,000 books in their holdings represent millions of chunks of content.

This is the real power of SGML and now XML: To support the creation of products that extract and combine types of information, allowing for repurposing of content in ways not possible in the print world. No one else may want that same combination of pieces, but it doesn't matter. If your data is ready for the future, this is an exciting time.

Seaman shared several anecdotes about the unexpected worldwide demand for digital content. One major initiative is the Early American Fiction Collection. Much of this is not great fiction, but it now has the veneer of history and is not widely available, certainly there are rarely classroom editions available. The center decided to publish as Web and e-book versions 80 available works from UVa, not just those of well-known authors, and this has produced some dramatic results. An 1830 novel, *Nix's Mate* by Rufus Dawes, was downloaded 2,000 times the first two months it was posted and more than 6,000 times to date. The lesson here is that "The world finds users for things you would never imagine." In a second example, the center took over the publication of a 40-year-old scholarly history journal. Its content would be appropriate for and should be available to students, including those in high school. In print, this journal had 400 subscriptions annually. Now that it is only electronic, it receives 77,000 document views in a peak month. In March 1994, an article about Jack the Ripper was published and now receives as many as 5,000 downloads a month. (We have to tenure this guy whether he wants it or not!) These examples demonstrate a lot of evidence that if we make information available at an "appropriate cost" (not necessarily free), there is a real market for it.

Which brings us to a third and final major point: returning to format and data portability considerations. The world of books has changed during the last two or three years, with enormous growth in digital publishing and the advent of delivery media other than the Web. In libraries, we've seen only Web-based publishing in our vision and peripheral vision–although we say "build once and use many," we have really just meant the Web. The acceptance of e-books and e-book readers, however, is growing in the consumer market. In March 2002, Stephen King sold 400,000 copies of an e-book at $2.50 each. Although we should be cautious about assuming that copyright and intellectual property debates will be resolved in the favor of libraries and their patrons (see Lawrence Lessig, *The Future of Ideas: The Fate of the Information*

Commons in a Connected World, ISBN 037550584) we can see that the Web is a great finding tool, but not the medium of choice for reading. Portable readers, including Palm Pilots or other PDAs, provide "a surprisingly not terrible" reading experience. Consumer acceptance of e-books is real, but too many producers overprice their products. The value must be in the reader's favor: When Barnes and Noble tried to charge $20 a book, they had few sales.

For a project sponsored by Microsoft and using their e-book reader, the center converted one of its existing digital collections to the e-book format. They were able to convert 1,000 texts to e-books in a week, demonstrating that this is just a new output format for the center, not a labor-intensive new production process. The project was launched in August 2000; by November 2000, one million e-books had been downloaded. Currently, 1,800 free e-books from many collections are available, and 6.6 million have been distributed from the Electronic Text Center.

There are many non-Web electronic readers available. About one-third of the downloads from the site are for Palm Pilots, for those Seaman refers to as having a "high pain threshold." Various manufacturers also produce a Pocket PC, running a pocket version of MS Windows, a device which supports page turning, highlighting, drawing, and editorial marking up. It holds up to 100 books and was used in a pilot study at UVa that preloaded a semester's worth of reading for students. Based on this study, he believes people will buy e-books for pleasure reading, but will not pay more than print equivalents. They don't care that it dies–that is, that the content expires after a set time period. Many other technologies are coming. Another recent example is a Microsoft audio book format that does a decent job of converting text to speech. Several firms are working with print-on-demand technologies that would produce perfect-bound books one at a time.

With the end of the conference approaching all too quickly, there was time for a closing thought: "Libraries are fabulously well placed to (create full text that is standardized and can be repurposed), because we think in the long term." The only negative aspect of this engaging and thought-provoking presentation was the lack of time for questions and that no reactor was built into the program schedule. It would have been interesting to explore the limitations copyright places on such activities and how publishers who handle content that is not in the public domain address these restrictions, or the challenges of supporting innovative technologies on the one hand while cooperating with Microsoft on the other. Perhaps these issues can be explored in Portland at the next conference. Nevertheless, the enthusiastic audience (this reporter included) was happy to close the conference on a note of optimism and high expectations, even without having all the answers.

SELECTED URLS

Electronic Text Center: *http://etext.lib.virginia.edu/*
E-books Collection: *http://etext.lib.virginia.edu/ebooks*
Modern English (aggregated) Collection: *http://etext.lib.virginia.edu/modeng/modeng0. browse.html*
Early American Fiction: *http://etext.lib.virginia.edu/eaf/*
Mark Twain in his Times: *http://etext.lib.virginia.edu/railton/*
Salem Witch Trials: *http://www.salemwitchtrials.org/*

CONTRIBUTORS' NOTES

David Seaman is Director, Digital Library Foundation. October Ivins is a consultant based in Sharon, MA.

CONCURRENT SESSIONS

Scholarly Journals Should Be Treated as a Public Good

Steve Black

Presenter

Note: This paper was presented in a concurrent session with Dr. Keith Seitter, entitled "Scholarly Publication: Business and Public Good?"

SUMMARY. The thesis that scholarly journals should be treated as public goods is based on five arguments. First, scholarly journal articles have many public good characteristics, and many of their private good characteristics are created by choice. Second, our current system undersupplies students with scholarly journals. Third, the supply chain for journals from publisher to user is burdened by many deadweight losses. Fourth, online publishing might reduce those deadweight losses enough to fund a system freely available to scholars. Finally, treating scholarly journals as public goods can meet the needs of all stakeholders. Explanations of the economic concepts of public good, deadweight loss, and Pareto optima are given to support the arguments. *[Article copies available for a fee from The Haworth Document Delivery Service: 1-800-HAWORTH. E-mail address: <docdelivery@haworthpress.com> Website: <http://www.HaworthPress.com>]*

[Haworth co-indexing entry note]: "Scholarly Journals Should Be Treated as a Public Good." Black, Steve. Co-published simultaneously in *The Serials Librarian* (The Haworth Information Press, an imprint of The Haworth Press, Inc.) Vol. 44, No. 1/2, 2003, pp. 53-63; and: *Transforming Serials: The Revolution Continues* (ed: Susan L. Scheiberg, and Shelley Neville) The Haworth Information Press, an imprint of The Haworth Press, Inc., 2003, pp. 53-63. Single or multiple copies of this article are available for a fee from The Haworth Document Delivery Service [1-800-HAWORTH, 9:00 a.m. - 5:00 p.m. (EST). E-mail address: docdelivery@haworthpress.com].

http://www.haworthpress.com/store/product.asp?sku=J123.
10.1300/J123v44n12_07

Online scholarly periodical literature naturally lends itself to be treated as a public good. Public goods are consumer goods that, when made available to anyone, can be made available to others at no additional cost. Since essentially all public goods have private goods characteristics, collective choices are made to treat schools, roads and other things with social value as public goods. While aggregations of producers' journals into large databases and organization of libraries into consortia are moving us in the direction of treating scholarly journals as public goods, we are in danger of creating an oligopoly that fails to adequately serve the needs of publishers, libraries, and scholars. Market forces alone will not adequately fund the social value of scholarly publications. The stakeholders in scholarly publishing should investigate what it would take to create an adequately funded, equitable system that serves all scholars as efficiently and effectively as possible.

My thesis that scholarly journals should be treated as public goods is based on five arguments. First, scholarly journal articles have many public good characteristics, and many of their private good characteristics are created by choice. Second, our current system undersupplies students with scholarly journals. Third, the supply chain for journals from publisher to user is burdened by many deadweight losses. Fourth, online publishing might reduce those deadweight losses enough to fund a system freely available to scholars. Finally, treating scholarly journals as public goods can meet the needs of all stakeholders.

SCHOLARLY LITERATURE HAS MANY PUBLIC GOOD CHARACTERISTICS, AND MANY OF ITS PRIVATE GOOD CHARACTERISTICS ARE CREATED BY CHOICE

Since we have only recently reached the point where the infrastructure in the U.S. allows convenient online delivery of journal articles to end users, path dependency has carried a print pricing model into a new market where it may not fit. Print journals, by their nature, have private good characteristics that must be artificially recreated online.

As stated earlier, a public good is a commodity or service that if supplied to one person can be made available to others at no extra cost. A pure public good, as defined by Paul Samuelson, is non-rival in consumption (one person's consumption of the good does not reduce its availability to anyone else), and has the characteristic of non-excludability (once the good is provided the producer is unable to prevent anyone from consuming it). [1]

It is likely that no pure public goods exist in the real world. A typical limitation to a public good is geography. A local public good is restricted to a limited area, an example being a fireworks display or a broadcast radio station. Public goods can be limited by congestion. A roadway is non-rival and non-excludable if traffic is not heavy, but congestion reduces the road's availability to drivers. Similarly, the public good nature of volumes in a library is limited by physical access to the collection and the fact that a volume cannot be used by more than one person at a time. Since "pure" public goods are extremely rare, provision of public goods is a matter of collective choice.[2]

It is critical to recognize that "public good" refers to nonrivalrous, nonexcludable consumption attributes, and *not* to whether a good is produced by the public sector. For instance, a broadcast radio program is a public good. My listening to a radio station does not lessen your ability to listen (nonrivalrous), and within its range the radio station does not limit who can pick it up (nonexcludable). Whether a station's broadcast is paid for by public funds or by advertising or by government is not relevant to the broadcast being a public good. Since the source of funding is not a defining characteristic of public goods, one can accept the premise that scholarly journals should be treated as public goods without assuming anything about how or by whom the production of journals is financed.

Also worth emphasizing is that a public good need not have the same benefit to all, even though the availability is the same to all. Publicly available weather forecasts may be of more value to pilots than miners, but forecasts are still a public good. A radio station's signal is a public good, even though some people have no radio, or no desire to tune in. The fact that some people have no interest in scholarly journals doesn't affect their public goods characteristics.

Collective choice to treat something as a public good makes sense when the costs of creating the first unit are very high, but the cost of making one more unit available is very low. Typically, public goods are "lumpy." They require large up-front infrastructure expenditures greater than any individual would be willing to pay. Think of the cost of building a radio station or a library or a new interstate highway. A large lump of funding is needed for the start-up, and relatively less to produce additional units or to maintain the good.

According to an economic principle called the Pareto optimum, society as a whole derives the greatest benefit from a good when no possible reallocation of the good can make anyone better off without making someone else worse off.[3] The optimal, most efficient allocation of a public good is achieved, in theory, when the total marginal cost to all consumers is equal to the total marginal cost of production. Therefore the ideal level of spending on a public good is essentially the equilibrium of costs after the "lumps" have been paid for. But since the marginal cost of producing another copy of an online journal article is trivial, publishers create online articles with basically all lump and no marginal cost. To provide articles at the Pareto optimum would be to provide them for free. So how would the first-copy costs be paid for?

Online journal articles can be public goods just as radio broadcasts are public goods. A journal article retrieved from a database is nonrivalrous, since one person's viewing and downloading of an article does not affect another person's ability to do the same (unless the provider imposes limits). But print journals are slightly rivalrous, since only one person can use an issue at a time, and use is limited by physical access to the volume.

A journal article online is excludable only to the degree chosen by the provider. A publisher can choose to exclude no one and make articles freely available on the Web, or a publisher can create a system that restricts access to paying users. In contrast, print journals are exclusive to those who pay subscriptions. Library subscriptions make journals less excludable, but people still have to gain physical access to the copy. The change in excludability from print to online has fundamentally upset the journals market. In the online environment, free access to journals is technologically simpler, but it doesn't pay the bills. So publishers, of necessity, spend effort and resources to make their products excludable like print subscriptions.

Society chooses to treat something as a public good when it would be under produced without group intervention. That choice is typically made when the social value of something is recognized as being worth paying for. Information found in journals has both a primary value and a social value. The primary value is the gain individuals enjoy from using the information. The social value is the benefit to society derived from the education gained from use of the information. Unless an organization able to act in the public's interest becomes involved, the social value of information is not funded. Public funding of education reflects the recognition of the social value of an informed populace.[4]

OUR CURRENT SYSTEM UNDERSUPPLIES STUDENTS WITH SCHOLARLY JOURNALS

A study of users of the *Bryn Mawr Classical Review* and *Bryn Mawr Medieval Review* showed that 65% and 45%, respectively, of users are faculty.[5] It's no news that the one million college faculty members in the U.S.[6] are important consumers of peer-reviewed scholarly periodicals. However, that means that if *Bryn Mawr Review*'s use is typical of scholarly journals, from 35% to 55% of use is by students and other scholars. There are 15,203,000 college students in the United States.[7] Two thirds of them work either full time or part time, and about 18% of them are over 35 years old,[8] so for many students finding time to access journals is difficult. The Bryn Mawr study also found 5-10% of users had no academic affiliation.[9] This large population of individuals who are not faculty could benefit from more convenient access to the scholarly journals they want or need to read.

Academic reference librarians know that many students feel underserved by their journal collections. We operate a gift economy, where we make our best guesses as to what the students will need to use, and purchase subscriptions for their use. Our guesses leave many patrons without the articles they would like.[10] The huge volume of interlibrary loan requests is concrete evidence of unmet need, and student use of journals made available online that their library never owned in print is high.[11]

THE SUPPLY CHAIN FOR JOURNALS FROM PUBLISHER TO USER IS BURDENED BY MANY DEADWEIGHT LOSSES

A deadweight loss is the gap between the price buyers pay and the price sellers receive. A market is optimally efficient when consumer surplus and producer surplus are maximized. That is, the consumer feels he's getting a good deal, and the producer makes a profit. Deadweight loss reduces market efficiency. The classic example of a deadweight loss is a sales tax. The price consumers pay for a taxed good is higher than the price received by the producers, so the tax hangs like a dead weight on the producers' income and the consumers' willingness to pay. This causes consumers to buy less, therefore reducing producers' ability to set prices as high as they would prefer.

The deadweight losses in the journal supply chain are mostly in the time and effort spent to distribute, organize, and access journals. Unlike a sales tax, these deadweight losses are not immediately apparent, and some are so diffuse as to be easily overlooked. Scholars (including students) spend enormous amounts of time accessing journal literature. Sweetland calculated that it takes 5.12 minutes to retrieve a bound journal volume, and 6.17 minutes to retrieve an article on microfilm.[12]

That's after the citation is in hand. If, for example, the 15 million college students in the U.S. can earn an average of $10 an hour, and retrieve 10 journal articles per year (on average), the direct time cost alone of retrieving articles would be $8.53 per student. That's a total of student time worth $12,800,000 per year. That figure does not include patrons' time getting to the library, or direct and indirect costs imposed by the time spent in the library (i.e., not at work, or home with the kids, etc.). A full accounting of the deadweight loss of scholars' time spent retrieving articles in print versus downloading online articles from any Web-connected computer would require a well-designed research project.

The funds libraries spend on serials acquisition, organization, and maintenance reduces funds available to pay for subscriptions. In theory, the difference between the total cost of managing a serials collection and the price paid to publishers is the deadweight loss in the system. Having scholarly journals online will not eliminate overhead costs for libraries, but the per-title cost of maintenance can be much lower.[13] Over time, the shift to online access may allow libraries to shift resources from binding, reshelving, and processing to paying subscription or license fees.

The portion of publishers' total expenses for marketing, invoicing, responding to claims, and handling physical volumes also represents a deadweight loss. Research is needed to determine the price publishers would be willing to receive for their journals if they only had to pay for first copy production. The costs of activities not related to editing, peer review, and first copy production may be borne more efficiently by organizations other than publishers.

ONLINE PUBLISHING MIGHT REDUCE THOSE DEADWEIGHT LOSSES ENOUGH TO FUND A SYSTEM FREELY AVAILABLE TO USERS

This premise is based on a hypothetical model, where funding from library consortia, foundations, governments, and/or other organizations pays for scholarly journals. The funding would cover publishers' first copy costs, the infrastructure for access to and storage of journal content, bibliographic databases that link to the content, and a system of peer-based quality control oversight. Details of how such a system might be created lie beyond the scope of this paper. In principle, though, considerable efficiencies can be gained by not processing physical volumes, reducing administrative costs, and saving the time of scholars.[14]

TREATING SCHOLARLY JOURNALS AS PUBLIC GOODS CAN MEET THE NEEDS OF ALL STAKEHOLDERS

Some aspects of a public goods model are already in place. For many years, publishers have received indirect support via subscription revenues from governments, foundations, and other bodies concerned with funding the social value of information. While the method of funding does not define a public good, the use of public funds for subscriptions through grants and library support indicate a history of public support for scholarly journals.

Consortial purchasing of online content represents a move from a market of private, excludable goods to quasi-public "club" goods. A club good is a public good made exclusively available to a defined group of users. For example, the library at The College of Saint Rose licenses access to about 800 journals in Elsevier's Science Direct via the Pi Squared consortium. Before our participation in the consortium, we subscribed to only 10 of the titles in Science Direct. The library is paying Elsevier the same as before (plus inflation), and Elsevier is receiving the same revenue from the Pi Squared members. By treating the journals in Science Direct as a club good, Elsevier is giving the students at my institution online access to eighty times as many journals as before.

State-wide consortia are actively working to increase the online journal content available to all library users in the state, effectively making them all members of a club granted access to full-text content. Just one example of state-wide funding of a full text database is the Health Reference Center, a Gale database provided to all libraries in New York State under the auspices of the New York State Library, backed by federal funding.[15] While this database includes full text from other types of sources, it does include articles from many scholarly journals.

While it appears that the journal market may be moving towards a public goods model, or at least a club goods model, important needs of stakeholders are not being adequately addressed. Since there is no direct support for publishers' first-copy costs, uncertain revenue to publishers threatens the stability of content in aggregated full-text databases. EBSCO, a leading vendor of online journals, holds the position that aggregated full text databases complement, but should not replace, individual journal subscriptions.[16] Apparently, payments by full text aggregators to publishers are not sufficient to cover first-copy costs.

Smaller libraries lack the necessary resources to adequately support subscriptions to individual online journals. Because of the work involved, it is feasible for a smaller library to administer an aggregated database of a few thousand titles, but not feasible to administer access and logins through dozens of publishers to the same number of titles. Similarly, small publishers may not have the resources to provide online content in a competitive manner. Managing individual online journal subscriptions may be as costly as managing print journals.

Since there are so many publishers and vendors of online content, and therefore myriad search interfaces and methods of linking to full text, getting from citation to online full text can be quite bewildering to users. Finally, the issue of reliable archival storage of online content is not yet resolved.

While alternative models have been proposed, it is my opinion that they fall short of meeting all stakeholders' needs. Bypassing publishers is a mistake, because they deserve to be adequately compensated for the very real value they add to scholarship. The Open Archives Initiative, for instance, may work, but I do not believe it can support first-copy production of high quality articles over the long run.[17] However, a public goods model is certainly capable of reducing the costs to publishers not related to the first-copy costs of creating content.

Insofar as publishers set creation of high-quality content as their top priority, reducing the cost of overhead is in their interest. There are almost 2000 active, refereed, scholarly journals with library subscription rates of less than $50, and another 1000 have rates less that $100.[18] If it costs $50 to gain a new subscriber to a periodical,[19] surely those publishers would be quite interested in having their first-copy costs paid for, and the content made readily and reliably available to scholars.

Librarians, working in the interest of scholars, desire to increase access to journals. This is certainly true for smaller, less wealthy institutions. Consortial deals and aggregated packages have dramatically improved student access at The College of Saint Rose, but there remains much unmet need. More disturbing is that patrons' need for journals for which we do have online access sometimes goes unmet. Each interface and method of linking to content may be rational, but our users face a very complicated system filled with potential for failed connections. To be able to assist patrons, librarians need a stable, predictable, explainable system for retrieving journal articles online. Libraries also need to minimize the administrative overhead associated with managing access to online journals.

Scholars clearly desire access from a convenient location to as much information as possible via understandable, navigable systems that allow efficient searching.[20] Scholars also have a stake in maintaining, and perhaps even improving, the quality of journal content. Also important, but rarely if ever voiced, is a need to provide scholarly journals to independent and young scholars. There could be great social benefit in giving prodigies and curious laymen broad access to scholarship, to allow them to feed their curiosity with good information. After all, what good is it to tell students the great value of being life-long learners, but then tell them they have to be at a university to keep in touch with scholarship?

CONCLUSION

George Washington believed that periodicals were "more happily calculated than any other [type of publication] to preserve the liberty, stimulate the industry, and meliorate the morals of an enlightened and free people."[21] Washington wrote that in a letter expressing condolence for the financial failure of the *American Museum*. Now as then, scholarly periodicals are important; they should be more widely available, and they need to be more predictably supported.

Now that the Web enables online access, scholarly periodical literature naturally lends itself to be treated as a public good. While aggregations of producers' journals into large databases and organization of libraries into consortia are moving us in that direction, we are in danger of creating an oligopoly that fails to adequately serve the information needs of millions of people. Market forces alone will not adequately fund the social value of scholarly journals. Publishers, librarians and all organizations that support scholarship should choose to treat journals as public goods, and create an adequately funded, equitable system that serves all scholars as efficiently and effectively as possible.

NOTES

1. Agnar Sandmo, "Public goods," *The New Palgrave: A Dictionary of Economics* (New York: Macmillan, 1987): 1061.

2. David W. Pearce, Ed., *The Dictionary of Modern Economics* (Cambridge: MIT Press, 1981): 352-354.

3. Agnar Sandmo, "Public Goods," 1062.

4. Benjamin J. Bates, "Information as an Economic Good: Sources of Individual and Social Value," in Vincent Mosco and Janet Wasko, Eds., *The Political Economy of Information* (Madison: Univeristy of Wisconsin Press, 1988): 76-94.

5. Richard Hamilton, "Patterns of Use for the Bryn Mawr Reviews," in Richard Ekman and Richard E. Quandt, Eds., *Technology and Scholarly Communication* (Berkeley, CA: University of California Press, 1999): 195-204.

6. The most recent data for the number of faculty in the U.S. comes from the National Center for Education Statistics, *Fall Staff in Postsecondary Institutions, 1997*. U.S. Department of Education, November 1999. Available online: *http://nces.ed.gov/pubs2000/2000164.pdf*. Table 1 in this report shows a total of 1,020,786 faculty. Table 2 indicates there are 989,813 faculty classified as "instruction/research/public service."

7. Data on number of students is drawn from "Table A-10: Attendance Status of College Students 15 years and Over," in *Education Statistics of the United States*, 3rd. ed. Lanham, MD: Bernan Press, 2001.

8. U.S. Census Bureau, "Table No. 270: College Enrollment–Summary by Sex, Race, and Hispanic Origin: 1999." *Statistical Abstract of the United States: 2001* (121st Edition) (Washington, DC: U.S. Census Bureau, 2001). Of 15,203,000 college students, 33.1% work full time, and 30.3% work part time.

9. Hamilton, "Patterns of Use for the Bryn Mawr Reviews," p. 200.

10. The potential deadweight losses associated with gift-giving are analyzed in Joel Waldfogel, "The Deadweight Loss of Christmas," *American Economic Review* 83 (1993): 1328-1337. The basic premise Waldfogel investigates is how gifts may leave recipients worse off than if they made their own choices with equal funds.

11. High use of online journals not owned in print is stated clearly by K. Mulliner, Collection Development Coordinator, Ohio University Libraries, in his letter to the Editor of *D-Lib Magazine* "The Big Deal: I Beg to Differ," April 2001, available online at *http://www.dlib.org/dlib/april01/04letters.html*. For the context of that letter, an overview of the "Big Deal" controversy, and a bibliography of the issues surrounding library consortia and online journals in aggregated packages, see Thomas A. Peters, "What's the Big Deal?", *Journal of Academic Librarianship*, 27 (2001): 302-305.

12. James H. Sweetland. "User Access Time: Hard Copy and Microfilm Compared." *Microform Review* 24 (1995): 133-137. Sweetland noted that there were very few studies of access times, and this 1995 article appears to be the most recent quantitative study of user access times.

13. The potential cost savings to libraries of online access is described well by Kevin Guthrie, president of JSTOR, in his "Archiving in the Digital Age: There's a Will, But Is There a Way?", *Educause Review*, 36, no. 6 (2001): 57-65. Available online: *http://www.educasue.edu/ir/library/pdf/erm0164.pdf*

14. For an overview of potential cost savings, and a possible model for electronic publication, see Hal R. Varian, "The Future of Electronic Journals," presented at the Scholarly Communication and Technology Conference at Emory University, April 24-25, 1997. Available online: *http://arl.cni.org/scomm/scat/varian.html*.

15. Information about the New York State Library's activities to provide access to full-text databases and other initiatives, including an explanation of the role of federal funding, may be found in the Library's Division of Library Development document "Will Your Constituents Lose the Economic Advantage of 21st Century Libraries?" March 28, 2002, available online at *http://www.nysl.nysed.gov/libdev/lsta/fundlsta.htm*.

16. EBSCO's rationale behind the position that aggregated full-text databases are not a replacement for individual subscriptions is described by Sam Brooks in his "Issues Facing Academic Library Consortia and Perceptions of Members of the Illinois Digital Academic Library," *Portal: Libraries and the Academy* 2 (2002): 43-57.

17. The Open Archives Initiative and the issues surrounding its creation are described in Jean-Claude Guédon's *Oldenburg's Long Shadow: Librarians, Research Scientists, Publishers, and the Control of Scientific Publishing* (Annapolis Junction, MD: ARL Publications, 2001).

18. *Ulrich's Periodicals Directory* online, accessed February 6, 2002. Out of 16,758 records for active, refereed, scholarly journals, filtering for "<$50" retrieved 1941 records, and filtering for "<$100" retrieved 2913 records.

19. Shulevitz, Judith, "Eulogy for a Little Magazine," *The New York Times on the Web*, November 18, 2001. Retrieved November 18, 2001 from *http://www.nytimes.com*.

20. An overview of university student opinions about user access may be found in John Lubans' " 'When I'm all alone I'm in bad company': defining the user experience," *Library Administration and Management*, 13 (1999): 167-170.

21. Letter to Mathew Carey from George Washington of June 25, 1788, cited in Frank Luther Mott, *A History of American Magazines: 1741-1850*. (Cambridge, MA: Harvard University Press, 1939).

CONTRIBUTOR'S NOTES

Steve Black is Serials, Reference, and Instruction Librarian at the College of Saint Rose.

A Publisher's View of the Public Good: Aspects of Scholarly Publishing

Keith L. Seitter

Presenter

Note: This paper was presented in a concurrent session with Dr. Steve Black, entitled "Scholarly Publication: Business and Public Good?"

SUMMARY. While scholarly journals possess many public good characteristics, it is argued that the scholarly community may be better served in the long run if they are not treated as a public good. The relationships among scholars, academic institutions, and publishers that developed over decades in the era of print journals continue to have value in the era of online delivery and help to ensure quality in a variety of ways. Treating journals as public goods could upset the balance of those relationships in ways that would keep the online dissemination from reaching its fullest potential for the scholarly community. *[Article copies available for a fee from The Haworth Document Delivery Service: 1-800-HAWORTH. E-mail address: <docdelivery@haworthpress.com> Website: <http://www.HaworthPress.com>]*

[Haworth co-indexing entry note]: "A Publisher's View of the Public Good: Aspects of Scholarly Publishing." Seitter, Keith L. Co-published simultaneously in *The Serials Librarian* (The Haworth Information Press, an imprint of The Haworth Press, Inc.) Vol. 44, No. 1/2, 2003, pp. 65-72; and: *Transforming Serials: The Revolution Continues* (ed: Susan L. Scheiberg, and Shelley Neville) The Haworth Information Press, an imprint of The Haworth Press, Inc., 2003, pp. 65-72. Single or multiple copies of this article are available for a fee from The Haworth Document Delivery Service [1-800-HAWORTH, 9:00 a.m. - 5:00 p.m. (EST). E-mail address: docdelivery@haworthpress.com].

http://www.haworthpress.com/store/product.asp?sku=J123
10.1300/J123v44n12_08

INTRODUCTION

My role is to provide a counterpoint to Steve Black's presentation[1]– that is, to address this issue from the publisher's viewpoint rather than the librarian's. I am affiliated with the American Meteorological Society, a nonprofit scientific and professional society that publishes eight journals in the atmospheric and related oceanic and hydrologic sciences. As a member society, our mission is to serve the scientific community, and one aspect of that is ensuring broad dissemination of the research results that are published in our journals. We view our "clients" as being both the authors who publish in our journals and the readers (researchers and students) who use them to further their own scientific study. Both groups are served best if the journals are of high quality in terms of their scholarly content and editorial quality. Both groups are also served best if the journals are easy to obtain and use, which is consistent with what Black is saying. Despite a good deal of agreement, however, I find that the situation from the publisher's perspective takes on a somewhat different view. Although my background is in science and my experience is in working for a scientific publisher, I hope that the discussion provided here is applicable in the broader context of scholarly publication and not just in terms of science journals.

Let me begin by saying that the public good characteristics of scholarly literature are hard to dispute if you limit the discussion to electronic delivery of the content. In that case, it makes sense to draw the analogy to radio since a publisher could provide the content to all who chose to "tune in" through an open Web site. The cost to provide that service freely to all is not only identical to providing it to one through the same means, but is actually less expensive than restricting access to only paid subscribers because the subscription process requires some kind of authorization system that increases the complexity (and therefore cost) of that Web site. The public good argument is more difficult to support for the print publication of journals because that method of delivery depends on printing, postage, etc., that represent real expenditures for each additional user. Following Black's lead, this discussion will therefore concentrate on the public good argument as it applies to online delivery of scholarly journal content.

A LOOK AT THE PRINT WORLD
OF SCHOLARLY PUBLICATION

Before discussing online delivery and its public good aspects, it is useful to review a few aspects of the print world of scholarly publication because print journals have worked very well for a very long time. The infrastructure and publication processes that have developed in the print world of scholarly communication have been refined and honed in a number of ways, resulting in the state of journal publishing that existed at the advent of the online revolution. It is important to recognize that the large number of publishers and large number of print journals have contributed to their perceived value and utility over the years.

The imprimaturs of print journals carry varying levels of prestige, so in nearly any field, the practitioners know where the "best" work is published and authors may either self-select the journals they feel best match the quality of their work, or they may choose to start at the top and let a paper cascade down the ladder of journals until it finds a home in which it is acceptable for publication. To be sure, gems sometimes land in unexpected places, and in virtually every discipline one can cite seminal papers that for one reason or another were published in low-prestige or obscure journals. For the most part, however, the most important work appears in the most prestigious journals, and libraries and individual subscribers have been able to select a relatively small number of journals in any particular field with some confidence of missing only the occasional truly significant paper. Few institutions have ever had the resources to subscribe to more than a fraction of the journals in any discipline, but given the labor required to stay abreast of all that is published in a large collection of print journals, the restriction to having access to only the "top" journals may have been a hidden benefit to the scholars at those institutions.

Until very recent times, it can be argued that the economics of the print journals had also been honed to a delicate balance. I cannot speak for the humanities, but in the sciences, the structure in place has benefited the entire scholarly community in a number of ways. In the typical scenario, the university researcher receives a grant from a federal agency that often includes a line item for publication charges. The university takes its cut off the top as indirect charges, including its percentage of the funds tagged for publication, with some of these indirect funds earmarked (at least on paper, if not in fact) for support to the university library. The investigator does his or her work and submits the paper for publication, using the grant funds allocated for publication expenses to pay page charges to the publisher. The publisher uses the page charge revenue to cover at least part of the cost of publication, including the peer review so critical to the prestige of the journal, and recovers the rest of its costs through income from subscriptions, including probably a subscription to the university from which that paper had originated. So, the public funds used to produce the research help to maintain the university's infra-structure through indirect charges, which support the scholarly enterprise for even those scholars not carrying out funded research, and also provide the funding to get the research results into print and effectively dissemi-nated to the rest of the world through a journal.

At this point, some have suggested that public funds "pay for the re-search twice"–once with the grant money to produce it, and then again to buy it back from the publisher. This argument fails to acknowledge the role really played by the subscription to a journal. The university's sub-scription to the journal is not "buying back" the research of its own schol-ars, but rather, all the *other* research published in that journal. All these other research results are critical to the work of the institution's own in-vestigator, who must use and build upon this related research in order for his or her efforts to be of the caliber required for publication in a journal of that quality. In fact, the library is getting quite a deal on most journals (with a few notable exceptions) in that the journal provides a window into the research results of all those other scholars in a selected discipline at a cost that is typically only a few dollars per article.

So, over a number of decades, a complicated symbiotic relationship has developed between scholarly institutions, publishers, and, at least in the case of the sciences, public funding agencies. The scholarly institu-tions rely on the publishers and their journals to filter and "grade" the research as a means of judging the quality of the work of its scholars, the results of which then play a significant role in the tenure and promotion of those scholars. For grant-funded research, the competitive funding process uses an investigator's publication record, in part, as a measure of past performance, with success in that publication record helping to secure the grant. Then, once awarded, the grant funds help to support the journal publication through both direct and indirect funds in ways that support the infrastructure of the institution as well as supporting the publisher. Educational institutions (public and private) that do not have strong research programs take advantage of the lower subscription fees resulting from the public funds paid through the research institutions so that students may have access to the literature.

THE CHANGING WORLD OF JOURNALS
IN THE ONLINE ERA

In a very short period of time (when compared to the time scholarly journals have been around), the finely honed print journal structure has been upset irrevocably. This is the result not of the "online revolution" being experienced in the publishing world, but more significantly, it is the result of the exponential increase in scholarly output. The number of pages published has been growing at a rate far exceeding monetary inflation, so even for those publishers who have not increased the price per page of their subscriptions, the subscription prices have risen at a pace that has outstripped the library budgets across the country. Universities and other scholarly research institutions have found needs for the indirect funds generated by grants that have kept them from increasing funding to the libraries at a rate that would allow even those most prestigious of journals to continue to fill the shelves. So, libraries are forced to look at cutting "core" journals that are extremely important for their scholars and for students.[2]

In the midst of this "serials crisis," the online publishing revolution emerged as a possible solution. Suddenly, the dissemination of the scholarly research was "nearly free" and one could envision a time in which all barriers to scholarly results were removed.[3] Some argued that the publisher could now be removed from the process altogether, and for journals operating on a small scale (that is, small enough for dedicated volunteers to carry out the entire process) this was clearly shown to be possible. Others argued that while the publisher's imprimatur was still important, it was only the stringent peer review that was needed to make a journal one of "high quality," so publishers should abandon all else and allow the resulting savings to provide the journals online for free.[4] Still others acknowledged the role of editorial quality on the prestige of the journal, and did not advocate the abandonment of print, but encouraged authors to pay a little more to the publisher to allow their articles to be freely available online–even if in only a static PDF format.[5] Finally, still others claimed that publishers should recover their investment within six months and after that make the online version free to all.[6]

In the midst of all these calls for reform of one degree or another, most publishers found that abandoning print altogether would not save as much money as many thought, and that adding online access in addition to print was expensive.[7] What's more, many librarians began to rightly point out that it is not at all clear how to ensure access to electronic online journals for future generations of scholars.[8] Without an acceptable archival solution in hand, some of the same librarians grappling with the serials crisis are urging publishers to not abandon print too quickly.

WHERE THINGS STAND

While there are a number of ways that the Web can be used to make scholarly content freely accessible, such as author self-archiving into repositories that can be "mined" by open archive servers, the sheer volume of scholarly material produced every year makes the sorting and grading process carried out by the established publisher more important now than it ever was. The symbiotic relationship between scholarly institutions and publishers has not really changed, and even in the face of clear-cut pricing abuse by some publishers, the prestigious journals published by them still carry the most weight toward tenure and promotion decisions.

I began by saying that both authors and readers were best served if the journals ensured high quality in both scholarly content and editorial quality and if the journals were easy to obtain and easy to use. Stringent peer review helps to assure high quality of the scholarly content, while publishing professionals can help to ensure high editorial quality so that scholars and students work from error-free presentations of the information. Making the content easy to obtain and easy to use does not simply mean making it available from its primary source at an affordable price and in a readable format. It also means making the presentation work for the user in ways that save time and effort, and working to ensure that other scholarly resources draw users to the content even if they were not previously aware of it. Publishers are just beginning to exploit some of these concepts when they link reference citations in one journal to the full text articles in another.[9] Imagine the value to readers (especially students) if accessing an article launched an Amazon.com-like script saying "readers of this article also found the following related articles useful." Other examples of making the content work for the user include making the presentation optimized for reading effectively on the screen or for printing, at the choice of the users, and making the content accessible to the visually impaired.

SHOULD THE JOURNALS BE TREATED AS A PUBLIC GOOD?

As appealing as it is to view the online delivery of scholarly journals as a public good and argue in favor of journals being made freely available to all through long-term stable funding, this approach might not provide the most benefit to the scholarly community as a whole. Authors and readers will have maximum benefit if they can take full advantage of what online delivery can offer in its most value-added form. Providing these value-added features will require a continuing investment by publishers that will require a continued source of funding. Users of the journals should be willing to pay for these features because of the savings in time and effort they will experience as a result of them. The need to improve the value-added features continuously to justify the subscription rate will drive publishers to push the technology to its limits, and the users' feedback will drive the process toward those features that have the greatest impact. This is already evident in the cooperative efforts of publishers to implement cross-journal linking among even rival journals.

If publishers can expect stable funding without this pressure, there will be far less incentive to maintain high quality (in all its measures) and virtually no reason to push the technology. Mediocrity will be rewarded by higher profit margins compared to the publisher investing in making the journal better. So, as much as I would like to see a funding structure that would make my budget worries disappear, I know that the competitive pressure we feel as a publisher in these times of rapid change make us run a leaner operation and search for ways to make the final product better and more useful to our subscribers.

This does not resolve the issues of access faced by many, especially faculty and students at smaller institutions, that Black has articulated so well. There are some ways to address aspects of this, but none are wholly satisfying. One approach is already in place and already being taken advantage of by many—consortia pricing arrangements. These often deal with the large collections from commercial publishers rather than the journals produced by the smaller publishers because the investment in negotiations is so large that it only makes sense if the result includes many titles. Another approach that helps is for publishers to have differential pricing that gives a significant break to the smaller institutions who might otherwise not subscribe at all. This is a win-win situation since the smaller institution gains access at a low cost and the publisher picks up a subscription that, while smaller in income, is still an addition where there was nothing before.

Finally, it is worth mentioning that for all journal publishers, it is possible to construct a business model that includes the prospect of content reaching an age at which it has paid for its creation and at which it can be given away at no cost to the user with no impact on paid subscriptions. For some journals that might be six months, for others six years, but when content reaches that point it makes sense to open access to that content so that it is freely available to all. In that way, the public good characteristics of the journal content can be at least partially acknowledged.

NOTES

1. Black, Steve, "Scholarly Journals Should Be Treated as a Public Good," *The Serials Librarian* 44 (2003): 53-63.

2. For examples, see the Create Change Web site at http://www.arl.org/create/home.html.

3. Harnad, Stevan, "The self-archiving initiative: Freeing the refereed research literature online." *Nature* 410 (2001): 1024-1025.

4. A full discussion on the pros and cons of many of these approaches to freeing the literature can be gleaned from the archived electronic discussion list at http://amsci-forum.amsci.org/archives/september98-forum.html.

5. Walker, Thomas J., "Free Internet Access to Traditional Journals," *American Scientist* 86 (1998): 463-471.

6. See, for example, the Public Library of Science Web site at http://www.publiclibraryofscience.org/.

7. King, Donald W., and Carol Tenopir, "Economic Cost Models of Scientific Scholarly Journals." Presented to the ICSU Press Workshop, Oxford, UK, 31 March to 2 April 1998. Available online at http//www.bodley.ox.ac.uk/icsu/kingppr.htm.

8. A good overview of the issues involved for long-term preservation is provided on the Digital Library Federation Web site at http://www.diglib.org/preserve.htm.

9. See, for example, the CrossRef Web site at http://www.crossref.org/.

CONTRIBUTOR'S NOTES

Dr. Keith Seitter is the Deputy Executive Director of the American Meteorological Society.

Challenging Current Publishing Models

Jan Velterop
David Goodman

Presenters

Virginia A. Rumph

Recorder

Jan Velterop told the story of Vic Nodgudinov, whose non life-threatening ailment requires many expensive pills to keep his condition bearable. However, as the financial burden gets worse year after year, Vic is forced to cut back on some of the medicines. He must learn to live with the resulting pain and side effects. Vic's middle name is Tim, and his last name increasingly describes his condition: Not Good Enough. STM publishing is a gold mine for the publishers who acquire the material for virtually nothing and make $5,000 per article. What are the consumers' options under these conditions? They can negotiate, accept decreases in their collections or access, or think of something else. Besides the cost factor, the present model no longer suits scientific communication.

The wind of change is blowing. The publishing model must change, and it will become more efficient. What characteristics identify this wind of change? From print to electronic, limited access to unlimited access, slow to fast, low usage to high usage, paid access to free access, expensive to less expensive, and output paid to input paid. Infrastructure may have to change from reader paid to author paid, but either way, academia is ultimately paying the scholarly publishing costs. If the cri-

[Haworth co-indexing entry note]: "Challenging Current Publishing Models." Rumph, Virginia A. Co-published simultaneously in *The Serials Librarian* (The Haworth Information Press, an imprint of The Haworth Press, Inc.) Vol. 44. No. 1/2, 2003, pp. 73-75; and: *Transforming Serials: The Revolution Continues* (ed: Susan L. Scheiberg, and Shelley Neville) The Haworth Information Press, an imprint of The Haworth Press, Inc., 2003, pp. 73-75. Single or multiple copies of this article are available for a fee from The Haworth Document Delivery Service [1-800-HAWORTH, 9:00 a.m. - 5:00 p.m. (EST). E-mail address: docdelivery@haworthpress.com].

http://www.haworthpress.com/store/product.asp?sku=J123
10.1300/J123v44n12_09

terion we use to determine what share each institution pays becomes articles published, then publication becomes an extension of the research effort. Open access becomes possible. Velterop is sure the time has come for open access because the technology is mature, librarians are losing the budget battle, scientists are waking up to the severe disadvantages of restrictive access, and the old model is no longer suitable. Using BioMed Central as an example, how does open access work? An article is submitted for publication; peer-review is arranged; if the article is accepted, the author is charged $500 (less or free for developing countries); it is immediately published; fully-coded HTML and PDF are available one week later; there are no restrictions on access. Why is open access taking so long to gain critical mass? A cultural revolution is required to change deeply engrained habits. Enough researchers must choose to publish in open access journals for open access to succeed.

David Goodman posed the question "How long can the present STM journal system continue?" Using diagrams, he showed the current flow of money and work in the STM publishing model and the several disruptions that could occur. The public funding agencies that supply most of the money for STM research stop or slow the flow of funds; libraries cancel titles they can no longer afford; university administrations shift allocations from researchers or the library budget; researchers decide to boycott certain high-priced journals. Goodman mentioned several initiatives (Public Library of Science, Open Archive Initiative), facilitators (SPARC, OAI), and publishers (BioOne, BioMed Central) that are trying to change the current model. BioMed Central is a commercial initiative with open access for research papers, 75 open-access journals (and counting), authors paying to get published, and supplemental income from advertising and acting as sales agent for review journals published by sister companies. The Budapest Open Access Initiative is led by the Soros Foundation with the agreed outcome of stimulating self-archiving, open-access journals and funding plausible initiatives over the next three years. The OAI E-Print Archives (ArXiV) model is inexpensive, has rapid publication, is searchable, interoperable, has permanent redundant backup, is compatible with current publishing, is compatible with refereeing, is academically acceptable, and is proven to work.

Goodman examined four factors for change: user desire for e-prints, general economic conditions, desire for change in the academic world, and publisher options. Either article-based servers or a journal-based system could replace the current model. Based on the results of his analysis, Goodman outlined three potential scenarios. In the case of the exponential e-print growth model, journal usage drops off sharply and sooner. Using the linear e-print or BioMed Central growth model, conventional journal usage decreases gradually as e-print and open-access journal usage rises gradually. The stable publisher strategy model shows the most gradual shift from conventional journals to e-prints and open access journals. However, all the new models predict the demise of the conventional STM journal by 2008. It will happen; only the "when" is in doubt. Inertia will not continue indefinitely.

CONTRIBUTORS' NOTES

Jan Velterop is Publisher, BioMed Central Group. David Goodman is Biology Librarian, Princeton University. Virginia A. Rumph is Serials Librarian at Butler University.

The OpenURL and SFX Linking

Nettie Lagace

Prsenter

SUMMARY. Library users wish to navigate seamlessly between library resources, and librarians wish to provide this capability to them. The OpenURL is a newly emerging standard in the library world that will allow librarians to create their own local links between the resources they choose for their users. Link servers such as SFX help librarians manage upkeep and resolution of links. *[Article copies available for a fee from The Haworth Document Delivery Service: 1-800-HAWORTH. E-mail address: <docdelivery@haworthpress.com> Website: <http://www.HaworthPress.com>]*

WHY LINK?

Any library, no matter its size, its user population, or its specialization, will make many different kinds of material available to library users. Materials may originate from different vendors and could be library catalogs, abstract and indexing databases, full-text databases, and/or interlibrary loan and document delivery servers. Reasons for purchase of disparate materials may vary from subject matter and importance to researchers, to cost, to accessibility. Because materials are of different types, it is often difficult to organize and present these materials to users under one common interface or even with one research approach. Bib-

---

[Haworth co-indexing entry note]: "The OpenURL and SFX Linking." Lagace, Nettie. Co-published simultaneously in *The Serials Librarian* (The Haworth Information Press, an imprint of The Haworth Press, Inc.) Vol. 44, No. 1/2, 2003, pp. 77-89; and: *Transforming Serials: The Revolution Continues* (ed: Susan L. Scheiberg, and Shelley Neville) The Haworth Information Press, an imprint of The Haworth Press, Inc., 2003, pp. 77-89. Single or multiple copies of this article are available for a fee from The Haworth Document Delivery Service [1-800-HAWORTH, 9:00 a.m. - 5:00 p.m. (EST). E-mail address: docdelivery@haworthpress.com].

http://www.haworthpress.com/store/product.asp?sku=J123
10.1300/J123v44n12_10

liographic instruction classes become focused more around vendor-specific pathways than common-sense research approaches.

Though they are different types, materials contained in different places in the library environment are often closely related. A citation in an article reference or abstract database may have its full-text counterpart available in an electronic journal subscribed to by the library, via an aggregator database, or in a bound volume available in the library stacks. One article's authors may be cited by other related articles, which may be potentially useful to a library user. A document delivery service may be available for information not specifically held by the library. Book reviews, book jacket pictures, etc. may be available for book records in the catalog.

Linking to one resource from another in the library environment is a natural and suitable activity and one that already occurs in more than one way today.

"OLD-STYLE" AND VENDOR-SPECIFIC LINKING

It's not hard to set up an initial set of links from one library resource to another. All it takes is the knowledge of the URL (uniform resource locator, or Web address) of the item you wish to link *to*–let's call it a link "target"–and the ability to embed this URL in the item you wish to link *from*–let's call it a link "source."

This is often called "hard linking" and it is quite practical–that is, straightforward in initial setup–but often not very durable. Journals may move from publisher to publisher, or vendors may change the maintenance and makeup of their servers, and these hard-coded URLs may change. Then it becomes necessary to determine that the link is no longer working, and to find the location of the new, proper link, *and* to make the necessary update in the source record. Anyone who maintains 856 links in a catalog probably knows well about how this update process works.

Another effect of vendor-specific linking is that links to the items held by a local library appear differently to an end user depending on which vendor's interface you are starting from as a source. For example, ISI, Ovid, FirstSearch, and SilverPlatter display links to full text, but these links appear in different areas of the abstract page and all say slightly different things. Linking is not under the local control of the library.

Where outbound linking is under the control of a vendor rather than a local library, the library is subject to links in databases having certain qualities. Usually these qualities lead to negative effects for the library. For example, where links maintained by a vendor are available, they are often dependent on specific business agreements between that vendor and other vendors. The library may or may not subscribe to the specific journals to which the product links. Or, libraries are required to purchase access to the journals linked to in a database, whether or not these journals are part of their collection development policy. So, links that exist in a database are non-context-sensitive; they don't have a one-to-one relationship to what the library actually subscribes to, or wishes to link to.

Second, these links are of a few types, or to limited services; simply pointing to full text or possibly to the library catalog. These links do not take advantage of the other databases or services offered by the library that may be related to the item at which the user is looking.

Alternatively, vendors will allow libraries to localize links available from their product, but what this means in practical terms is that the library must continually update the information they maintain for *each* vendor whose abstract databases they subscribe to. Local holdings change too often for this task to be easy to attend to.

Enter a new way to link: using OpenURL to link *out* from source databases. The idea behind having databases become OpenURL-aware is that libraries may now set up links between the databases and materials that they subscribe to as *they* deem helpful for their users, not as vendors design. It is now possible to allow users to navigate seamlessly and meaningfully among the resources that librarians have selected for them.

METADATA ALREADY EXISTS IN DATABASE RECORDS

Metadata that exists in a record in a citation database can be used to supply creative types of services that are under the control of the local library. Here are a few examples of the general idea behind the relationship between metadata available in database records and *extended services* that libraries may wish to create:

- ISSN, year, volume, issue, start page can be used to create a link from the citation to the article at a publisher's Web site or in an aggregator database.

- ISSN or journal name can be used to check for print holdings in the library catalog, whether or not electronic full-text is available.
- Author names can be used to look up the authors in a citation or other abstract databases to see other articles they have written or how well-cited they are.
- Subject terms from the original citation can be re-used in other related databases or to link to Web sites that librarians judge potentially useful.
- ISSN or journal name can be used to look up the journal in a serials directory to find out more general information about the journal–its publication schedule, where it is indexed, publisher information, etc.

The important thing to remember is that the links created in these situations are *appropriate*–meaning that local librarians take an active role in their creation; they appear or do not appear subject to local decisions; *and* they link to material that is really available to the users of that library.

The same types of metadata that appear in citation databases also appear in references included in online full text articles. If the full text article database is made OpenURL-aware, the same sorts of extended services could be made available for *each reference.*

WHAT IT TAKES TO LINK
TO EXTENDED (LOCAL) SERVICES

The solution to allow libraries to control their own links is to throw the concept of hard-coded linking to the four winds and introduce local link servers. Link servers, also known as link resolvers, are necessary to maintain information about where librarians wish their users to link and to keep resulting target links up to date. These link servers come in different flavors, from different vendors, often with different capabilities and features and management options. My discussion will often refer to the SFX link server available from Ex Libris.

Under the "traditional" linking scenario, a source database contains a "hard" link to a target item. Resolution of links–making sure the user is sent where s/he ought to go–is the job of the source database, meaning that if the link changes, it must be updated *in the source record.* Also, hard links by their nature can go only to one target: one link, one target.

In contrast, link resolving using OpenURLs introduces a third component placed in the middle of the transaction: a local link server. The end user still sees a link in the source database and is prompted to click on it based on its appearance, words, etc. However, instead of being a URL that describes the target document, this URL is special: it is an *OpenURL* that describes, using metadata, *the item or citation that the user is looking at.*

An example of a simple OpenURL describing an article written by PM Colman published in the journal *Virology* in 2001 could be:

```
http://sfx.aaa.edu/menu?genre=article&issn=0042-
6822&volume=290&issue=2&spage=290&date=2001&aulast=Colman&auinit=PM
```

OpenURLs, unlike hard links, are not delivered directly to targets. They are pointed to a link server, an intermediary server that has the responsibility for determining to which target or targets the user should be delivered, and the addresses or URLs for those targets.

A crucial aspect of introducing the link server into the linking scenario is that the link server is maintained by the library and contains data on the journals, catalogs, document delivery servers, and other databases and services to which the librarians desire their users to be able to link. This is what we mean by "context-sensitive" linking: users of a particular citation database at Library A see their links; users of the same database at Library B see *their* links.

The library may subscribe to OpenURL-aware products from a variety of vendors. Although the vendors are different, each one sends its OpenURLs to the same library link server, so the library has to maintain data in a single place rather than many.

A link server receives metadata about items from where users come (referents) on the OpenURL and it can re-use this metadata to create new links to where users can be sent (appropriate targets). The OpenURL is simply a way to package metadata in a standard syntax and send it on a URL so that it can be used to create and resolve new links.

With a link server like SFX acting as an intermediary link resolver, librarians can create new pathways for their users. For example, a library user could begin her search in an abstract and indexing database. From a citation there, she could then be shown a menu of choices which would link her to the full text of her citation, a record in the library's catalog showing her where to obtain it in print form, or a Web-based document delivery form, already filled in for her. Other choices on the menu could be a search on the Web or a Web encyclopedia using title or subject words, or author searches in other related databases.

OpenURL linking has some important advantages over its hard-coded link counterparts:

- Link servers can enable the localization of links. No longer are librarians subject to vendor decisions on where to send their users.
- Link servers can provide extended services. Librarians can choose to simply provide links to full text, or choose new services based on the variety of metadata delivered on the OpenURL.
- Link servers furnish a single point of administration for the various services for potentially all data sources. Because all OpenURL-aware vendors will point their OpenURLs toward the library's one link server, it becomes the only place where librarians need to supply holdings information.
- Link servers set up standardization of services across resources, as defined by librarians. End users can see the same graphic button directing them to the library's link server via OpenURL and will experience the same service menu look-and-feel, no matter in which resource they start their search. Library users will know that their local librarians furnish the services.

MORE ABOUT THE OPENURL

The OpenURL syntax description was developed by Herbert Van de Sompel, Oren Beit-Arie and Patrick Hochstenbach. NISO accepted the OpenURL as a fast-track work item and formed the Committee AX to consider its adoption and implementation. More information about this committee's work and the OpenURL itself can be found at:

```
http://library.caltech.edu/openurl.
```

The existing draft syntax was adopted by Committee AX as OpenURL version 0.1. Version 1.0 has been written and will be tested by vendors and libraries in early 2003. It builds on the existing syntax description by introducing further mechanisms for extensibility–including further information about who the user is, where they are coming from, and further types of information they may be looking at. Version 0.1 is in use by vendors today.

OpenURLs can be composed in different ways, but the components of an OpenURL always are the base URL, which is the server address for the service component, and the query, which is a description of the object: metadata and/or identifiers supporting the delivery of link services. In the example given earlier in this article, the base URL is:

```
http://sfx.aaa.edu/menu?genre=article&issn=1234-
5678&volume=12&issue=3&spage=8&date=1999&aulast=Smith&aufirst=Paul
http://sfx.aaa.edu/menu?
```

and the query is:

```
genre=article&issn=1234-
5678&volume=12&issue=3&spage=8&date=1999&aulast=Smith&aufirst=Paul
```

This is a simple example of an OpenURL, where the metadata that is sent is described using a set of standard descriptors, ISSN, volume, author last name, etc.

An important aspect of the OpenURL syntax is that it can be constructed in different ways to accommodate a vendor's particular set-up or database system differences. So an OpenURL constructed by one vendor may differ significantly from an OpenURL constructed by another vendor.

A very important piece of information usually sent on an OpenURL is the "sid," or source identifier. It supplies the link server with the identification of the vendor and database sending the OpenURL, and it can be invaluable for providing accurate services.

Metadata can be sent on an OpenURL using its "object-metadata-zone" which includes a set of tags describing bibliographic information such as ISSN or ISBN, volume, issue, start page, title, etc. Metadata available in a record may extend beyond these available tags; for example, it may be desirable to send a patent number to a link server, or send information about multiple authors (the object-metadata-zone allows for only one author).

Therefore, the OpenURL has available a "local-identifier-zone"or "pid," meaning private identifier. Any kind of information, as long as it is URL-encoded, can be sent on a pid. The link server, using the sid as a means of identifying the source, can then use an internal program written especially for it to interpret the information sent on the pid. This information can then be used to present additional services. Alternatively, information sent on a pid could be used by the link server to conduct a Z39.50 connection back to the source database to retrieve additional metadata about the item the user is looking at. This Z39.50 session takes place "behind the scenes," server-to-server, and is not seen by the end user; it should not slow down the process of displaying the service menu.

Another useful zone of the OpenURL is known as the "global-identi-fier-zone." This zone can be used to transmit identifiers which are "globally" accepted by librarians as pertaining to a particular data type. For example, an acceptable OpenURL sending a direct object identifier (DOI) on the global-identifier-zone would be:

```
http://sfx.aaa.edu/menu?id=doi=10.1014/abcdefg
```

Because the DOI is itself nothing more than a string of numbers and letters, the link server can query (again, server-to-server, transparent to the end user) an outside database of metadata such as the CrossRef pub-lisher metadata database, and retrieve metadata associated with a DOI. It would then use this metadata to provide local services such as a link to the catalog using the journal ISSN, or a link to the full text either at the publisher's Web site or in another database licensed by the library.

The OpenURL is catching on in the library marketplace, in no small part due to the efforts of librarians who have spoken to their vendors to explain the benefits of incorporating this new standard.

Databases other than abstracting and indexing databases can be used as link sources, though these are an obvious good choice because of the fact that they usually contain only citations, no full text of their own. Library OPACs, if made OpenURL-aware by the integrated library system vendor, could also serve as link sources and then there would be no need to maintain 856 links since the link upkeep would be the job of the central link server.

E-journals, including the Institute of Physics (IOP) and ScienceDirect journals, are now OpenURL-aware. DOI links can also be redirected to point to a link server to enable localized DOI linking.

OpenURL-enabling is not limited to the vendor world; many of our SFX customers have set up their own local databases containing local faculty citations or company product literature to deliver OpenURLs.

A list of vendors which have made their databases OpenURL-aware appears at the SFX Web site at http://www.sfxit.com/sources.html. We have also included appropriate configuration files and source entries in the SFX product.

THE SFX FLOW

When a library has an SFX link server installed, its patron base can benefit from it, as this example demonstrates: a user finds a useful citation in a source database, in this case an abstracting and indexing database. He or she sees an SFX button, which is nothing more than a small graphic embedded in the HTML of the page, meant to get attention and signal the existence of extended services. Many vendors support button customization.

Behind the image (IMG) tag for that button in the page's HTML is an OpenURL which contains the metadata corresponding to the citation the user is viewing. When the user clicks this SFX button, the OpenURL is sent to the library's local SFX server, which consists of a local database and configuration files. The metadata sent in the OpenURL is compared to information contained in the local database 'describing' the library's holdings and targets, and the SFX server can output an "SFX Menu" of suitable local services, which have been decided on in advance by libraries at the institution. SFX will keep the metadata delivered on the OpenURL, for, when the user chooses an item from the SFX Menu, it will re-use it in order to create a new link, this time to the ultimate SFX target. For example, OpenURL delivered:

```
http://sfxserver.university.edu:8888/local?sid=vendorname:db
&genre=article&issn=0022-538X&volume=75&issue=23&spage=11868
&epage=11873&date=2001&part=&title=JOURNAL+OF+VIROLOGY
&aulast=Nakaya&auinit=T
&atitle=Recombinant+Newcastle+disease+virus+as+a+vaccine+vector
&pid=<authors>Nakaya,T|Cros,J|Park,MS|Nakaya,Y<authors>
```

SFX extracts the following metadata from the OpenURL:
Title: Recombinant Newcastle disease virus as a vaccine vector
Source: JOURNAL OF VIROLOGY [0022-538X]
yr: 2001 vol: 75 iss: 23 pg: 11868
Authors: Nakaya, T; Cros, J; Park, MS; Nakaya, Y
SFX uses this metadata to create a new link to the HighWire Press target using a prediction program written for that publisher:

```
http://jvi.asm.org/cgi/content/full/75/23/11868
```

If the link to the target should change, for example, if the journal moves or the publisher decides to change the server organization, then the prediction program will be changed, updating all links created subsequently.

References at the end of an online article could be obtained in full text in the same process. Each reference contains its own OpenURL. Even if electronic full text is not available the user can be offered an option to look up the journal in the library's catalog.

THE SFX LINK SERVER AND KNOWLEDGEBASE

An SFX server consists of a database and configuration files. When a library implements SFX, the local librarians decide what kinds of services they would like to present to a user "in a perfect world"–that is, if all metadata elements are present–and configure the SFX server accordingly. Examples of services that could be shown in an SFX Menu are "Full Text," "Holdings," "Document Delivery," "Web Search," etc.

The SFX link server:

- Accepts OpenURL as input from information resource
- Analyzes contents of OpenURL
- Evaluates appropriate Services to be shown on SFX Menu based on metadata received and contents of localized KnowledgeBase
- Creates SFX Menu
- Dynamically computes links to target Services chosen by end user, using metadata

On the other side of the picture, after an SFX Menu is created there appear SFX targets–places for a user to choose to go.

SFX comes with pre-defined target services covering not only electronic journal providers but also other extended services to link to; for example, a range of OPACs from different vendors, patent databases, and Internet bookstores.

A library is not limited to what is already configured in SFX; it's also possible to set up original, local targets in SFX; they work best if there is some kind of link-to or search syntax that can be imitated by a program. Note that there is no described standard for a link-to syntax (or "inbound linking") the way there is for the OpenURL or "outbound linking."

To date our customers have defined and implemented many different and interesting target services, for example, "Look for other books on this subject in Books in Print," "Look up this movie in the Internet Movie Database," "Look up this journal in Journal Citation Reports," etc. With OpenURLs delivering metadata contained within databases and available link-to syntaxes enabling re-use of that metadata, libraries can potentially link from anywhere to anywhere.

SFX works through the relationship of three major parts, all of which are managed centrally through a tool known to SFX customers as "KBManager" (KnowledgeBase Manager). The three parts are:

- Definition of *potential* services: the SFX KnowledgeBase, or underlying database, contains information on different information which is *generally* available–sources (databases which are OpenURL aware) and targets (journals, aggregator databases, catalogs, Web sites, etc. which can be linked to).
- Information about the local collections: librarians must localize their SFX database; that is, they must "activate" the items in the database which match their local subscriptions. For example, if a library subscribes to 500 journals from ScienceDirect, it must turn on the items in the SFX KnowledgeBase that match those journals.
- Rules supporting a decision on the relevance of services: These are rules placed on individual items in the database to ensure that the services returned on the SFX menu will resolve to "good" targets. For example, if an OpenURL contains information on a citation for a journal from 1990,and the library's electronic subscription to that journal begins in 1996, there needs to be a rule in the KnowledgeBase to prevent that full-text link from showing on the user's SFX menu, since the library does not have access to that journal for the time period that the user is seeking. Or, if users of the campus medical library should be shown a separate document delivery service than users of the main library, there needs to be a rule in the SFX database to show the proper document delivery service to the proper users.

The underlying SFX KnowledgeBase is regularly updated with changes in aggregator content, journal moves from publisher to publisher, and date updates as backfiles become available. These updates are then distributed to SFX customers.

Ex Libris provides Web-based tools for local administrators to manage the KnowledgeBase. Local collections can be reflected in the KnowledgeBase on a single basis, or by batch loading if local subscription information, particularly on e-journals, is available elsewhere, e.g., in an Excel spreadsheet or other database, or from a library's subscription agent.

A benefit of maintaining a central link server such as SFX is the ability to view the activity of this server. SFX usage is generated when OpenURLs are delivered and when target links are constructed. A few of the reports that can be generated from SFX are:

- How many times did users click the SFX button within a specific resource?

- How many times was the article's full text available via the SFX Menu?
- If the article's full text is available, how many times did users select other services from the SFX Menu?

Once a library localizes the SFX KnowledgeBase, the information contained there can be re-used in other ways. Ex Libris includes a script in the SFX package which exports and creates HTML pages listing the full-text journals to which the library subscribes, along with dates and publishers or aggregators where the journal is available. SFX customers can edit HTML templates used by the script, so the task of creating updated journal listings can be completed literally within a few minutes.

In response to ideas generated by librarians who came to our booth last year at ALA, we created a little tool called "Citation Linker" which allows library end users to create OpenURLs on the fly; perhaps users wander up to the reference desk or even to the library home page with a citation written down on a piece of paper. By inputting their own data into this form, they can create an OpenURL which will query the library's SFX server and create an SFX menu. This form can be used as-is or customized to be incorporated into a library's Web pages.

By using a central link server like SFX, what a library displays to its users is under its control. Ex Libris supplies an "out of the box" SFX Menu, but many customers have started to make the menu resemble their home pages, as an added reminder to end users that the services are presented by that particular library.

SFX also has an option *not* to show an SFX Menu. A library might be interested in using SFX to link only to full text, not to any other extended service, and in that case, no menu would appear, and rather the user would be redirected to the correct target link when s/he clicks the SFX button in the source database.

CONCLUSION

In summary, the OpenURL is an important mechanism that enables libraries to 'open up' the databases they subscribe to and make the information contained there available to other databases and applications. Though the OpenURL is about to be fully standardized, I believe we are only at the beginning of what can be achieved through the imagination and perseverence of librarians.

ADDITIONAL READING

Stephens, Owen. "SFX @ RHUL." UK Serials Group Annual Conference, April 2002. *http://www.sfxit.com/publications/presentations/SFX_UKSG_2002_Owen.ppt* (9 August 2002).

Blake, Miriam. "SFX at Los Alamos." VALA, Melbourne Australia. January 2002. *http://lib-www.lanl.gov/lww/articles/OpenURL_vala.pdf* (9 August 2002).

McDonald, John. "SFX @ Caltech." ALA Annual, San Francisco CA, 16 and 18 June 2001. http://library.caltech.edu/john/sfx/(9 August 2002).

Caplan, Priscilla. 2001. "A Lesson in Linking." Library Journal NetConnect supplement. Fall 2001. *http://libraryjournal.reviewsnews.com/index.asp?layout= article&articleid=CA177643* (9 August 2002).

Van de Sompel, Herbert and Oren Beit-Arie. "Open Linking in the Scholarly Information Environment Using the OpenURL Framework." D-Lib Magazine. 7(3) 2001. *http://www.dlib.org/dlib/march01/vandesompel/03vandesompel.html* (9 August 2002).

Van de Sompel, Herbert and Oren Beit-Arie. "Generalizing the OpenURL Framework Beyond References to Scholarly Works: The Bison Futé Model." D-Lib Magazine. 7(3) 2001. *http://www.dlib.org/dlib/july01/vandesompel/07vandesompel.html* (9 August 2002).

Beit-Arie, Oren et al. "Linking to the Appropriate Copy." D-Lib Magazine. 9(3) 2001. *http://www.dlib.org/dlib/sept01/caplan/09caplan.html* (9 August 2002).

CONTRIBUTOR'S NOTES

Nettie Lagace is SFX Librarian with Ex Libris (USA), Inc.

Seize the E!
The Eclectic Journal and Its Ramifications

Gerry McKiernan

Presenter

SUMMARY. In recent years, an increasing number of electronic journals have embedded audio, video, and other multimedia within their publication to augment their usefulness. In addition, some have further enhanced access and use with a variety of "eclectic" features, functionalities, and content, such as advanced navigation; font, format, and display control; modeling; personalization and customization options; and reader participation. In general, most cataloging records, however, do not reflect such components, depriving users of the necessary information and instruction that could facilitate use. A variety of recommendations and options are reviewed as possible solutions. *[Article copies available for a fee from The Haworth Document Delivery Service: 1-800-HAWORTH. E-mail address: <docdelivery@haworthpress.com> Website: <http://www.HaworthPress.com>]*

THE ELECTRONIC JOURNAL

For many in the academic environment, the concept of the "electronic library" is synonymous with electronic journal (or e-journal) collections. Overall, of the more than 164,000 serial titles reported in a

[Haworth co-indexing entry note]: "Seize the E! The Eclectic Journal and Its Ramifications." McKiernan, Gerry. Co-published simultaneously in *The Serials Librarian* (The Haworth Information Press, an imprint of The Haworth Press, Inc.) Vol. 44, No. 1/2, 2003, pp. 91-113; and: *Transforming Serials: The Revolution Continues* (ed: Susan L. Scheiberg, and Shelley Neville) The Haworth Information Press, an imprint of The Haworth Press, Inc., 2003, pp. 91-113. Single or multiple copies of this article are available for a fee from The Haworth Document Delivery Service [1-800-HAWORTH, 9:00 a.m. - 5:00 p.m. (EST). E-mail address: docdelivery@haworthpress.com].

http://www.haworthpress.com/store/product.asp?sku=J123
10.1300/J123v44n12_11

recent edition of an international periodicals directory, 27,083 were available exclusively online or in addition to a paper counterpart,[1] an increase of more than 260 percent over a three-year period.[2] In the academic arena, the number of peer-reviewed electronic journals has grown from seven titles in 1991 to nearly 4,000 titles in 2000, an increase of more than 28,500 percent![3] As noted in this directory, "most scholarly publishers now provide an electronic version of print journals because the World Wide Web has proven to be a convenient, cost-effective, and reliable resource."[4] Indeed, "there has [clearly] been a dramatic increase in the use of the Internet as a publishing medium . . . [with] new breeds of serials" emerging every day.[5]

MULTIMEDIA E-JOURNALS

Earth Interactions

Earth Interactions (earthinteractions.org) is a Web-only e-journal jointly published by the American Geophysical Union, the American Meteorological Society, and the Association of American Geographers. Begun in 1997, this e-journal serves researchers from universities, government, and industry that work in various areas of the Earth-systems sciences, a broad discipline that includes the atmospheric, oceanic, hydrologic, solid-Earth, and biological sciences.[6] From its conception, *Earth Interactions* was intended to be more than an electronic publication that would only reproduce what could be printed in the conventional paper scholarly journal.[7] In creating this e-journal, the goal was to "exploit the [digital] medium" and to "go beyond the capabilities of the printed page." *Earth Interactions* encourages authors to include sophisticated graphics, and raw data, as well as computer code with their submissions.[8]

Earth Interactions supports MPEG (Moving Picture Experts Group) and QuickTime™ files that allow authors to include image loops and animations within the text of their articles. It also permits authors to include audio narratives with these presentations so that a reader need not consult the written text. The journal allows authors to include small datasets as an integral part of an article and provides access to larger datasets by allowing links to external data-archive facilities. *Earth Interactions* also supports the inclusion of *Mathematica Notebooks* (www.wolfram.com/products/mathematica/tour/page10.html) interactive documents that allow a reader to enter data for equations within an article to create graphs for these values. In addition, authors can provide the numerical code for models that enable readers to interact with authors' data and observations to verify and expand upon their results.

Earth Interactions is not unique in its use of embedded multimedia; an increasing number of e-journals incorporate a wide variety of multimedia as an integral or adjunct part of their publications.[9]

Benefits of Multimedia

Although many e-journal publishers remain conventional in their use of the World Wide Web, others clearly recognize that Web "technologies permit us to move beyond the traditional features of the print-based paradigm to explore new ways of using e-journals."[10] In addition to "textual extensions," some e-journal publishers are becoming keenly aware that "there is room for other media . . . to make the basic information clearer or the reading more attractive . . ."[11] Furthermore, there is growing appreciation that the multimedia environment provides an opportunity to present information that by its nature could not be conveyed on the printed page.[12] Overall, as inherently interactive media, multimedia offers an opportunity for the reader to more fully interpret and analyze to facilitate the communication of research.[13]

Common Multimedia Formats

While there has been an increased development and refinement of Web-based multimedia in recent years,[14] several types are used more often in current e-journals. Based upon a review of known multimedia e-journals in 1999, McKiernan identified animation, audio, modeling, and video as the more common types of multimedia utilized. He found that animated GIFs, Shockwave Flash™, MIDI (Musical Instrument Digital Interface), QuickTime™, ReadAudio™, RealPlayer™, Chime™, MPEG (Moving Picture Experts Group), and RealVideo™ were among the more common formats and plug-ins.[15] Among the journals using one or more of these multimedia types are *Expert Reviews in Molecular Medicine* (www-ermm.cbcu.cam.ac.uk) (ShockWave Flash™, *Interactive Multimedia Journal for Computer-Enhanced Learning* (imej.wfu.edu) (QuickTime™), the *Journal for MultiMedia History* (www.albany.edu/ jmmh/) (RealPlayer), and *Videre* (mitpress.mit.edu/e-journals/Videre/) (MPEG)[16] (see Figure 1).

FIGURE 1. Screen print of main page of *M-Bed(sm): A Registry of Embedded Multimedia Electronic Journals* <http://www.public.iastate.edu/~CYBERSTACKS/M-Bed.htm>.

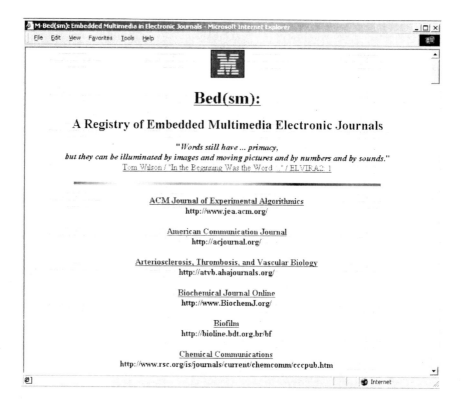

OBSERVATION I

As multimedia electronic resources become more available and are candidates for inclusion in local collections, their multifaceted nature raises significant issues for catalogers who seek to describe them appropriately. In a review of multimedia e-journals in summer 1999, McKiernan[17] found that of 41 identified titles, 34 had records in the OCLC WorldCat database. Of these, only five–less than 15%–noted the availability of a multimedia component. From this review, he concluded that catalogers in general were not aware of the multimedia dimensions of such journals. For those cataloging records with a description of the multimedia content, McKiernan found no standard or uniform descriptions of such components (the five records that mentioned multimedia did so in the 516, 520, 538 MARC fields). Later in spring 2002, the OCLC WorldCat records for these multimedia e-journals were reviewed again, with no difference. However, while a significant percentage of cataloging records for the select multimedia e-journals lacked adequate notes describing relevant multimedia content, some librarians are indeed cognizant of these additional components, and include explicit and appropriate descriptions and other notes for these "new breed" serials.[18]

ECLECTIC JOURNALS

[1]*eclec.tic*
Etymology: Greek eklektikos, from eklegein to select, from ex- out + legein to gather–more at LEGEND. Date: 1683

1: selecting what appears to be best in various doctrines, methods, styles
2: composed of elements drawn from various sources; heterogeneous[19]

An "eclectic" journal may be defined as

A Web-based resource that at its core provides access to the conventional content of a digital form of a journal, but also provides or permits interaction with novel and innovative features and functionalities (e.g., reference linking, cross-publisher searching, page customization, open peer review, etc.), and/or novel and innovative content (e.g., e-books, pre-publication history, electronic discussions, translation services, e-prints, bibliographic databases, etc.).[20]

The variety of eclectic features, functionalities, and content can range from embedded computer code; "dynamic" articles; font, format, and display control; and three-dimensional subject indexes, to interactive models, "reactivity," reader participation, and supplemental data[21] (see Figure 2).

FIGURE 2. Screen print of *EJI(sm): A Registry of Innovative E-Journal Features, Functionalities, and Content* <http://www.public.iastate.edu/~CYBERSTACKS/EJI.htm>.

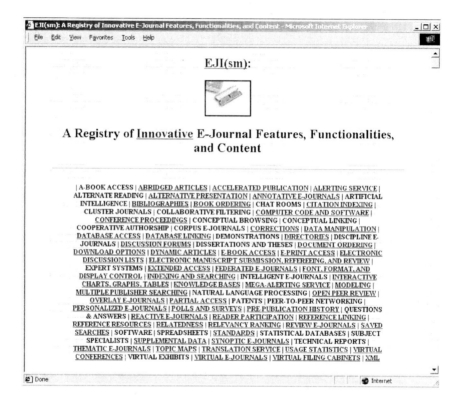

Computer Code

To complement or supplement the contents of select articles, an increasing number of e-journals encourage authors to provide supplemental data or resources. One of the more noteworthy supplemental materials found is computer code or programs. A notable example is the computer software provided as an appendix to a recent article in *Conservation Ecology* (www.consecol.org). The program, *Nonpoint*, allows a reader to simulate the interaction among key stakeholders in the management of a lake vulnerable to pollution. Actors in the simulation include scientists, economists, regulations, farmers, the lake and its environment, and the reader. In addition to the program, full documentation for the use of the program is provided.[22]

Dynamic Articles

Unlike the print medium, the Web offers authors an opportunity to augment a previously published work with current findings and new observations. For example, in *STKE Reviews*, a section with *Science's STKE: Signal Transduction Knowledge Environment* (stke.sciencemag.org), authors can update reviews as circumstances warrant.

Font, Format, and Display Control

To reduce the information overload of readers, some e-journals enable readers to specify the journal titles to be read on a regular basis from a collection of available titles. For example, the Institute of Physics (www.iop.org) allows readers to create a "Personal Main Menu" in which the reader can customize a main menu that includes only journal titles selected by the reader and not all titles subscribed to by his or her library. Personalization and customization of e-journals, however, are not limited to the selection of e-journal titles or topics. The *Internet Journal of Chemistry* (IJC) (www.ijc.com), for example, offers a variety of options for reader configuration of its content structure, reference link style, journal title format, author name order, footnote display, and other components and content[23] (see Figure 3).

Indexing and Searching

A select number of e-journals have embraced the potential of the digital environment, providing novel and innovative access to their content. One, *J.UCS: The Journal of Universal Computer Science* (www.jusc.org), provides access to its articles using the alphanumeric subject category codes of the *ACM Computing Classification System*.[24] Articles are assigned one or more subject codes as well as keywords, and subject codes are hotlinked within an abstract, allowing a hyperlinked search of all articles assigned the same code. *J.UCS* is a joint publication of the KNOW Center in Graz, Austria and Springer-Verlag. It covers all aspects of computer science and was one of the first electronic journals, having been published without interruption since its founding in 1995. A second e-journal, the *Astrophysical Journal*, offers a "self-organized" visual index (simbad.u-strasbg.fr/ApJ/map.pl) to more

FIGURE 3. Schematic depicting optional page layouts for the *Internet Journal of Chemistry.*

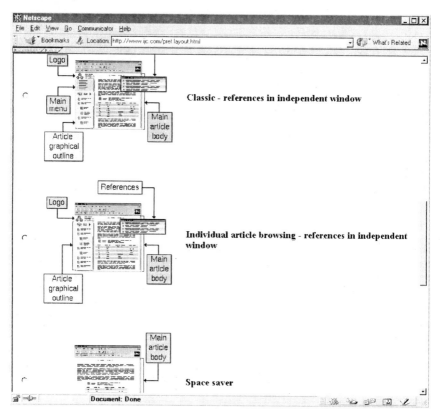

than 16,000 recent articles (1994-2000) created by the application of a Kohonen Self-Organizing Map (SOM) algorithm. SOM is an artificial intelligence technology based on neural computing developed by Teuvo Kohonen of the Helsinki University of Technology. The algorithm automatically organizes indexing terms (or documents) and clusters them within a two-dimensional grid.[25, 26]

Models

Of the various media types embedded within the *Internet Journal of Chemistry*, perhaps the most impressive are interactive chemical 3-D structures created with the Virtual Reality Markup Language (VRML) and with Chime, the chemical structure plug-in provided by MDL Information Systems (www.mdli.com). With Chime models, using the mouse pointer or mouse control options, readers can rotate the molecular model; display the structure as a wire frame, sticks, ball and sticks, or space fill, or other appropriate structure; change the rendering from three-dimensional to two-dimensional; change the coloring; or cluster components, among numerous options. VRM models have similar display and manipulation options (see Figure 4).

FIGURE 4. A three-dimensional model of benzene used to illustrate an article in the *Internet Journal of Chemistry*. The interactive model was created using VRML, the Virtual Reality Markup Language.

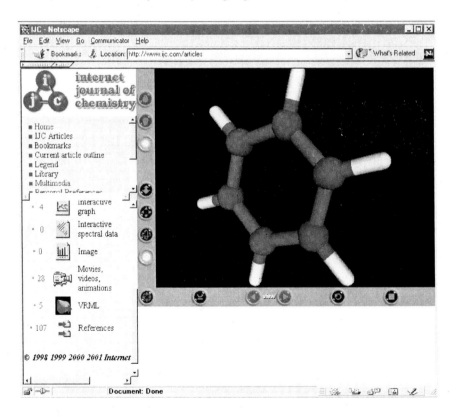

Reactivity

Journals have long encouraged readers to respond to articles and other components. Such responses typically have taken the form of letters to the editor or companion articles that support or oppose published items. In the digital environment, a number of publishers are continuing this tradition by providing Web-based forms to facilitate submissions. For example, *bmj.com* (bmj.com), through its "Rapid Responses" feature, allows readers to comment on articles, editorials, and other content, as well as on previously published letters. The IDEAL Online Library (www.idealibrary.com) publishes a *Forum* column that provides critiques of published papers within the scope of its individual journals (e.g., *Animal Behaviour Forum* (www.academicpress.com/anbehav/forum).

One of the most innovative e-journals incorporating a variety of novel features, functionalities, and content is the *Journal of Interactive Media in Education* (JIME) (www-jime.open.ac.uk), a journal that seeks to "foster a multidisciplinary and intellectually rigorous debate on the theoretical and practical aspects of interactive media in education." Through its "document-centered discourse interface," JIME enables readers, reviewers, and authors "to progressively enrich JIME documents with . . . interactive demonstrations, video and audio clips, evaluation instruments, discussions, and pointers to related or future work."[27] Within framed windows, readers may opt to display editor, reviewer, and public comments beside an original article.

Reader Participation

Unlike the print medium, the Web permits journal publishers to dynamically solicit and ascertain reader opinion about a variety of professional and publication issues. Using the Web, bmj.com solicited reader preferences about the publication of articles in its paper journal. Specifically, it requested that readers rate the importance of "readability" versus "appraisability" of proposed shortened articles. In a second questionnaire, it solicited reader opinions about nine paper versions (www.bmj.com/cgi/content/full/319/7220/DC1/1) with links to examples of the particular versions. Among these were a "traditionally structured short version with emphasis on methods," "journalistic style," and "diary style."

As a distributed, interactive environment, the Web can empower readers to develop resource collections of significant benefit to their community. For example, readers of the *MRS Internet Journal of*

Nitride Semiconductor Research (nsr.mij.mrs.org) can contribute relevant references to journal articles, books, conference papers, or unpublished work, for inclusion in its Web-accessible database (nsr.mij.mrs.org/refs/Default.html).

Supplemental Data

In addition to offering computer code and software programs, some e-journals allow authors to include such supplemental materials as output files from programs, data sets, as well as text appendices. Within an article in *Internet Archaeology* (intarch.ac.uk), the "first fully refereed electronic journal for archaeology," readers may search data sets using a variety of specialized query forms.[28] Search results with relevant data are displayed in an HTML table. In some cases, links are provided from within tables to an interactive map. A reader can export data sets, including underlying geospatial data, to a local database or to a geographic information system (GIS).[29]

OBSERVATION II

In a review of the OCLC WorldCat cataloging records for a sample of eclectic journals (n = 8) conducted in late Spring 2002, only one (15%) included mention of relevant eclectic components of those with cataloging records (n = 7).[30] From this random review, one may conclude that catalogers in general are also not aware of the eclectic features, functionalities, and content of these "new breed" serials journals.

RAMIFICATIONS OF MULTIMEDIA AND ECLECTIC JOURNALS

As the online catalog continues to become "the hub for information discovery," it is essential that the "catalog become comparable with other tools so it can provide maximum support for users." As observed by Hsieh-Yee, "[T]o serve remote . . . [and other catalog users], catalogers . . . [should] . . . include technical information or requirements specific to a resource so that . . . users would know if they have the necessary setup to use the resource. Indeed, [t]he implications for catalogers [of evolving and emerging electronic information forms and formats] are that they must have an efficient way to produce resource descriptions that can assist users in searching, identifying, selecting, and accessing [these] resources."[31] With the development and use of an ever-evolving variety of multimedia and other components, one can expect over time that authors will create and submit their contributions with embedded multimedia and eclectic features, functionalities, and content not currently accepted by e-journals.

New components would have an impact not only on the nature of the e-journal, but on library staff as well. To appropriately and adequately identify and describe the multimedia and eclectic components of "new breed" e-journals will require that a cataloger's workstation be equipped and configured to allow for the retrieval of these components. This responsibility raises numerous technical, professional, and service issues, of which the currency and accuracy of a catalog record may be paramount.

To maintain accurate and current catalog records, catalogers would need to be notified or be required to revisit an e-journals routinely to identify any new components. Cataloger description of multimedia and other eclectic components could be greatly facilitated if publishers noted these in an explicit location on an e-journal's Web site.

SOLUTION I

While clearly beneficial to both the cataloger and user, recommendations about the nature, structure, and content of e-journals that could facilitate use and description raises the issue of the implementation of appropriate standards for e-journals in general, and those for multimedia and eclectic journals, specifically.

Standards

"A standard is generally intended to be a level of attainment. The American Library Association (ALA) describes a standard for libraries as 'a rule or model of quantity, quality, extent, level of correctness . . . intended as a criterion by which current judgments of value, quality, fitness and correctness are conformed.' Technical standards in library work are similar to industrial standards, and typically provide a measure of excellence or adequacy for a product or a thing."[32]

The international standard for the presentation of periodicals, ISO 8: 1977, "sets out rules intended to enable editors and publishers to present periodicals in a form which will facilitate their use; following these rules should help editors and publishers to bring order and clarity to their own work. These requirements are of varying importance and may go against certain artistic, technical or advertising considerations." The standard addresses such components as:

- References
- Title of periodical
- Issue
- Numbering
- Volume
- Date
- Layout
- Running title
- Pagination
- Presentation of articles
- Contents list of issue[33]

For "layout," it notes that:

> Typographic uniformity should be used in similar issues of a periodical. A variety of sizes and weights and other typographic and editorial methods should be used for distinguishing different issues of the text. The typography of articles, abstracts, abstracts sheets and bibliographical identification should follow the appropriate International Standard.[34]

A more recent publication offers recommendations of "good practices" for publishing printed journals and other serial publications that cover similar aspects as the ISO standards:

- Title
- Information about the serial
- Issues
- Articles
- Format and presentation
- Standards, commercial, and legal requirements[35]

For "format and presentation," it notes that:

> The choice of formats may depend on the nature and contents of the serial. Factors to be considered include the number and types

of illustrations and tables and the number of columns per page . . .
The choice of printer and prices will also be factors determining
format.[36]

SERIAL STANDARDS COMPLIANCE

While there have been national and international standards and recommendations for the presentation and layout of periodicals for several
decades,[37, 38, 39, 40, 41, 42, 43, 44] adherence has never been uniform nor universal.

A recently published in-depth review and analysis of the degree of
standards compliance by several dozen biomedical journals published
in Spain is illustrative of the current situation. Using a sample of 221
biomedical journals published in Spain, López-Cózar assessed compliance using a checklist of 136 elements derived from standards for the
presentation of periodical publications developed by the International
Organization for Standardization (ISO) and from recommendations
published by UNESCO, the International Committee of Medical Journal Editors, the Council of Biology Editors, and E. J. Huth.

For most parameters in this assessment, three aspects were evaluated: presence, presentation, and location. Based on his analysis,
López-Cózar concluded that about one-third (34.3%) of the Spanish biomedical journals complied with the recommended standards and practices. This reflected the complete absence of specific elements relating to
the volume (e.g., cover, contents list, index) and abstract sheet, more than
a general neglect of a large number of standards. López-Cózar observed
that the poor degree of compliance with standards by Spanish biomedical journals was due in part to the lack of familiarity with standards on
the part of authors, editors, and publishers, and in part by the fact that
these individuals and organizations are rarely involved in the creation
and development of standards.

López-Cózar concluded his review with several appropriate generalizations regarding compliance and standards in general, most notably that:

- standards for the presentation of periodicals are infrequently used
  and inadequately used;
- publishers are understandably reluctant to implement standards
  that are technically complex; and
- the gestation and birth of a standard is an excruciatingly slow and
  complex problem.[45]

Such observations and conclusions are not unique. In a study published in 1971, 168 of the most-cited British scientific serials were examined to evaluate the differences in their presentations. In this review, the British standards for presentation of serial publications (B.S. 2509: 1970)[46] and Bibliographic References (B.S. 1629: 1950)[47] were used as the bases of comparison. The investigator found that while the majority of the serials followed the standards for bibliographic references, fewer complied the standards for presentation. Interestingly, serials in the fields of Chemistry and Medicine adhered less to the standards requirements than serials in other fields.[48]

BEST PRACTICES

In the forthcoming revised edition of guidelines for "good practice" in publishing printed and electronic journals,[49] there is explicit acknowledgment of the proliferation of electronic journals and their significance:

> Like the first edition, the book provides practical guidelines for all those involved in publishing journals. . . . However, the focus has changed in some important ways. The exclusion of electronic journals is no longer justified; in the intervening years, parallel print and electronic publication has become the norm for the vast majority of journals, and the separation has become artificial. Material on electronic publication has therefore been added throughout the book.[50]

Of particular note is recognition of the existence of the variety of "eclectic" features, functionalities, and content:

> In many cases, the electronic version of a serial will be more than just a straight copy of the print version. It may contain more content, have links to further information, additional datasets, images, sound or video. . . . Alternatively, moving images and three-dimensional pictures can also be accommodated.[51]

In addition, the guidelines note that

> electronic serials may contain links to other sites, e.g., linking from a citation to an abstract or full-text database. They may also link to the author's primary datasets or executable files. . . . [A]

number of medical and scientific journals have links into the medical database Medline/PubMed . . . and to the DNA and protein database GenBank. . . . Links to computer programmes and data sets are also being setup.[52]

SOLUTION II

Regina Romano Reynolds of the National Serials Data Program (NSDP), Library of Congress, is among many who recognize that e-journals pose significant issues for publishers and librarians alike, noting that "publishers are experimenting with a new medium and need the freedom to try new approaches and models."

She further notes that "traditional bibliographic rules which governed the print world have not responded rapidly enough to the electronic environment," recommending that "publishers must keep librarians informed" and that "librarians must realize that e-journals are in a state of transition and should expect experiment and change" and that "neither side should forget the user."

To facilitate the bibliographic management of electronic serials she recommends that publishers:

- carry "masthead" information on the journal homepage, including issuing body, publisher and place of publication;
- show consistency in title presentation;
- maintain stable URLs; and
- give information about differences between print and various electronic versions

More importantly, she insightfully recognizes that "this is the right time to consider a standard or set of guidelines addressing the presentation of e-journals, " noting that "[d]efining 'best practices' would guide new e-journal publishers on 'how to do it better' and help established publishers provide reliable and predictable information to secondary publishers and librarians, their business partners."[53]

SOLUTION III

To facilitate the identification of essential bibliographic data, the International Organization for Standardization established a standard that would provide "a concise summary of bibliographic reference data." Known as the "Bibliographic Strip" it was to be "printed at the foot of the front page of the cover of a periodical" to facilitate "on the one hand, the arrangements of the periodicals and, on the other, the compilation of citations."[54] One might consider the creation of analogous features for electronic journals–an "Eclectic Strip" which would serve as an index of eclectic features, functionalities, and content available in a specific electronic journal. The Eclectic Strip would be visible and prominent on the main page of the e-journal, where on the one hand it would facilitate the identification and use of eclectic components, and on the other, it would facilitate the proper cataloging of the serial.

SOLUTION IV

Bibliographic Control of Web Resources: A Library of Congress Action Plan

In mid-November 2000, the Library of Congress Cataloging Directorate sponsored the *Bicentennial Conference on Bibliographic Control for the New Millennium: Confronting the Challenges of Networked Resources and the Web* "as a working meeting of experts from the various communities that play a role in the creation, retrieval, and cataloging of Web resources. The primary goals of the conference were:

- to develop to an overall strategy to address the challenges of improved access to Web resources through library catalogs and application of metadata; and
- to identify attainable actions for achieving the overall strategy.

"The aim of the conference . . . was to generate recommendations for the Library of Congress, in collaboration with the larger library community, to use as a blueprint for action to improve bibliographic control of the Web."

Participant deliberations resulted in eleven sets of recommendations that were subsequently distilled into an "Action Plan." For these, a number of over-arching objectives for the framework of the plan were extracted and include several related directly and indirectly to the management of embedded multimedia and eclectic e-journals:

- 1.2. Explore ways to re-purpose/reuse metadata received under programs for registration, acquisitions, cataloging, copyright, and related activities.
- 3.2. Identify and publicize existing registries of metadata schemes to establish points of convergence among them, to promote the consistent labeling of fields, and to facilitate mapping of fields.
- 3.6. Convey and reiterate the need for the continuing development of AACR2 to provide principles and practices for bibliographic access to and control of the full array of electronic resources on a timely basis and in harmony with other descriptive cataloging standards.
- 4.2. Develop specifications for a maintenance tool to provide mechanisms for detecting and reporting changes in resource content and associated metadata. Communicate the specifications to the vendor community and encourage their adoption.
- 4.3. Develop specifications for a metadata creation tool for authors that can support various metadata standards. Communicate the specifications to the metadata community and encourage their adoption.
- 4.5. Promote OAI (Open Archives Initiative) standard for harvesting metadata.
- 5.2. Sponsor a series of open forums on metadata needs to support reference service in conjunction with various professional association meetings to include catalogers, reference librarians, vendors, systems developers, publishers, and administrators.[55]

SOLUTION V

New Generation Journals

On February 14, 2002, the Budapest Open Access Initiative (BOAI) was formally launched.[56] The BOAI is a public statement and plan of action that calls for "open access to peer-reviewed research articles in all academic fields and the preprints that might precede them." 'Open access' is characterized by the free availability on the public Internet of peer-reviewed journal articles, as well as non-reviewed preprints of potential interest to the scholarly community.[57]

The BOAI endorses two strategies for achieving its overall goal: (1) author self-archiving and commitment to offering open access to the full content of publications, and (2) the establishment of "a new generation of journals."[58] The first strategy advocates that authors deposit a digital copy of their publications or pre-publications in a publicly accessible Website, while the second calls for the founding of new research journals that do not charge for a subscription or impose access fees.[59]

Web-based Journal Manuscript Management and Peer Review Software and Systems

In an effort to provide and promote open and wide dissemination of articles, the BOAI proposes that new journals no longer invoke copyright to restrict access or use of journal content. Significant savings can be expected for open-access journals by publishing only online and by dispensing with the costs associated with managing subscriptions of authorized and unauthorized access.[60] In addition, free or affordable software for electronic journal publishing would also reduce the cost and expedite the production of open-access journal.[61]

In recent years, a variety of experimental and commercial systems have been developed that facilitate the management and review of scholarly manuscripts for electronic and paper publication. Among the established and recent Web-based systems are:

- AllenTrack™ [www.allentrack.net]
- Bench>Press™ [benchpress.highwire.org]
- EdiKit[SM] [www.bepress.com]
- ESPERE [www.espere.org]
- Journal Assistant™ [www.journalassistant.com]
- ManuscriptCentral [www.scholarone.com/products_manuscriptcentral. html]
- Rapid Review™ [pc.cadmus.com/rapidreview/][62]

The increasing interest in and adoption of Web-based journal manuscript management and peer review software and systems[63] presents an unprecedented opportunity to facilitate the incorporation of multimedia and eclectic features, functionalities, and contents by authors. More importantly, such software and systems also hold the potential to concurrently facilitate the explicit presentation of multimedia and eclectic components within actual publications, thus facilitating appropriate cataloging that would significantly enhance access and use of these "new breed" serials.

The future of scholarship will be both diverse and complicated, with rich options for publication using a variety of multimedia and eclectic features, functionalities, and content. To facilitate access and use, catalogers and cataloging should identify and delineate these components.[64]

NOTES

1. *Ulrich's international periodicals directory*, 37th ed. (New Providence, N.J.: R. R. Bowker, c1998), vii.

2. Ulrich's international periodicals directory, 40th ed. (New Providence, N.J.: R. R. Bowker, 2001), vii.

3. *Directory of scholarly electronic journals and academic discussion lists*. Washington, DC: Office of Scholarly Communication, Association of Research Libraries, 2000), vii.

4. Ibid.

5. *Ulrich's international periodicals directory*, 40th ed., vii.

6. Judy Holoviak and Keith L. Seitter, "*Earth Interactions*: Transcending the Limitations of the Printed Page," *Journal of Electronic Publishing* 3, no. 1 (September 1997). <http://www.press.umich.edu/jep/03-01/EI.html> (18 August 2002).

7. Keith L. Seitter and Judy Holoviak, "*Earth Interactions*: An Electronic Journal Serving the Earth System Science Community," *Bulletin of the American Meteorological Society*, 77 no. 9 (September 1996): 2095-2100. <http://www.agu.org/ei/bamsei.html> (18 August 2002).

8. Keith L. Seitter and Judy Holoviak, 2096.

9. Gerry McKiernan, "Embedded Multimedia in Electronic Journals," *Multimedia Information and Technology* 25, no. 4 (November 1999): 338-343.

10. Peter J. Murray and Denis M. Anthony, "Current and Future Models for Nursing e-Journals: Making the Most of the Web's Potential," *International Journal of Medical Informatics* 53 no. 2/3 (February-March 1999): 152.

11. Dirk Schoonbaert, "Biomedical Journals and the World Wide Web," *Electronic Library* 16 no. 2 (April 1998): 99.

12. C. J. Hildyard and B. J. Whitaker, "Chemical Publishing on the Internet: Electronic Journals–Who Needs Them?" In *Online Information 96: 20th International Online Information Meeting: Proceedings, London, 3-5 December 1996*, edited David I. Raitt and Ben Jeapes (Oxford: Learned Information Europe, 1996), 146-147.

13. Alan Griffiths and Edie Rasmussen, "The Future of Multimedia in Research," in *Workshop Proceedings: Digital Libraries Conference and Multimedia Workshop: Multimedia for the Information Professional: An Interactive Workshop for Librarians and Information Managers, 29-30 March 1995, Raffles City Convention Centre, Singapore* (Singapore: Library Association of Singapore (?), 1995), 68-74.

14. Allison Zhang, *Multimedia File Formats on the Internet: A Beginner's Guide for PC Users*, 1999. <http://www.lib.rochester.edu/multimed/contents.htm> (18 August 2002).

15. Gerry McKiernan, "Embedded Multimedia in Electronic Journals," *Multimedia Information and Technology* 25, no. 4 (November 1999): 340.

16. Gerry McKiernan, "M-Bed(sm): A Registry of Embedded Multimedia Electronic Journals," 2001. <http://www.public.iastate.edu/~CYBERSTACKS/M-Bed.htm> (18 August 2002).

17. Gerry McKiernan, "Cataloging of Multimedia E-Journals," Posting to Web4Lib electronic discussion list, August 18, 1999, <http://sunsite.berkeley.edu/Web4Lib/archive/9908/0145.html> (18 August 2002).

18. Beatrice L. Caraway, "Notes for Remote Access Computer File Serials," *Serials Librarian* 41, nos. 3-4 (2002): 157-178. <http://www.public.iastate.edu/~gerrymck/SLv41n3-4.pdf> (18 August 2002).

19. yourDictionary.com. 2001. <http://www2.yourdictionary.com/index.shtml> (18 August 2002).

20. Gerry McKiernan, "EJI(sm): A Registry of Innovative E-Journal Features, Functionalities, and Content," 2001. <http://www.public.iastate.edu/~CYBERSTACKS/EJI.htm> (18 August 2002).

21. Gerry McKiernan, "E is for Everything: The Extra-Ordinary, Evolutionary [E-]Journal," *Serials Librarian* 41, nos. 3-4 (2002): 293-321.

22. Stephen Carpenter, William Brock, and Paul Hanson, "Ecological and Social Dynamics in Simple Models of Ecosystem Management. NonPoint Software Documentation," *Conservation Ecology* 3, no. 2, article 4 (December 1999). <http://www.consecol.org/Journal/vol3/iss2/art4/> (18 August 2002).

23. Steven M. Bachrach, Anatoli Krassavine, and Darin C. Burleigh, "End-User Customized Chemistry Journal Articles," *Journal of Chemical Information and Computer Sciences* 39, no. 1 (1999): 84.

24. Association for Computing Machinery, "ACM Computing Classification System," c2000. <http://www.acm.org/class/1998/ccs98.html> (18 August 2002).

25. Teuvo Kohonen, *Self-Organizing Maps.* 3d ed. (Berlin: Springer, 2001).

26. Phillipe Poinçot, Soizick Lesteven, and Fionn Murtagh, "A Spatial User Interface to the Astronomical Literature," *Astronomy and Astrophysics. Supplement Series,* 130 (May 1998): 183-191.<http://www.edpsciences-usa.org/articles/astro/full/1998/10/ds1464/ ds1464.html> (20 August 2002).

27. Simon Buckingham Shum and Tamara Sumner, "JIME: An Interactive Journal for Interactive Media," *FirstMonday* 6, no. 2 (February 2001). <http://www.firstmonday.org/issues/issue6_2/buckingham_shum/index.html> (18 August 2002).

28. Martin Millett, Francisco Queiroga, Kris Strutt, Jeremy Taylor and Steven Willis, "The Ave Valley, Northern Portugal: An Archaeological Survey of Iron Age and Roman Settlement Ave Valley Data Sets–Data Help, " *Internet Archaeology* 9 (autumn/winter 2000). <http://intarch.ac.uk/journal/issue9/millett/data.html> (18 August 2002).

29. Ibid.

30. Gerry McKiernan, "Seize The E!: The Eclectic Journal and Its Ramifications" (PowerPoint presentation at NASIG 2002: Transforming Serials–The Revolution Continues, the 17th Annual Conference of the North American Serials Interest Group, June 20-23, 2002, College of William and Mary, Williamsburg, Virginia).

31. Ingrid Hsieh-Yee, *Organizing Audiovisual and Electronic Resources for Access: A Cataloging Guide* (Englewood, Colo.: Libraries Unlimited, 2000), 257.

32. Charlotta C. Hensley, "Serials Standards (and Guidelines): Who Cares," in *Library Serials Standards: Development, Implementation, Impact: Proceedings of the Third Annual Serials Conference,* edited by Nancy Jean Melin (Westport, Conn.: Meckler Publishing, c1984), 87.

33. International Organization for Standardization, *Documentation-Presentation of Periodicals* (Geneva: International Organization for Standardization, 1977).

34. International Organization for Standardization, *Documentation-Presentation of Periodicals* (Geneva: International Organization for Standardization, 1977), 3.

35. Association of Learned and Professional Society Publishers, *Serial Publications: Guidelines for Good Practice in Publishing Printed Journals and other Serial Publications* (Witney, Oxfordshire: United Kingdom Serials Group, 1994).

36. Association of Learned and Professional Society Publishers, *Serial Publications: Guidelines for Good Practice in Publishing Printed Journals and other Serial Publications* (Witney, Oxfordshire: United Kingdom Serials Group, 1994), 29.

37. American National Standards Institute, *American National Standards for Periodicals: Format and Arrangement* (New York: American National Standards Institute, 1977).

38. American Standards Association, *American Recommended Practices for Reference Data for Periodicals* (New York: American Standards Association, 1935).

39. American Standards Association, *American Standard Reference Data and Arrangement of Periodicals* (New York: American Standards Association, 1943).

40. British Standards Institution, *British Standard for Layout of Periodicals: A Guide for Editors & Publishers* (London: British Standards Institution, 1954).

41. British Standards Institution, *British Standard for Periodicals of Reference Value: Form and Presentation* (London: British Standards Institution, 1959).

42. British Standards Institution, Specification for the Presentation of Serial Publications, Including Periodicals (London: British Standards Institution, 1970).

43. International Organization for Standardization, *Layout of Periodicals* (Geneva?: International Organization for Standardization, 1955).

44. United States of America Standards Institute, *USA Standard for Periodicals: Format and Arrangement* (New York: United States of America Standards Institute, 1967).

45. Emilio Delgado López-Cózar, "ISO Standards for the Presentation of Scientific Periodicals: Little Known and Little Used by Spanish Biomedical Journals, *Journal of Documentation* 55 no. 3 (June 1999): 288-309.

46. British Standards Institution, *Specification for the Presentation of Serial Publications, Including Periodicals.* 3rd ed. (London: British Standards Institution, 1970).

47. British Standards Institution, *Bibliographical References* (British Standards Institution, 1950).

48. Jacqueline Hills, *Presentation of British Scientific Serials* (London: Aslib, 1971).

49. Diane Brown, Elaine Stott, and Anthony Watkinson, *Serial Publications: Guidelines for Good Practice in Publishing Printed and Electronic Journals.* 2nd ed. (Association of Learned and Professional Society Publishers, 2002).

50. Association of Learned and Professional Society Publishers, "Serial Publications: Guidelines to Good Practice in Publishing Printed and Electronic Journals (2nd Edition)," 2002. <http://www.alpsp.org/pub3.htm> (20 August 2002).

51. Diane Brown, Elaine Stott, and Anthony Watkinson, *Serial Publications: Guidelines for Good Practice in Publishing Printed and Electronic Journals.* 2nd ed. (Association of Learned and Professional Society Publishers, 2002), 1.

52. Ibid., 2.

53. Priscilla Caplan, "E-Journals Report: Report on the NISO/NFAIS Workshop: Electronic Journals–Best Practices, Held February 20, 2000, Philadelphia, PA," 2002. <http://www.niso.org/news/events_workshops/e-jrnl-report.html> (20 August 2002).

54. International Organization for Standardization. Information Centre, "Bibliographical Strip," in *Information Transfer: Handbook on International Standards Governing Information Transfer: Texts of ISO standards* ([Geneva]: International Organization for Standardization, 1977), 172-173.

55. Library of Congress, "Bibliographic Control of Web Resources: A Library of Congress Action Plan," 2001. <http://www.loc.gov/catdir/bibcontrol/draftplan.html> (20 August 2002).

56. Ivan Noble, "Boost for Research Paper Access," *BBC News. Sci-Tech* (February 14, 2002). <news.bbc.co.uk/hi/english/sci/tech/newsid_1818000/1818652.stm> (20 August 2002).

57. Open Society Institute, "Budapest Open Access Initiative," c2002.

58. <www.soros.org/openaccess/read.shtml> (20 August 2002).

59. Gerry McKiernan, "Open Access and Retrieval: Liberating the Scholarly Literature, in *E-Serials Collection Management: Transitions, Trends, and Technicalities*, edited by David Fowler (Binghamton, New York: The Haworth Press, Inc. (forthcoming).

60. Open Society Institute.

61. Peter Suber, "Budapest Open Access Initiative: Frequently Asked Questions," 2002. <www.earlham.edu/~peters/fos/boaifaq.htm> (20 August 2002).

62. Ibid.

63. Gerry McKiernan, "Web-based Journal Manuscript Management and Peer-Review Software and Systems," *Library Hi Tech News* 19, no. 7 (August 2002): 31-43.

64. "Scholarly Reviews Through the Web," *New York Times*, 12 August 2002, sec. C, C3.

ACKNOWLEDGMENT

The author is grateful to Steven M. Bachrach, editor in chief of the *Internet Journal of Chemistry* and Dr. D. R. Semmes Distinguished Professor of Chemistry, Trinity University, San Antonio, Texas, for permission to reproduce selected screen prints.

CONTRIBUTOR'S NOTES

Gerry McKiernan is Science and Technology Librarian and Bibliographer at Iowa State University Library.

Management of Electronic Serials, Outsourcing, and Bringing New Products to the Marketplace

Peter McCracken

Presenter

Greetings and welcome. Together, Mike Markwith and I have created an approach to this presentation that we hope will highlight some very important issues in the ever-growing area of managing e-journals, as well as encourage discussion on the topic.[1] We developed a set of seven questions that we feel cover many of the salient issues and that we believe librarians should ask. We will each take 20 to 25 minutes to offer our insights into these questions, and the remainder of the time is set aside for questions, answers, and much more importantly, *discussion* of these ideas, and the introduction of any relevant issues and ideas not presented.

In exploring answers to the following questions, we expect that our opinions will differ, and ideally our comments will lead to a group discussion that will fill the remaining time and will lead to many more ideas than either of us has presented individually. I think we both welcome questions of clarification or items for further discussion during the course of the presentation.

[Haworth co-indexing entry note]: "Management of Electronic Serials, Outsourcing, and Bringing New Products to the Marketplace." McCracken, Peter. Co-published simultaneously in *The Serials Librarian* (The Haworth Information Press, an imprint of The Haworth Press, Inc.) Vol. 44, No. 1/2, 2003, pp. 115-123; and: *Transforming Serials: The Revolution Continues* (ed: Susan L. Scheiberg, and Shelley Neville) The Haworth Information Press, an imprint of The Haworth Press, Inc., 2003, pp. 115-123. Single or multiple copies of this article are available for a fee from The Haworth Document Delivery Service [1-800-HAWORTH, 9:00 a.m. - 5:00 p.m. (EST). E-mail address: docdelivery@haworthpress.com].

http://www.haworthpress.com/store/product.asp?sku=J123
10.1300/J123v44n12_12

The seven questions we've posed are:

1. Is there a need for an e-journal management system?
2. If so, should an institution do it in-house, or find someone on the outside to do it?
3. What do we, as vendors, see as the benefits of either doing it in-house or outsourcing this work?
4. What does a librarian risk by outsourcing this work?
5. Assuming one decides to outsource, what options are now available, and what may be available in the future?
6. How can librarians assess the value of work from a particular vendor, and how can they improve the vendor's product?
7. What's next?

Not surprisingly, we believe the first question will be an easy one: "Is there a need for an e-journal management system?" Given that we both sell such systems, this is a little like asking a car salesman if there's a need for cars. Certainly, we believe there is a need for e-journal management systems.

I think there *is* a critical need for a system that tracks these resources. The discussion surrounding this issue at this conference alone is sufficient evidence of the need. Aggregated databases were originally populated with content to facilitate quality topic-based searching, not for accessing content from specific journals. But the resources were there, and librarians and patrons naturally sought them out.

Today, these databases offer hundreds or occasionally thousands of journals in a single database, and they provide a particular value in accessing specific journals and articles, particularly for off-campus users, or in situations when a patron cannot or will not go to another library–or microfilm or the stacks, for that matter–to get the article they need. With the growing availability of full text e-journals from publishers and subscription agents, the number of journals continues to increase, and so too does the number of potential sources for a journal. Some of the libraries that subscribe to our service have access to more than 25,000 journals through as many as a hundred sources. This is, indeed, a collection that requires a comprehensive management system if one is to get the most out of it. If you want to approach this collection from the point of seeking a specific title or article, rather than using the collection solely for subject searching, you simply cannot effectively manage these data alone.

The second question we posed is "If there *is* a need for e-journal management systems, should an institution do it in-house, or find someone on the outside to do it?" The answer depends somewhat on the size of the collection, but in my opinion, anything over a handful of databases can be managed better, and more cost-effectively, by an outsourced provider. It is simply a question of economies of scale. Because Serials Solutions is providing this service for so many institutions, we can spread the not-insignificant cost of building the software, collecting the data, doing quality control, etc., over more than a thousand libraries, instead of just one.

As we get to the third question, perhaps we are beginning to get into areas where our company philosophies diverge from each other. The third question is "What do we, as vendors, see as the benefits of either doing it in-house or outsourcing it?" Without sounding too repetitive, I think that clearly this is an instance where it makes great sense to outsource most of this work. The library community tried to create a cooperative approach to solving the problem, through the development of Jake, but while everyone wanted to use the resource, no one wanted to do the grunt work of downloading and updating the data. E-journal management solutions are able to amortize the high cost of tracking these data across all subscribers.

Accurate data are critical to this process, and we must continually work to improve their accuracy. E-journal management solutions improve these data by developing relationships with all of the aggregators and publishers, which in turn improve the access we and others have to their data, as well as the accuracy of those data. This is an area where our work benefits the entire library community. This is not a one-way street, where we receive data from the aggregators and go no further. We help aggregators themselves in identifying potential data collection problems, or help them identify errors in their own data lists. This improves the services they provide to all libraries, whether they use a management service or not.

I have been asked before about the issues of outsourcing this work, since outsourcing is often considered a dirty word to many librarians. Clearly, there have been situations where outsourcing has been the cause of frustration, dissent, and a reduction in patron service in libraries across the country. But in this case, we're taking grunt work out of the library, but leaving all decisions within the institution, so I believe it is, in fact, an ideal candidate for outsourcing.

But outsourcing any work does present legitimate concerns a library should keep in mind, which leads to our question four: "What does a library risk by outsourcing this work?" The primary concerns, as we see it, relate to the inter-connected issues of *reliability* and *control*.

If a library is having someone else provide a service that its staff used to do themselves, or that they consider critical, I believe it is incumbent upon the library staff to review carefully the reliability of the service. This applies to every service and product a library contracts for or purchases. In the case of e-journal management systems, what happens if you lose access to the site two weeks before the end of the term and patrons can't find data they need? What if the data provided are not accurate and librarians have to deal with frustrated patrons? These are legitimate concerns; when you hand over responsibility for doing the work, you hope your vendor will be reliable. In terms of control, every library is different, and natural questions to ask include the following: Will the data be presented in the way that best suits my patrons? Will they track all the data we want tracked? What happens when we make changes to our subscriptions? Can we elegantly remove all traces of this service if we so choose?

These are all issues that most vendors work hard to address, and our long-standing philosophy is to offer our library partners as much control as possible. Ensuring that a vendor will listen and will respond is one way of reducing the risk when outsourcing this–or any–work. The core of *our* service, for example, has been a single comprehensive list of e-journals. Virtually every library we work with hosts the HTML pages we provide on *their* servers, because *they* want to retain these levels of control. They maintain control of when the servers are up, control of the aesthetics and page presentation, and control over how this resource integrates with the library's Website and other resources.

If you outsource this or any work, is the service provider unduly controlling how the final product appears, and thereby taking control and credit away from your library? Do your patrons need an e-journal management system? My company doesn't think so, so we don't advertise to them: You'll find our name in plain type at the very bottom of each HTML page, but that's it, and that was an important point to me, as a librarian. This issue, like many others, came from my experiences with library vendors, and my sincere hope that I, as a vendor, would act how I, as a librarian, would like me (the vendor) to act.

We work hard to address these issues, but we don't succeed 100% of the time. For example, we're working on offering several new products or services, including volume enumerations and subject headings. Like other vendors, when we do introduce our solutions, they may not be exactly what some individual libraries want most. I have talked with enough librarians to know how much their requests vary, and I expect that our solutions will fulfill the expectations of the vast majority of librarians, but I know they won't fill expectations for all. Doing this work in-house ensures that (assuming you can get complete agreement within your own library) your service will look exactly as you intend, and work exactly as you expect. While most vendors try to provide you with as many features as you want, they can rarely provide you with every feature, every time, in the exact format you request. If you can agree on a format, and have the resources to create and implement it, then you will probably get something that more closely matches what you seek. Of course, the tradeoff is the comparison between what a vendor can offer at a certain price and in a certain timeframe, and what your institution can create, given your available time and money.

As a perfect example of this, at breakfast this morning I spoke with a librarian who felt very strongly about how we should handle a specific issue regarding one of our new projects. I understand her points, and I understand her concerns, and I think they are very good ones, but *I* have to go back to our technology department and look for another systemic solution to solve this problem in the manner she would like to see. I'm certainly going to give it a try, but I don't quite know what my brother the "tech guy" will say about it.

As with any decision surrounding the use and application of limited resources, librarians in this situation must make decisions based on the best use of those limited resources. Since they probably cannot have it all, what can they have at the best price available to them?

The next question more specifically addresses the differences between our companies and their solutions to this problem. This conference gives you the opportunity to hear directly from vendors, ask questions, and hear specific details, rather than generic speculations.

Serials Solutions has been providing print, HTML, MARC-ready, and spreadsheet reports for the past two years. Our reports include all of the journals available at an individual institution through electronic publishers, subscription agents and database aggregators. Our goal, however, ever since conceiving of the company about four years ago, was to put these data in the OPAC. This has taken many months, and more money than I care to consider, to make happen. We have, however, done it, and this is a point of great pride for me. Institutions have been talking for a number of years about several different approaches to incorporating these records into the catalog: one is a single record approach, in which all electronic access points for a journal are added to a single MARC record, usually representing the print version of a journal.

We have offered a MARC-ready product for some time–electronic holdings data presented in a format designed to be cut and pasted into the specific journal's record in the OPAC. While this has been helpful for libraries that have already traveled far down the "single record approach" path, it is quite labor intensive, and also requires that the library acquire bibliographic records for e-journals that are not already in their catalog. For these reasons, this is a service we do not particularly promote.

Another approach has been to make a separate record for every single version of the journal, under the belief that each version of the journal is a sufficiently different representation to justify additional cataloging. The version of *Journal of American History* in JSTOR is certainly a different bibliographic beast than the version that appears in ProQuest databases or through History Cooperative. I don't believe this opinion is wrong, but I do believe it confuses the user who is faced with half a dozen or more possible records to investigate when they're seeking a specific journal. On the other hand, I see a significant difference between print and electronic versions of a journal; this is a difference anyone seeking a specific journal from home can quickly comprehend.

So Serials Solutions is developing what we describe as the "dual record" approach in creating MARC records for journals available through database aggregators. In fact, it closely parallels the plan that Regina Reynolds, Becky Culbertson, and Naomi Young have raised in the last year within CONSER, and which has been the subject of much discussion at ALA and here. Your existing records appear in the OPAC for your print or microfilm copies of a journal, and we don't impact, influence, touch, or affect those records in any way. Instead, we provide a full MARC record, drawn from the CONSER serials database, to which we attach the electronic holdings data relevant to your library. We draw from our extensive database of holdings data, including journal coverage dates, embargo periods, journal-specific links, and other relevant data, to apply only that information specific to your library.

Because we understand the importance of *control by* and *variation between* libraries, we have developed the capability to allow libraries to implement whatever changes they request to the MARC records we deliver to them. We can delete fields, such as 510s that indicate where a journal is indexed–why include this data, if you know it's often out of date, and the record in question is leading someone to full text anyway? In another example, we might delete listings of additional physical forms represented in the 530 field. We can also add fields, such as notes that a journal is only available to patrons of the institution, or add a genre field indicating it is an "electronic journal." We can also modify fields, such as change the 245 title field to include a subfield h for "[electronic resource]" or add an "(Online)" qualifier to the uniform title field. All of this work is done at the specific request of the subscribing institution.

I mentioned before the investments we've made in this project, and much of it has related to our decision to build extremely flexible and robust technologies. This allows us to offer these customizations, which are developed through a profile we create with the library.

Of course, this information is no good if it's not regularly updated. We offer updates as often as every month, or more commonly every other month. Records are overwritten if there is any change in the data we are generating for the library, from coverage dates or URLs that result from changes in the aggregators' data, to changes in the original CONSER record. Using an annual subscription pricing model, we offer an easy, manageable, and affordable system for tracking the journals available through a library's database aggregators.

As I hope you can tell, I am very excited about this service, and I think it has the opportunity to bring a great resource to users at many institutions. Librarians and their patrons can better know just what is available through their databases, and make the most of the resources for which they are paying so handsomely. More importantly, the OPAC remains the primary source for locating information regarding a library's resources, regardless of format.

Having heard what is available, the next question we think you should ask is, "How can librarians assess the value of work from a particular vendor, and how can they improve the vendor's product?" I think the easy answers to this question are, *look very carefully*, and *talk back*. As a vendor, I stand behind our product, and take pride in delivering a quality product. Indeed, this is, to us, an inescapable necessity in the tight-knit library community. For example, we have done very little advertising of our product, and instead have relied on word-of-mouth to spread knowledge of our services. We view users' opinions as being critical to the success of our services. When I was making purchasing decisions for a product I was unfamiliar with, I often looked to librarians who were more knowledgeable than I about the specific products. This happens everywhere. Ask librarians who are using these services "Are you happy with it? Is it what you expected?" It's simple but effective, and it provides real pressure to the vendors to deliver what was promised.

For those who have a system in place, talk to your fellow librarians candidly, and talk to your vendor as well. This is critical. In a sector that is this complex and so rapidly evolving, some things are done well and some are not. Not every product issue can be resolved, but the services improve best when people tell vendors what they think. With librarians at over a thousand institutions looking at our various products, we hear a lot about potential improvements, and almost all of our upgrades have come directly from input from librarians and users. Also, when we make a mistake (and we don't claim to be perfect) you can believe that we hear about it immediately. It keeps us on our toes and keeps everyone honest.

The final question is "What's next?" The easy answer here is, "Lots and lots of really cool stuff is next." We've been developing relationships with related services, such as Ulrich's, for improved searching from both our service and from theirs. Mutual subscribers can link to our reports from their UlrichsWeb pages to learn if they have access to a specific journal, or link to a journal's bibliographic data, drawn from UlrichsWeb, directly from their Serials Solutions report.

Linking is an important area, as these URLs with UlrichsWeb take patrons directly to specific journal information within a database, instead of confusing the patron with another search. We've seen a tremendous increase in the availability of journal level linking since we began, and we believe this trend will continue, along with article level linking. Where journal level links are in place, we're now regularly seeing lists of volumes and issues and tables of contents provided by publishers and aggregators.

Serials Solutions will continue to explore and develop technology in this area, and I believe that everything we do will improve the services we offer to librarians. As our services improve, librarians will be able to provide better and better resources to their patrons, which, in the end, is truly the most important service.

I started as a reference librarian, and this product began with public services in mind. With integration into the OPAC, we've needed to add a strong technical services component to what we do. In either case, our goal has always been to make the best and most useful product possible. It is a rapidly evolving process, but the key word there is "evolving." We'll never be "done" with this product–we'll always find or hear of a new way to improve it. We cannot do that without input from other librarians, and I am sure that Mike feels the same way.

Thank you very much for your attention. I am pleased to have been invited to present here today, and I believe that the services provided by e-journal management companies significantly benefit patrons and library staff alike. I'm pleased to be involved in development of these resources, and I thank you again for your interest in our discussion of them.

NOTES

1. The NASIG Executive Board believes that this paper conveys a level of commercialism that is inappropriate for a NASIG presentation. NASIG conferences are not marketing opportunities, and we regret this break with our well-established traditions. The paper is printed in full as it was presented at the conference.

CONTRIBUTOR'S NOTES

Peter McCracken is co-founder of Serials Solutions.

Management of Electronic Serials, Outsourcing, and Bringing New Products to the Marketplace

Michael Markwith

Presenter

The NASIG conference this year has been filled with a lot of good conversation on issues specifically related to e-journal management. My talk is going to focus on what I think some of the key issues are and I will say up front that my remarks come from my personal perspective not necessarily from my company's perspective. The purpose of this concurrent session is to share and address the issues about choosing an e-journal management system.

This morning I will discuss some practical and pragmatic issues. We have been told that a third of the attendees at this conference are first-timers to NASIG. This is fantastic not only for the organization, but it also shows how important the "world of serials" is to librarianship. In this presentation, I will address the same issues that Peter raised. These are issues that all of us in this room have been talking about in nearly every conversation throughout this conference. It is incredible; it is wonderful stuff.

[Haworth co-indexing entry note]: "Management of Electronic Serials, Outsourcing, and Bringing New Products to the Marketplace." Markwith, Michael. Co-published simultaneously in *The Serials Librarian* (The Haworth Information Press, an imprint of The Haworth Press, Inc.) Vol. 44, No. 1/2, 2003, pp. 125-130; and: *Transforming Serials: The Revolution Continues* (ed: Susan L. Scheiberg, and Shelley Neville) The Haworth Information Press, an imprint of The Haworth Press, Inc., 2003, pp. 125-130. Single or multiple copies of this article are available for a fee from The Haworth Document Delivery Service [1-800-HAWORTH, 9:00 a.m. - 5:00 p.m. (EST). E-mail address: docdelivery@haworthpress.com].

http://www.haworthpress.com/store/product.asp?sku=J123
10.1300/J123v44n12_13

The questions/issues that we are addressing this morning are:

- Is there a need for e-journal management systems?
- If so, should an institution do it in-house, or find someone on the outside to do it?
- What do we, as vendors, see as the benefits of doing it in-house versus outsourcing it?
- What does a librarian risk by outsourcing this work?
- Assuming one decides to outsource it, what options are now available and what may be available in the future?
- How can librarians assess the value of work from a particular product and how can they improve the vendor's product?
- What's next?

Is there a need for e-journal management systems? I will establish the context for this question with the bold assertion that there is a definite "confusion of convenience" for library users today. I coined this phrase after hearing Ken Frazier speak at IFLA about how the students at the University of Wisconsin were "choking" on too much information and so the C words made sense to me. What has happened in the world of publishing is that information is provided traditionally or it is packaged by aggregators. It is purchased by individual libraries or through consortia and/or agents. To the end user it is a very confusing world. Also, this is all under the rubric of making access to information more convenient, so that there is more and better information for everyone. I would like to suggest a different conclusion.

One more important note of context: In 1995 I was working for Swets in the US and participating in their annual International Seminar. The topic for one of the sessions was "How are we going to handle all of these electronic journals?" and at the time there were approximately only 200 titles. In seven short years we see that the number of electronic journals has just mushroomed. It is now all types of journals and formats. When I started in this current job in 2001, we were managing 14,000 journals and now we are managing 39,000. This is a pretty dramatic leap and reminds me of this quote: "Until vendors can find and relieve user pain points, many e-products will continue to be solutions in search of a problem."[1]

What are the pain points? My initial proposal for this concurrent session was to involve a number of customers and non-customers to discuss the issues librarians feel are most important when selecting an e-journal management system. I reviewed my e-mail from customers and non-customers to try to determine their most frequently mentioned and relevant pain points.

The first is the volume and velocity of change data: what the URL is at any given moment, whether the title is in or out of any aggregator's full-text databases this week, and whether the coverage period has changed. Another point I identified from librarians is how does the agent fit into what we are doing? I hear comments such as "We want to support them and we need them to help manage the actual publisher subscription transactions." "If we are going all electronic, are they coming with us?" Established relationships and historic value have been the strength of the agent in the print world. With the format and the nature of the information changing, there is concern about how we are going to deal with all of this. The role of the subscription agent is an issue that is on serials librarian's minds and this has to be acknowledged as we move forward.

The second and third questions follow the first with discussion about librarians' perspectives on outsourcing and the vendor's response. First of all, from our professional perspective it is not an easy decision. Often this decision may be clear to the library leadership who have the responsibility and authority to save money or reallocate resources. But it's not necessarily clear to those of you who are doing the actual work. Sound familiar? Committees are convened. Discussions that I am very familiar with usually reveal this is not just an issue of outsourcing serials work, and it's not just a matter of outsourcing cataloging functions: This is a decision that affects the entire library.

In her introduction Eleanor mentioned my "shady past" as an acquisitions/serials librarian. In 1975 we were fighting the battle of outsourcing cataloging. We purchased single main-entry cards for a few pennies. Some thought this was cheaper than spending a dollar or so on getting a complete OCLC card catalog set with the machine-readable record. What we renegades pointed out was that although the main-entry card was less expensive it actually cost more to create a catalog record from the single main-entry card. Library money was spent on staff to create or find the subject headings, verify author information, and all the other requisite "metadata. Then the copying and typing on additional cards was required to complete a full card set. Sounds so bizarre now, doesn't it? And, of course we know that those who did this work did not necessarily lose their positions; they were redirected to do other important jobs in the library.

It is this issue of job security and control that is very important in the library's decision to outsource work such as e-journal management.

With a locally developed system there is a positive feeling that the staff knows the content and use of the entire collection. So it is very important that the library has total control over customizing every development. This is important for consistency for the user population. Conversely, there are not necessarily the software capabilities or the technical capabilities in all libraries to achieve these local goals. Although there are very bright people working in institutions, the institution is still limited to the local staff for a local solution. This involves a lot of time, money and resources. It then becomes a library leadership issue with the library directors saying, "Yes it's going to cost more if we are going to do something locally. Then we need the staff and the money to support the staff." Or, conversely, the library leadership chooses to outsource and use this money for other purposes.

The fourth question is "What do libraries risk when e-journal management is outsourced?" I agree with what Peter said about economies of scale. The economies of scale, of course, are what created the library vendor business. It is the intermediary, the third party, the bookseller who consolidated all of the books from various publishers and brought them into one warehouse, consolidated library orders, customized library specific shipments, and then produced a customized weekly or monthly library invoice. There was the serials agent who took all of the subscription invoices and put them together to form one annual invoice with occasional library specific supplemental invoices. Vendors put it all together in terms of reducing the clerical work that people do. So, in fact, by doing these things themselves, libraries do risk losing the value of the economies of scale. They risk the loss of familiar work patterns. Some original catalogers from 1975 still are not happy about the fact that some of their work has been taken away. Still, I think libraries lose valuable time and staff resources that could be better spent helping users deal with the confusion of convenience.

The fifth question we ask is what services are available "commercially?" In terms of outsourcing there are various options. There are A-Z lists, Web development, and the often misunderstood topic of open URL and newly emerging linking technologies. The various options form conversations that we (all 250 of us in this room) have on a daily basis because they are very important to us. We know that there is a lot of change happening, and we wonder how we are going to make all this information available. How are we going to manage all we have licensed and how are we are going to allow our users to access this information? Also, modules are being developed now through ILS vendors as components of their company's services. Some subscription agents have a long and valuable history of providing answers or services for librarians and are developing new services that merit consideration. Thus, a wide range of commercial options does exist and rather than speak specifically about the various companies involved, I want to discuss the issues that help inform a library's decision when choosing one of them. The strength of the commercial solution, in addition to the economy of scale issues, is that by definition they are in business to help libraries manage information as well as to free staff from basic tasks. In e-journal management this means tracking links, resolving links, and providing statistical information necessary for justifying the money spent on e-journals, all in a customized environment. The commercial companies that say it's "my way or the highway" usually find they are the ones left behind! The weakness of commercially provided services is the perception of the lost local look and feel that is so important. There is the feeling of transferring control that cannot be denied. And, finally, the commercial vendor is not able to provide real time updates of local OPAC records.

The sixth question we ask is that the librarians assess the vendor value. I think that the "r word" is very important. Relationships. The conclusions of conversations between vendor and librarian are what develop products. This is a new definition of a business relationship: understanding that librarians have need for services, we have products, and making the two come together. It is not necessarily the buy/sell relationship as much as it is the service development relationship. This has been a real breakthrough in terms of how the commercial and the library world work together especially in e-journal management. This is very different from experiences that I had in other services provided by library vendors. Another way that vendors get assessed besides direct feedback, whether direct conversation or e-mail, is to include feedback mechanisms in the basic service. The Web is a wonderfully interactive tool that allows communicating suggestions or complaints directly with the provider. Finally, I think it's very important that the vendor should be assessed on how their service enables the library in an economic and timely way to make available all of the electronic information that has been purchased in a convenient and non-confusing manner.

The seventh and final question: What is next? Where we are going with these e-journal management services? Most of us in this room recognize that how we use information is changing. We are not confined to purchased books, journals, or commercial databases. Information abounds on locally created Word documents, or an internal memo, or an e-mail. The world has changed dramatically in terms of scholarly communication and it's going a lot faster than many of us in this room want it to. What is going to happen next in this business, I think, is that we are going to get out of our traditional ways and look at ways to integrate all forms of electronic information. What is next is finding a way to drive that information in a customized way to end users so that they control their own e-journal lists, their own e-book lists, their own content lists, their own document sources, and their own e-mails in one customized environment. I think that we are going to see companies collaborating and not trying to create solutions on their own. We will be doing it in partnerships with businesses like ILS vendors, subscription agents, primary publishers, and with libraries. And we will use the technology and services created thus far to move towards e-content instead of just e-journal management systems.

Thank you!

NOTES

1. Outsell, Inc: "Outlook 2002: Information in the Marketplace," *Information About Information*, v. 4, n. 57 (December 21, 2001), p. 18.

CONTRIBUTOR'S NOTES

Michael Markwith is President of TDNet, Inc.

Historical Messages in the Digital Medium

Roger Matuz
Nancy Godleski

Presenters

Christine Ericson

Recorder

SUMMARY. The presenters addressed the ongoing effects of technology on scholarly communications and serial publications, specifically the digitization of serial archives. The manufacturing process of historical periodical databases, librarian-vendor relationships and criteria for evaluating digital archives were covered. *[Article copies available for a fee from The Haworth Document Delivery Service: 1-800-HAWORTH. E-mail address: <docdelivery@haworthpress.com> Website: <http://www.HaworthPress.com>]*

Rapidly changing technology has had an enormous impact on scholarly communications and publications, especially in the digitization of serial archives. Recent advances in the last few years have made it possible to develop increasingly sophisticated databases of historical content. There are many factors to consider, however, when deciding whether or not to digitize serial collections. Roger Matuz, who develops

[Haworth co-indexing entry note]: "Historical Messages in the Digital Medium." Ericson, Christine. Co-published simultaneously in *The Serials Librarian* (The Haworth Information Press, an imprint of The Haworth Press, Inc.) Vol. 44, No. 1/2, 2003, pp. 131-134; and: *Transforming Serials: The Revolution Continues* (ed: Susan L. Scheiberg, and Shelley Neville) The Haworth Information Press, an imprint of The Haworth Press, Inc., 2003, pp. 131-134. Single or multiple copies of this article are available for a fee from The Haworth Document Delivery Service [1-800-HAWORTH, 9:00 a.m. - 5:00 p.m. (EST). E-mail address: docdelivery@haworthpress.com].

databases of historical periodical content for Proquest Information and Learning, briefly outlined these factors and then discussed the manufacturing process in the creation of digital archives.

Matuz began his discussion with examples of digitized images and articles from periodicals dating back to the eighteenth century. But why, he asked, should this content be digitized? Magazines are full of cultural artifacts and can be very useful in scholarly research. Old issues, however, are often very fragile and researchers may have to travel great distances to use these primary sources. In addition, microfilm holdings are often inconvenient to use.

Digital databases, in contrast, offer full-page images and text in their original context, robust search capabilities and increased retrieval speed. Fragile paper documents can be better preserved through less frequent handling and through digitization, historical content can be made readily available to a wider range of people. Library patrons, who are becoming increasingly computer literate, are expecting higher levels of service and more electronic products. Also, databases are often stored on remote servers and thus do not take up library space, other than the terminals used for accessing the library's electronic information.

Matuz then went on to discuss the process by which print is converted into electronic form. There are basically three methods of capturing historical content. One way is to re-key the original source, which results in full-text search capability, but loses often crucial images. This method is most appropriate for monographs or scholarly journals, which are mainly text. The second method is to scan the print source. This method retains the original context of the page, but results in a lower optical character recognition (OCR) rate and thus decreased search capability. The third method, which Matuz discussed in further detail, is to scan the original microform. This method, which is the most costly, is the most attractive in that it offers full-text search capability while retaining the context of the full-page image. This method also offers enhanced tools that allow for better searchability such as index links and bibliographic records.

Prior to any work, however, there are many pre-production decisions to be made–editorial decisions as to how to display the content, how the end product will be searched, and the addition of added-value features that might enhance or supplement the content. From the outset, librarians, subject specialists, and faculty should be consulted in the creation process in order to meet the expectations of the end user.

The digitization process begins with the check-in stage. The scanning operator prepares the microform by capturing bibliographic information on each article according to the pre-set editorial guidelines. With the help of scanning software, the operator captures each image separately, cropping out any extraneous material that could slow down retrieval time.

Once the images have been scanned and saved as TIF files, the digitization begins. In a process called "zoning," each image is separated from its original source, cleaned up and "tagged." There are basically three types of tags: an article tag covers anything that is text-based; an article can be tagged as fiction, for example. The second kind of tag covers images such as illustrations, photographs, comics, etc. The third kind of tag describes non-article textual information such as a table of contents or acknowledgements. Tagging allows for much more robust search capabilities. For example, users can search the database for photographs or advertisements on a particular subject. In another example, especially in light of the Tasini decision regarding copyright issues, articles and photographs can be given "yes/no" tags that can be activated, blocking their retrieval from the database.

Each stage of the digitization process is subject to stringent quality control checks to ensure high image quality and OCR rates. In the final stage the retrieval speed and accuracy of the database are tested. User feedback is solicited upon the release of the database and any changes or updates can be added relatively easily.

Following Matuz's presentation, historian and librarian Nancy Godleski of Yale University discussed the criteria used in selecting and evaluating databases. Basically, there are three criteria: content, usability and accessibility, and cost. Librarians need to determine the value of the content and how it would enhance their collections. Does the database offer a coherent collection? Is it a full run of one serial title or is it a group of selected serials? Does it duplicate existing holdings and if it does, what value does it add as a research tool? There are also many questions to ask in terms of usability and accessibility. Is the database easy to use? Does it have an intuitive search engine? Does it have indexes and full-text searching? What are the equipment requirements? Are MARC records available? Can it be used as a pedagogical tool? Cost is also an important issue in selecting a database. Do the features of the database justify the cost involved? Librarians need to decide whether to subscribe to a database or purchase it outright. Pricing structures and negotiations can be very confusing, especially for consortia.

Both Godleski and Matuz stressed the importance of communication between the librarian and the vendor in the development of historical periodical databases. Reference librarians know what kind of research tools their patrons want and need and must convey this information to the vendors. User groups, advisory boards, beta testing, and numerous trials are all essential in determining whether or not a database will fulfill needed requirements. Librarians need to work closely with vendors to ensure a useful, cost-effective product, without all the fancy "bells and whistles" that merely drive up the cost of the database. Vendors need to solicit feedback from librarians and their users as they develop their products to ensure customer satisfaction.

As the presentation concluded, audience members asked many questions. One concern was what happens if a publisher goes out of business. License agreements should contain contingency plans for continued storage and access. Also, can a database really serve as a long-term archive? In her role as a historian, Godleski stressed the importance of realizing that a digital database is just a research tool–it is not the "real thing." Audience members also wanted to know how commercial vendors select collections to digitize and how they can get their own collections digitized. Demand for a product must be high enough to justify the cost and time involved in creating a digital database. As technology improves and costs decrease, more historical archives can be digitized, which will allow libraries to offer even higher levels of service to their patrons

CONTRIBUTORS' NOTES

Roger Matuz is Product Manager at Proquest Information and Learning. Nancy Godleski is the Kaplanoff Librarian for American History at Yale University. Christine Ericson is Serials Assistant, Consortium Library, University of Alaska, Anchorage.

Get Hip to E-Journals
and Forget About the Print:
Inciting a Faculty Revolution?

Janet Palmer
Mark Sandler

Presenters

Sarah E. George

Recorder

SUMMARY. This project studied the attitudes and behaviors of sixty-one social science professors at the University of Michigan. Qualitative interviews were conducted to determine faculty preferences for print and electronic use of journals. Preliminary data analysis indicates a general acceptance of electronic journals despite significant concerns for the loss of print journals. *[Article copies available for a fee from The Haworth Document Delivery Service: 1-800-HAWORTH. E-mail address: <docdelivery@haworthpress.com> Website: <http://www.HaworthPress.com>]*

The University of Michigan Libraries, like many academic libraries, felt pressure on its storage space and acquisitions budget and wanted to explore options for addressing these issues. Causes of this pressure in-

[Haworth co-indexing entry note]: "Get Hip to E-Journals and Forget About the Print: Inciting a Faculty Revolution?" George, Sarah E. Co-published simultaneously in *The Serials Librarian* (The Haworth Information Press, an imprint of The Haworth Press, Inc.) Vol. 44, No. 1/2, 2003, pp. 135-142; and: *Transforming Serials: The Revolution Continues* (ed: Susan L. Scheiberg, and Shelley Neville) The Haworth Information Press, an imprint of The Haworth Press, Inc., 2003, pp. 135-142. Single or multiple copies of this article are available for a fee from The Haworth Document Delivery Service [1-800-HAWORTH, 9:00 a.m. - 5:00 p.m. (EST). E-mail address: docdelivery@haworthpress.com].

cluded the proliferation of scholarly publishing and of information in print and electronic formats. This scenario is especially true for serials budgets. Studies published in the literature point to the growing acceptance of electronic journals within the science, technology, and medical fields; however, studies of humanities and social science professors have typically shown reluctance in using electronic journals. What are the implications of these user needs in light of the pressures experienced by the library?

Mark Sandler and Janet Palmer designed this project to explore options for reducing the duality of formats and the possible effects of these options on collection development policies. They elected to study social science disciplines as a "middle ground" between science and humanities. Taking Sandler's idea, Palmer developed the research design and conducted the interviews. The project sought to answer three main questions:

1. Among which disciplines, disciplinary concentrations, and/or methodological orientations might users be most receptive to electronic-only access to journals?
2. What concerns do users have regarding electronic-only access to journals?
3. What do faculty responses suggest for future collection development policies?

METHODOLOGY, SAMPLE, AND INTERVIEW PROTOCOL

Palmer used qualitative, semi-structured, face-to-face interviews as her method for obtaining data. Questions were intended to generate in-depth, semi-exploratory discussions. Face-to-face interviews, lasting thirty to ninety minutes each, afforded an improved response rate and a richer quality of discussion.

The purposive sample consisted of sixty-one faculty members. The professors represented three different departments–twenty in economics, twenty in sociology, and twenty-one in anthropology. The sample was limited to tenured or tenure-track faculty. Variations in the sample occurred in subject specializations, research methodology employed, disciplinary expectations for output, age, rank, and gender.

Each interview consisted of questions arranged into ten categories:

1. Subject focus and research methods
2. Publishing and disseminating
3. Journal/book use ratio
4. Access/use of current journals
5. Access/use of journal backfiles
6. Three hypothetical scenarios regarding choice electronic or print journals
7. Perceptions about current mode of access that colleagues and students are using
8. Projections about future mode of access and use by graduate students
9. Index of "computer cosmopolitanism" (e.g., purchasing airline tickets online)
10. Final thoughts?

Some categories consisted of multiple questions; for example, several questions about computer and Internet use fleshed out the concept of computer cosmopolitanism.

SELECTED RESULTS

Sample demographics included gender, faculty rank, date of Ph.D., and type of research methodology employed. The majority of faculty interviewed were male (44 out of 61). All ranks were represented: 2 emeritus, 28 professors, 17 associate professors, and 14 assistant professors. The faculty also represented a diverse range of ages, as measured by the year the Ph.D. was earned. Twenty-five percent earned their doctorate in the 1960s; eleven percent in the 1970s, 23% in the 1980s, and 36% in the 1990s. Overall, these data support the study's selection of highly influential and productive faculty members. There was equal representation between quantitative and qualitative research methodology, and 10 percent employed a combination of the two. For individual departments the distributions of methodologies were 55% quantitative, 20% qualitative, 25% mixed methods for economics; 50% quantitative and 50% qualitative for sociology; and 33% quantitative, 62% qualitative, and 5% mixed methods for anthropology. One area of initial interest was the comparison between perspectives of faculty using cultural or historical methodologies and of faculty using more scientifically oriented ones. However, such comparison proved difficult because many faculty did not easily fit into these methodological categories, and disciplines differ in the interpretation of the categories.

Palmer then presented specific data for two interview questions–dealing with journal format preference and projecting future access, respectively.

The first question, "Do you prefer accessing current journals in print or electronic form?", elicited many qualified answers and proved difficult to categorize. Comments included access to and use of journals generally, rather than just current journals. Comments were categorized into four preference tendencies: those that prefer print, those that prefer print but accept electronic, those that like electronic but also want print, and those that prefer electronic with less concern for print. These categories describe a continuum of preferences rather than discrete opinions. A general ambivalence prevailed regarding the options, even among those who were less concerned about print.

Four faculty members indicated that they had strong preferences for print journals. These men have senior rank and represent each department studied. All received their degrees in the 1960s, and three of them rely on qualitative or historical research methods. They exhibited less familiarity and use of computer-based information than their colleagues.

An additional nine professors preferred print but accepted the electronic format, although at times begrudgingly. Two-thirds of these professors received their degrees in the 1960s or 1970s; seven of nine employ cultural or historical research methods. Additionally, seven of nine still used the older, telnet version of the library's online catalog.

Four professors favored electronic journals but wanted print copies available; some explicitly stated that the print copy would serve as a permanent archive. This group consisted of senior professors but their degree dates were not consistent. They also had a range of library skills.

Forty-two faculty members liked electronic journals and were less concerned about print copies. However, they acknowledged their colleagues' need for print and their preference for books in print over electronic editions. All of them assumed the existence of a print archive.

Faculty concerns about the loss of print and electronic access emerged during the interviews. Print journals were considered "the proven archive" and a necessity for more obscure and non-English titles. At least one professor attributed his preference for print journals to his imminent retirement and the resulting lack of motivation to learn new things. An anthropologist who received her doctorate in the 1970s described her feelings about the enduring value of print:

It's so personal. I guess as an anthropologist, the one thing that always strikes me about the medium in which this stuff is conveyed, says a lot about the social relationship between the person doing the reading and the people who produced the thing. I guess I feel like it's more direct when you have the actual thing they produced rather than another iteration of it in a different form. I guess it's that. And . . . like to some people it doesn't matter, but for an anthropologist, you know, *who did it* matters. So even seeing the drips and drops on the page or whatever is part of what it's all about.

Other faculty stated that electronic access was desirable yet added several qualifications: availability of journals in both formats, option to print out the electronic articles, and access to top of the line technology. On the other hand, one professor predicted that the library "will have a revolt on your hands if you take this [e-access] away now."

The second question was "Do you have any sense as to which mode accessing journals your graduate students–say the faculty of the future–will be choosing for their research and teaching?" Faculty overwhelmingly predicted that current graduate students would use electronic journals (90%). Three professors believed there would be a mix of electronic and print access. Only one thought that print journals would be the more prevalent form. Responses to this question reflect some disciplinary bias. For example, 95% of the Economics faculty predicted electronic journals for future use by graduate students, whereas 86% of Anthropology selected electronic-only access to journals.

Other representative comments by faculty include the following:

- [S]ince most of graduate students do ethnography and history I can't imagine they'll give up paper. You need to find old things, you know, traveling to other countries and bringing stuff back with them.
- Well I think it's going to be both . . . there are those who are still, sort of, digging their heels in, you know, and insisting on the print . . . it's really a function of convenience, economy, a whole variety of things.
- My guess is it will depend on their disciplinary belongingness . . . I think people are moving to electronic, but some people feel quite strongly about remaining with the print format . . . so there'll be some resistance.

- I don't know how these things will develop . . . right now it may be that electronic subscribers are free-riding on the money that paper subscribers pay . . . everything will depend on what the prices are.
- I expect that most of the younger people are more into online than the hard copies.
- I'm sure they're going to be entirely electronic. No doubt.
- Electronic more and more, assuming it's available, freely available.

CONCLUSION

The majority of faculty interviewed expect that electronic journals are readily available and they appreciate the convenience and immediacy that the electronic format provides. However, they valued access to print journals and were clearly concerned about its potential loss, even among those who most appreciated electronic journals. Attention to these faculty concerns when possible will facilitate the adoption of new collection development policies when necessary.

Data analysis for this project has already provided the library administration with a clearer understanding of faculty concerns and their appreciation for print and electronic access. Future analysis of other interview questions should broaden these findings and provide links to similar projects conducted at other institutions.

DISCUSSION

Audience discussion after this presentation was lively. Some questions sought corroboration for anecdotal evidence from other institutions. Others inquired about faculty perspectives on a few "hot topics" in serials.

A librarian from the University of Maryland reported on an upcoming article that discusses faculty preferences for non-core journals.[1] In that study seventy percent of faculty surveyed preferred electronic access for these journals. However, faculty who used fewer core journals and more peripheral titles were concerned that journals will be dropped because they are not available electronically.

When asked about archiving, Palmer reported that most faculty wanted "the real thing" as the archival copy, which she interprets to mean a paper copy. Faculty also believed that journals must be archived somewhere. However, many faculty were not interested in the archival debates among the major players. Those professors who are strong supporters of the library expressed more concern about the archival dilemma and the limitations of state funding.

Palmer's analysis of faculty opinions and behavior boiled down to a common thread–that most faculty are concerned simply with doing their work and being productive. They appreciate assistance from the library to correct their misconceptions about the number of journals available electronically or about how much such access costs. Most of the faculty interviewed did not initially report differences in content between print and electronic journals. They did comment on the gaps in coverage of electronic journals; for example, a journal included in JSTOR may have a gap between the older coverage included in JSTOR and the more recent material available through another provider. Once they were made aware of issues relating to completeness of online journals, they noticed such differences more frequently. As for reading online, most choose to print out the articles because reading online hurts their eyes or they are tired of sitting at their desks.

Are these preferences for electronic journals transferable to books? Although the focus of this study did not include electronic books, Palmer said that e-books were often mentioned in the interviews. Generally, faculty were not enthusiastic about e-books. Reasons included the longer length of time required to skim an online book and the inability to flip pages. One faculty member declared his ambivalence to which format was chosen for journals so long as books remained in the paper format. When asked why, he replied, "I like the bookness of books."

How do the faculty's perspectives change when they move from the role of researcher to author? Some professors felt that their work is more freely available when it appears in electronic form. Others were concerned about plagiarism. Still others mentioned that publishing in electronic form does not yet have the same stature as a print publication.

Palmer closed with the admonition to "get hip!" Electronic journals are fast, easy, and accepted by the faculty of the future.

NOTES

1. Dillon, Irma F., and Karla L. Hahn. "Are Researchers Ready for the Electronic-Only Journal Collection? Results of a Survey at the University of Maryland." *portal: Libraries and the Academy*, 2 (July 2002): 375-390.

CONTRIBUTORS' NOTES

Janet Palmer is University Library Research Fellow, University of Michigan, Ann Arbor. Mark Sandler is Collection Development Officer, University of Michigan, Ann Arbor. Sarah E. George is Serials Librarian, Illinois Wesleyan University.

Cataloging:
The Good, the Bad and the Ugly

Regina Romano Reynolds

Presenter

JoAnne Deeken

Recorder

SUMMARY. Regina Romano Reynolds of the Library of Congress gave a wide-ranging presentation on the current state of cataloging. She praised the good things the catalog does, and pointed out problem areas and intractable problems. She proposed some solutions to the problem areas. Periodically in the presentation she asked for (and received) audience reactions and additional suggestions. *[Article copies available for a fee from The Haworth Document Delivery Service: 1-800-HAWORTH. E-mail address: <docdelivery@haworthpress.com> Website: <http://www.HaworthPress.com>]*

Mary Page introduced Regina Romano Reynolds by saying "[She] makes any topic interesting . . . I could listen to her reading the phone book." Ms. Reynolds lived up to the high expectations of Ms. Page.[1]

[Haworth co-indexing entry note]: "Cataloging: The Good, the Bad and the Ugly." Deeken, JoAnne. Co-published simultaneously in *The Serials Librarian* (The Haworth Information Press, an imprint of The Haworth Press, Inc.) Vol. 44, No. 1/2, 2003, pp. 143-153; and: *Transforming Serials: The Revolution Continues* (ed: Susan L. Scheiberg, and Shelley Neville) The Haworth Information Press, an imprint of The Haworth Press, Inc., 2003, pp. 143-153. Single or multiple copies of this article are available for a fee from The Haworth Document Delivery Service [1-800-HAWORTH, 9:00 a.m. - 5:00 p.m. (EST). E-mail address: docdelivery@haworthpress.com].

http://www.haworthpress.com/store/product.asp?sku=J123
10.1300/J123v44n12_16

Ms. Reynolds stated that the purposes of her talk were to stimulate thinking, challenge assumptions, and propose possible solutions. We, as catalogers, must demonstrate the worth of our work and that we can change as different needs arise. Only by becoming flexible marketers can we survive in this world of change and competition.

The talk was outlined as dealing with five areas. These were the "good" (defined as "examples of things done well"); the "bad" ("examples of things we can do better"), the "ugly" ("examples of complex, intractable problems"); how technology can help, and the follow-up (organizations for referral of ideas). Audience input was solicited (and obtained) in each of these areas.

Before jumping into these areas, Ms. Reynolds discussed the nature of cataloging. It can be costly, unresponsive to users' needs, threatened by alternative search mechanisms and is unable to keep up with the increasing number of resources. However, cataloging is vital to the retrieval of material. All present liked OCLC's button stating "Cataloging IS public service." Cataloging (or perhaps "catalogers") must change in response to the new demands or be replaced. Alternatives to cataloging are already available for some types of materials; for example, many libraries have Web lists of electronic journals instead of full cataloging for them. At this conference there were sessions on alternatives to creating individual MARC records for e-journals. Catalogers are becoming more versatile and inventive; we need to continue this innovative thinking.

One of the greatest achievements of the cataloging community is authority control; our national authority file is a magnificent accomplishment. Other information providers are becoming aware of the need for, and existence of, such files. Our classification systems are thoroughly realized and can be used in the Web environment. With its logical structure, the Dewey Decimal Classification is particularly suited for providing access to materials in this new environment. Library catalogs demonstrate the advantages of a controlled vocabulary over keyword searching. On her overhead, Ms. Reynolds likened LCSH to a gold mine.

An example of Ms. Reynolds ability to weave humor into a situation and still make a valid point is her analogy regarding the quality, accuracy, and standardization of our catalogs. She said the cataloging underlying these was "like underwear." It provides support and is a foundation of library access. It's also something people don't like to talk about. "Think about this the next time someone says cataloging isn't sexy."

Our libraries provide access to a breadth and depth of information that cannot be matched in the Web world. We cover material going back centuries, most of which will never be digitized, although access to this older material is often crucial for research. The catalog is the gateway to the material in the libraries–researchers will not locate this information if they don't use the catalog. Bypassing the catalog will become the norm if we aren't able to provide some of the user-friendly features found in Web searching.

One of our responsibilities is to champion the role of the catalog. The catalog should be determining the shape of information retrieval systems, not vice versa. At the same time, we have to realize the library no longer stands alone. We need to partner with Web developers in creating new access mechanisms. We can contribute our expertise in information retrieval, our authority files and our controlled vocabularies. Our partners can contribute descriptive, structural, and other metadata. An example of an area where a partnership opportunity exists is the recently developed ONIX standard that publishers are using to provide information to vendors and booksellers like Amazon.com. The Library of Congress has been very successful in an experiment to add table of contents information extracted from publisher ONIX records to existing catalog records.

LCSH is a wonderful tool, but we have to acknowledge that its structure is too complicated for anyone except librarians. We need to create and make available a simplified version of LCSH for use outside the library catalog. Publishers could then create the subject headings for their material as it is produced. This metadata would be as widely available and usable as CIP. Lois Chen is working on a simplified syntax for LCSH that may meet this need.

At this point, Ms. Reynolds asked for audience input on the good portions of our catalogs. She specifically asked for groups with which we should partner.[2] The audience felt we needed to be involved in both university and library strategic planning. These groups are shaping the future and we need to help in that process. We also need to partner with vendors and the WWW consortium in the development of search engines and Web standards. It's also important for us as catalogers to touch base with our public services librarians to find out what works or doesn't work with the catalog. We need to be leading library instruction classes not just for the patrons, but for our staff and clerks as well. A staff unable to use a catalog ensures ineffective and time-consuming searches by patrons.

Ms. Reynolds then went on to describe things the catalog does badly. The first was our use of inscrutable terminology and notes. We need to use common terms (CD-ROM, DVD) in our records. Catalogers should not be spending time composing notes in "cataloging style." Notes are not prescribed by AACR2. Catalogers are free to compose notes in natural language; we need to encourage ourselves to use this option. The abbreviations used in cataloging were developed to conserve space on the physical card. In an electronic environment, adding a few more characters increases understanding and use of the information.

Current cataloging rules require exact transcription from an item to the catalog record. Does a user care about a "prescribed source of information" or understand our particular use of brackets? In a traditional catalog, we transcribe what a resource says it is and may not describe the essence of what it is. The layout we so painstakingly transcribe is often unintentional since a book designer concentrates on visual appeal while creating it. In cataloging digital materials, the type of browser used and the date one looks at the site affect what is seen. In an electronic environment, exact transcription is probably unnecessary and confusing.

The emergence of electronic resources has caused other problems for the catalog. Should we be creating traditional catalog records for these resources or are new solutions possible? Any new solution would require the creation and acceptance of standards so that access could be assured. Search engines are becoming better and are much more user friendly than are catalogs, and we need to incorporate some of those user-friendly features into our catalogs. We should be looking for ways to display cover images, user recommendations and related works. If we don't provide them, users will bypass the catalog. Many of us are trying to cover the entire digital universe in our catalogs. How can we partner with each other and with other interested groups to share this work?

There is a tension between AACR2 and MARC. AACR2 is written as if MARC didn't exist; MARC gets blamed for many problems that are really AACR2 problems. AACR2 is tied to the card environment. The 3x5 card assumes one looks at an entire record at once. Conventions such as main entry, order of notes, and abbreviations are all tied to the appearance of the card. But MARC and our current on-line catalogs operate in a database environment, and databases expect fields of information to be accessed independently. Presentation of the information from a database is established independent of the order in which it is created. The view of an entire record at once is not the norm. As we take advantage of the freedom offered by database technology, following the rules related to a 3x5 card is counterproductive. MARC may well outlast AACR. It is a flexible format that can handle other metadata schema, such as Dublin Core.

The further examples of the "'ghost' of the 3x5 card" Ms. Reynolds mentioned included ISBD punctuation, main and added entries, the construction of a "body of the description" instead of separate, independent fields, and the requirement (even in the revised Chapter 12) that the description of a serial all come from the same issue, and abbreviation. The Joint Steering Committee (JSC) will be looking at some of these issues.

Ms. Reynolds suggested some strategies for improvement. We should continue revising AACR, but make revision continuous and always include implementation timelines. JSC might consider contracting a study of the vocabulary and elements of catalog records. We also need better OPAC displays for both the expert and novice. Technology can help us capitalize on the effort we put into cataloging by allowing us to take better advantage of the wealth of information in them.

Members of the audience suggested other strategies. In order to preserve information that is valuable to the cataloger, but not to the public, there could be an entirely different staff view from public view. The public view would have the information meaningful to the patrons in a more unformatted display and the staff view would be more like the formatted view we have today. A problem with trying to describe the essence of material is the subjectivity needed to describe what a resource *is* versus what it *says* it is. How can we incorporate subjectivity without losing the objectivity provided by our rules? The Functional Requirements for Bibliographic Records (FRBR) model was suggested as an approach to balance objectivity and subjectivity.

There were five areas of the "ugly" discussed–multiple versions (format variations), multiple ISSNs, titles in aggregations, latest vs. successive entry, and conference proceedings. Creating a separate record for each format of a title is prescribed, but many libraries are ignoring this rule because the separate records are expensive and time-consuming to create and confusing for users of the catalog. There are also disadvantages to using one record for all formats in that rules do not yet exist that allow us to *describe* all formats on one bibliographic record. Some libraries have developed local practice for description; these local practices could become the basis of a future standard. An alternate suggestion has been to put the descriptive information in the holding record. While this makes logical sense, currently there is no way to share this information with other libraries and gain cataloging efficiency. Many libraries purchase catalog record sets, especially for microform or electronic formats. How could these be used in conjunction with a single record? And, if we use the print record as the basis for description, what does a library do if it doesn't own the print?

A JSC task force is exploring use of the Functional Requirements for Bibliographic Records (FRBR) to solve the multiple format dilemma by cataloging serials at the expression level, but preliminary results are not positive. With only a manifestation in hand it is difficult to create a record for the expression. Sometimes the expression evolves after, and based upon, the various manifestations. FRBR assumes the expression exists before any particular manifestation of it.

The ISSN has become a manifestation level identifier. The publisher needs this unique number to control its products and subscriptions necessitating a separate ISSN for each format of a journal. Indexing and abstracting services want the ISSN to be assigned at the expression level since this makes the identification of articles separate from their format. The assignment of ISSN by format also causes problems with the one record policy.

Titles in aggregations are major headaches for everyone. Exactly what is an aggregator–a publisher? A distributor? Some other entity not yet described? Currently there is no standard for describing aggregators. Because of the lack of standards and changes in practices, our national databases have a "jumble" of records. Some of these records show the aggregator as the publisher and others show them simply as the access method. CONSER is discussing these issues and developing a possible solution.

Ms. Reynolds next "braved the dragon" and talked about latest versus successive entry cataloging. With latest entry cataloging, the entire history of a serial and a library's entire holdings for that serial are on one record and are thus easier for a patron to use. However, there is a conflict with the ISSN standard that requires successive entries. Also, latest entry records can grow long, complex, and become difficult to interpret, even by trained serialists. The records cannot be separated easily into successive entries. According to Ms. Reynolds, successive entries are shorter, and easier to create and maintain. Additionally, successive entry records can be combined into a latest entry record and they are compatible with ISSN. However, the history of the serial and each library's holdings are spread over multiple records.

The final "ugly" problem in serials cataloging Ms. Reynolds discussed was conference proceedings. These can be handled as straight serials, as analyzed series, or as monographs. No one way is correct and a library often makes different decisions on how to catalog based on the conference. Treatment as a straight serial is less costly, but one loses individual subject and title access. Treatment as a monograph is the most costly alternative, but does give a complete description of each conference. An analyzed series is the cross between the two, but the cost savings are minimal at best.

After discussing the "bad" and the "ugly" issues, Ms. Reynolds suggested some solutions. The three types of solutions she mentioned were: changing the cataloging rules, abandoning cataloging, and exploiting technology. There are obvious problems with the first two. Although we keep changing cataloging rules, we can't change them often enough and quickly enough to keep up with the changes in our world. Abandoning cataloging would be "throwing out the baby with the bath water." According to Ms. Reynolds, the third possibility is the strongest. Currently most of our online systems mimic the card catalog. Using computer technology can provide assistance, but ILS vendors won't build change into their systems without a demand from libraries for the changes.

Matthew Beacom has spoken of some cataloging issues as questions of "lumping vs. splitting." Latest entry cataloging of serials is an example of lumping: all the information about a title is put together on one record. Successive entry cataloging is an example of splitting: separate records are created for each title and are linked together. Neither of these solutions works perfectly. We need to find a system that allows us to do both.

Catalogers could create records at the finest level of granularity. These records would be shorter and easier to create than our current records and they would be easy to remove from the catalog if necessary. Lumped records would be created by the system when a coarser level of granularity is desired. The individual records for each title could be used for purchase orders, for check-in records, and for use by technical services staff. These "split" records would also be part of global shared databases (e.g., OCLC, RLIN.) But the local holdings, the local OPAC displays, and the records of shared holdings could be pulled together into one consolidated display record. One of the items on the Action Plan resulting from LC's *Conference on Bibliographic Control in the New Millennium* is to

> [d]efine functional requirements for systems that can manage separate records for related manifestations at the global level and con-

solidate them for display at the local level. Communicate the requirements to the vendor community and encourage their adoption."[3]

Ms. Reynolds then showed a mock-up of screens a local catalog might display. The particular journal she used as an example did not have title changes, but it had holdings in multiple formats. The first screen would show the title, selected descriptive fields from the bibliographic record and a list of available formats with dates of coverage for those formats. Choosing one of those formats would pull up a screen with essential elements from the catalog record for that format. The call number, holdings, and circulation status for that particular format would appear at the bottom of the record. Underlying this record, and available in an advanced view, would be a complete catalog record for the individual format.

Ms. Reynolds believes that the "multiple versions" or "format variations" problem is really twofold, and that solving the display problem solves only half of the problem. The other half is the time and effort needed to create multiple records when multiple formats are received at the same time. Current record "cloning" techniques are perhaps not the most efficient approach. Ms. Reynolds proposed that a combined input screen be developed to solve this problem. She showed a mock-up of a template-based input screen that would allow for the creation of the multiple records at once. Such a template would allow the cataloger to choose a primary format for input purposes and specify the other formats.

A lumping and splitting approach could help solve the "latest entry" vs. "successive entry" discussion. We could use successive entry for cataloging, purchasing, and claiming the title. The system would pull the records together for a latest entry display to the public. The holdings would be in one holdings statement.

Regarding the identification of individual titles, we need to consider the possible impact of the International Standard Textual Code (ISTC), a draft standard from ISO for a work-level identifier. The ISTC could identify the serial work (however that is defined), with the manifestations being the individual titles and associated individual ISSN.

Reynolds showed a screen mock-up of "split and lumped" title change solution. If a patron did a search on a title that had undergone a succession of changes, the first display would be a list of the sequential titles together with the years of coverage. A patron would choose the title s/he wants based on title and year and then get the brief description with all available formats and dates of coverage for that title.

Thinking outside our usual lines, we could consider a graphic solution to the linkage issue, instead of relying on the verbal linkages we currently use. The ISSN Network has developed a display of a complex "serials family." This sample screen is complicated to view, but with better screen design and the ability to click on any part of the graphic, this could be a useful approach.

One of the issues identified as problematic with serials cataloging is dealing with multiple ISSNs. Can lumping and splitting help us with this issue? To reiterate the problem, libraries use the unique ISSN for ordering and claiming. Publishers use them for keeping track of subscriptions and for catalogs. All current cataloging rules assume one ISSN per title and format. A single ISSN is needed/wanted by A&I services, for document delivery, and for linking services such as Cross-Ref and SFX. Even though it is not officially sanctioned, many libraries are using a "one record" approach to cataloging. In doing this, they must choose the primary ISSN for the record.

An alternate suggestion would be for the cataloger to use repeatable 776 (other physical forms available) fields to enter the multiple ISSN associated with each title. NSDP and other ISSN centers are encouraging publishers to list all the ISSN appropriate to the title on each format published. Tables transparent to the user could list all ISSN for a title, or the ISTC could be used as the linking identifier. Ms. Reynolds then showed examples of each of those possible solutions.

Titles in aggregations are a real issue. Creating a separate record for every title in every aggregation is overkill, as these are not different resources. They are the same resources accessed through a different interface. We need an "aggregator neutral" record. Ms. Reynolds suggested lumping at the national level, with information for each aggregator in a specified field(s). An individual library would choose whether to have one or more records, depending on their individual situation. It is imperative that these records be constructed so that they can easily be identified and titles added or removed by services such as Serials Solution, TDNet, or SFX and that individual aggregators of a title can be added and removed. As an example, the 130 field for a title could have a generic |h (Online). There could be separate 856 fields listing separate Web addresses for each aggregator.

The problems related to conference proceedings were the last of the ugly problems addressed. Ms. Reynolds felt that the best possible solution from the patrons' point of view is to have separate records for each conference. But if separate records are not available, then there are lump or split options for them as well. They can be cataloged as serials or not-analyzed series or the series record can have an 856 field with a link to the individual title information. This link could be to a Web page maintained by the group sponsoring the conference or it could be a Web page maintained by the library.

Before turning the discussion over to the attendees, Ms. Reynolds had suggestions for new cataloging systems. She would like to see systems that were further developed to include templates with pull down menus for either novice or experienced users. These systems would eliminate having to input punctuation; the system should be able to display the correct punctuation for the specific tags used. Reciprocal linking should be automated; that is, if you put a link in one record, the link in the other record is automatically created. A cataloger would be able to override this linking if necessary. It should be possible to create non-standard records–such as listings of the individual titles and locations of conferences–and make that searchable along with standard catalog records. There should be a continuous link between local and national systems so that when the national record is changed, the library is notified to change their individual record. When updating in this fashion, local fields would be protected. Librarians and system vendors should also look into incorporating other tools and models such as Extensible Markup Language (XML) or Resource Description Framework (RDF) to address some of the problems inherent in our current catalogs.

Ms. Reynolds then asked the audience what they wanted from new cataloging methods and systems. The audience liked the idea of notification from a national utility when a record has been modified, but stressed local information would need to be retained. The California Digital Library will implement a type of automatic merging of records in which each member of the consortium will have its own bibliographic record for each title, but the CDL system will automatically merge these records into one record with separate holdings statements when the union catalog is searched. Another participant suggested using the 776 field for related ISBNs and ISSNs (especially with dual publications). In a non-public linked record, systems should have licensing and other non-public information. Users should have the ability to display whatever elements they wish to see; that is, a personalized view and not just a novice or advanced view. Systems should be able to fully embrace and work with FRBR at the level of works, expressions, and/or manifestations. If a patron has a citation, s/he should be able to search by that citation. Even if the title has changed, the date information should be able to retrieve the correct bibliographic record. As a last comment, an audience member remarked that we were all still thinking textually. We haven't broken away from the card mentality ourselves and we won't be able to fully exploit technology until we do so.

Ms. Reynolds was concerned that all the good information and ideas coming from this and other meetings not be lost. Could we identify ways to follow up? One participant thought that grant funding might be available for a library/libraries to work with vendors to make some of these ideas a reality. NASIG itself might be able to provide channels for us to follow developments or exchange ideas. LC has many task forces working as a result of their *Conference on Bibliographic Control for the New Millennium*. Any audience members present were urged to take these ideas to those groups. We all need to work to change the current "good, bad, and ugly" to the future "great, brilliant, and beautiful."

There was a very large audience for this presentation, but the size did not hinder audience participation. Large numbers of people either contributed ideas or were prohibited by time constraints from doing so. At the end of the lecture, not only was there sustained applause, but also large numbers of people coming forward to continue the discussion with Ms. Reynolds and each other. It was an extremely successful session.

NOTES

1. The majority of this report was based on a copy of the power point presentation given by Ms. Reynolds at this conference. Wording can often be attributed directly to that copy.

2. Mary Page recorded all audience comments on flip charts. Many thanks to her.

3. "Bibliographic Control of Web Resources: A Library of Congress Action Plan" *Bicentennial Conference on Bibliographic Control in the New Millennium: Confronting the Challenges of Networked Resources and the Web, sponsored by the Library of Congress Cataloging Directorate.* July 2002. *http://lcWeb.loc.gov/catdir/bibcontrol/actionplan.pdf* (August 6, 2002).

CONTRIBUTORS' NOTES

Regina Romano Reynolds is Head, National Serials Data Program, Library of Congress. JoAnne Deeken is Head, Technical Services and Digital Access, at the University of Tennessee, Knoxville.

WORKSHOPS

E-Journal Subscription Management Systems and Beyond

Gregory Szczyrbak
Louise Pierce

Workshop Leaders

Karen Matthews

Recorder

SUMMARY. York University of Pennsylvania, like many libraries, has been grappling with the issue of serials control for titles in aggregator databases. Historically the librarians have adapted the methods they used (word processing lists, lists on Web sites, online catalog, etc.) to provide journal access as technology has advanced. However, as the number of titles has increased beyond the capabilities of the staff, other options needed to be reviewed. In 2001 a task force was set up to evaluate three management systems: Serials Solutions, JournalWebCite, and TDNet. The librarians reviewed the technical requirements, the display and organization, searching capabilities, how often the systems are updated, usage statistics, management reports, cost and other special features. *[Article copies available for a fee from The Haworth Document Delivery Service: 1-800-HAWORTH. E-mail address: <docdelivery@haworthpress.com> Website: <http://www.HaworthPress.com>]*

[Haworth co-indexing entry note]: "E-Journal Subscription Management Systems and Beyond." Matthews, Karen. Co-published simultaneously in *The Serials Librarian* (The Haworth Information Press, an imprint of The Haworth Press, Inc.) Vol. 44, No. 3/4, 2003, pp. 157-162; and: *Transforming Serials: The Revolution Continues* (ed: Susan L. Scheiberg, and Shelley Neville) The Haworth Information Press, an imprint of The Haworth Press, Inc., 2003, pp. 157-162. Single or multiple copies of this article are available for a fee from The Haworth Document Delivery Service [1-800-HAWORTH, 9:00 a.m. - 5:00 p.m. (EST). E-mail address: docdelivery@haworthpress.com].

http://www.haworthpress.com/store/product.asp?sku=J123
10.1300/J123v44n34_17

BACKGROUND

Serials control has always been an issue for libraries due to the "regular irregularities" of these publications. York College of Pennsylvania has gone through the various steps of trying to provide their users with an up-to-date list of journal holdings. Initially the librarians provided a WordPerfect listing of their journals, which they updated quarterly. They then moved to an online periodicals holdings list that they were able to update any time. When the library migrated to an online catalog, the librarians were able to input all their serials titles and have the holdings update dynamically as issues were checked in. The initial online journals were easily input into the catalog with the addition of a 690 field to indicate an online journal, and the addition of an 856 field to denote the URL. Also, these online journals could be added to subject-based Web pages as a continuation of their online periodicals holdings list.

The situation became more complicated with the addition of full-text databases. For their first databases, Expanded Academic ASAP and Business Index, holdings for titles were added to the online catalog. Their online system did not allow open entries, so periodically the databases were checked and the holdings updated. More full-text databases were added a couple of years later. The librarians did not have the time to add these holdings to the catalog, so instead their technical services staff downloaded records from Gale and Proquest into the catalog. These records provided links to the database but they could not provide direct links from a database search to any article in any full-text database or to online journals owned by the library.

At this point the librarians believed they had exhausted the capabilities of their catalog with the current staffing available to work on electronic resources. Other in-house options would require more staffing; however it was not feasible to hire the necessary staff. The librarians became aware of three software systems that could help with providing access to full-text journals in aggregator databases. These three systems are Serials Solutions, JournalWebCite, and TDNet. The librarians decided to evaluate the three systems to see which would best meet their needs.

SERIALS SOLUTIONS

Serials Solutions was founded by librarian Peter McCracken who was aware of the problem of managing serials in the electronic age. Discussing these issues with his brothers, they designed and marketed a system to track and report full text journals in aggregator databases. Along with these aggregator database titles, Serials Solutions also reports individual electronic journal subscriptions if the library provides this information. Customers may receive these reports in HTML, PDF, spreadsheet, MARC-ready or customized formats. Serials Solutions provides an alphabetical list of the library's titles, which can then be loaded onto a local server. Serials Solutions updates the library's listing bimonthly and can be loaded on the server in less than five minutes. MARC-ready records cost thirty-five percent more that the other reports. These MARC records are not in full MARC format, but they will allow the library to incorporate holdings information into their catalog by cutting and pasting the data into the 856 field. They must be deleted manually if the aggregator discontinues access to a journal.

All the various reports include title, ISSN, dates of coverage including embargoes, and the database in which the title can be found. The list is sorted by title, and includes all the databases in which it is located rather than having multiple entries for one title. Searching functionality includes "title," "title begins with," "title contains phrase," and other search parameters. In March 2002 Serials Solutions began a strategic partnership with Harrassowitz to develop a better understanding of individual e-journal subscriptions. They are also working with EBSCO Online, SwetsBlackwell and Information Quest.

Serials Solutions sends reports to the library in a zipped HTML file via e-mail. They included twenty-nine files–one for each letter of the alphabet and one each for an index page, a page for titles with numbers, and a style sheet for the library's Web page. The library's systems administrator then unzips the files and adds them to the library's Web page. The reports provide links to the journal if journal-specific links are available and stable. They do not provide links to specific articles. Serials Solutions also offers an Online Client Center which permits librarians to add or subtract databases and make other administrative changes.

Serials Solutions does not provide usage statistics. They believe these statistics would not be useful since users access e-journals from other places such as from Web pages and online catalogs, as well as through Serials Solutions. They do not provide management tools that would help evaluate the collection.

Serials Solutions pricing is based on number of full-text titles and ranged from $900 for under 7,000 titles to $3,150 for over 25,000 journals. Consortial pricing is also available. Consortia with a single billing office and a minimum of five libraries will get a fifteen percent discount. If the consortium has a single billing office and twenty or more libraries they get a twenty-five percent discount. There is also a price break for multi-year contracts.

Possible ideas Serials Solutions is considering for the future are keyword searching (within the lists), subject breakdowns, and reporting free online journal within the institution's list.

JOURNALWEBCITE

The second management system evaluated was JournalWebCite. JournalWebCite hosts the database listing aggregator e-journals on their site, not locally as Serials Solutions does. They update their database quarterly. They offer two versions, lite and standard. The major difference is usage statistics; the lite version does not provide any statistics, while the standard version provides statistics by database, listing the top ten databases used. Searching functionality is by title, source, and subject. The subjects are the same as used in Ulrich's, although they plan to implement Library of Congress subject headings. JournalWebCite can track 40,000 titles.

JournalWebCite provides management reports, among which are a database overlap report, cost analysis reports (cost per title), provider analysis reports and usage reports. The usage reports provide monthly statistics and year-to-date statistics.

Pricing is based on full-time equivalencies (FTEs), with the lite version's pricing between $660 and $1,980. If the FTE is below 2,000, the library will get the lowest price; if the FTE is above 5,000, the library will pay the maximum amount. If FTEs are above 20,000, the library will need to call for a price quote. For the standard version, the pricing varies between $2,000 and $6,000. Consortial pricing is available. As with Serials Solutions, the library selects from a list of databases.

The administrative area is password protected. The systems administrator can make changes to the lists to account for title changes, subscription changes, etc.

TDNET

The last of the three management systems to be evaluated was TDNet. The TDNet database may be hosted locally or at TDNet's site.

TDNet provides weekly updates and provides links to approximately 30,000 titles. While TDNet's product is a database, other formats are available upon request. TDNet provides usage statistics based on title, vendor, user profiles, unique IP addresses accessing the database, and peak usage, thus providing more usage information than either Serials Solutions or JournalWebCite. However, it does not provide any management reports.

Its search capabilities include some unique access points not included by the other systems. Searching may be done on title, vendor, publisher, or ISSN; but the user may also search tables of contents by authors (the most recent year), plus Library of Congress subject headings, journal titles, article titles, volumes, and years.

TDNet has other unique features. It includes tables of contents and will allow linking to document delivery. It also has an SDI (selective dissemination of information) system which allows the user to set up MyTDNet profiles.

TDNet is more expensive than the other two systems, with price varying between $5,000 and $30,000 depending on the number of unique titles in the databases. Discounts are available for consortia and for development partners. The price per title decreases as the number of titles rises.

COMPARISONS AND CONCLUSIONS

Each of the three systems offer some different features which may influence librarians' decisions about which system is best for their library. For example, TDNet works with a proxy server (York uses EZProxy) to provide off-campus access. For ease of cataloging, Serials Solutions is working to provide full MARC records from the CONSER database which will integrate with various ILS systems by providing a separate record for the electronic journals which libraries will not modify, since these records may be replaced at any time. TDNet has more searching functionality than the other two systems; however it also costs more. Serials Solutions requires the reports to be hosted locally; JournalWebCite hosts the database on their server, and TDNet allows the option of locally loading the database or hosting it on TDNet's server. TDNet provides more usage statistics than the other two systems; however, JournalWebCite provides management reports that the other two systems do not provide. Serials Solutions is more flexible in the display by offering several formats (HTML, PDF, printed lists). Updating varies, with TDNet being weekly, Serials Solutions updating bimonthly, and JournalWebCite quarterly. The librarians at York liked TDNet's My TDNet Profiles feature.

Other features that are not currently included in these systems but which some librarians would like to have are classification numbers (050, 090) included in the records, the 130 field stripped out of print records to cut down on confusion for users, extra indexed fields for statistics, plus the capability to change fields in records that need to be amended rather than replacing the entire record.

Other libraries are trying different options for providing access to serials in aggregator databases. Among these options are: homegrown systems such as Journalfinder at the University of North Carolina at Greensboro, cataloging the titles in the online catalog, and alphabetic and subject lists on Web sites.

WEB ADDRESSES FOR COMPANIES MENTIONED

Serials Solutions: *www.serialssolutions.com*
JournalWebCite: *www.journalWebcite.com*
TDNet: *www.tdnet.com*

CONTRIBUTORS' NOTES

Gregory Szczyrbak is a Reference Librarian, York University of Pennsylvania. Louise Pierce is Periodicals Specialist, York University of Pennsylvania. Karen Matthews is Coordinator of Technical Services at the Dana Medical Library, University of Vermont.

Conducting Serials Surveys: Common Mistakes and Recommended Approaches

Susan Gardner

Workshop Leader

Susan B. Markley

Recorder

SUMMARY. In the changing world of serials, there is a continuing interest in knowing how other libraries are managing their e-journal collections and how these journals have affected the organizational structure and workflow of their institutions. Specifically, has the workload increased when dealing with the ordering, processing, licensing negotiations, serial maintenance, and perpetual access issues of electronic journals? As part of her graduate library studies, Susan Gardner developed a simple seventeen-question Web-based serial survey that addressed some of these issues. She used a "mixture of multiple-choice nominal and ordinal queries supplemented by one open-ended question that allowed the respondent the opportunity for a free response." Her objective was "to identify developing standards or common practices used by libraries to handle e-journals." Gardner submitted her survey to 110

[Haworth co-indexing entry note]: "Conducting Serials Surveys: Common Mistakes and Recommended Approaches." Markley, Susan B. Co-published simultaneously in *The Serials Librarian* (The Haworth Information Press, an imprint of The Haworth Press, Inc.) Vol. 44, No. 3/4, 2003, pp. 163-170; and: *Transforming Serials: The Revolution Continues* (ed: Susan L. Scheiberg, and Shelley Neville) The Haworth Information Press, an imprint of The Haworth Press, Inc., 2003, pp. 163-170. Single or multiple copies of this article are available for a fee from The Haworth Document Delivery Service [1-800-HAWORTH, 9:00 a.m. - 5:00 p.m. (EST). E-mail address: docdelivery@haworthpress.com].

http://www.haworthpress.com/store/product.asp?sku=J123
10.1300/J123v44n34_18

ARL serial librarians and received thirty-four responses. Her presentation detailed how she constructed this viable survey, how she compiled
the data, and some of the results. However, the main focus of Gardner's
workshop was her insightful commentary on the design flaws she discovered within the survey that may have skewed her results and how these
mistakes could be avoided in future surveys. *[Article copies available for a fee
from The Haworth Document Delivery Service: 1-800-HAWORTH. E-mail address:
<docdelivery@haworthpress.com> Website: <http://www.HaworthPress.com>]*

INTRODUCTION

As an introduction to her workshop "*Conducting Serials Surveys:
Common Mistakes and Recommended Approaches,*" Susan Gardner,
Instruction/Reference Librarian at East Carolina University, administered to the session attendees a brief true-or-false questionnaire to test
their knowledge of designing a successful serial survey. She then focused most of her presentation on some of the design flaws she encountered in her own survey, addressing specific problem questions and
suggesting how these common mistakes could be avoided in future surveys.[1,2]

One of the initial problems she discovered as she collated her data
was that by not pre-testing her survey instrument on an unbiased third
party, she lost an opportunity for constructive feedback on the wording
and conciseness of the questions. For example, in survey question #3,
which asked: "*The literature reports many changes in staff patterns as a
result of electronic journals. Compared to the number of staff members
who worked with print journals before your library started receiving
electronic journals, have the number of staff who work with electronic
journals increased or decreased?*"[3] The failure of her survey to specify
"professional" staff rather than all staff skewed the results because she
was really trying to chart the changes affecting only the professional librarians. Since respondents did not know which staff was to be included
in the answer, responses given tended to be misleading. Gardner admitted that a pre-tester, even one with no serials background, would have
recognized the inconsistencies in that question. They would also have
recognized a problem when the survey inadvertently interchanged the
terms "upper level staff" with "professional staff" in question #9: "*Do
electronic journals or print journals require a higher number of professionals to become involved in the ordering process?*"[4] Possible answers
referred to "*upper-level staff members*"[5] instead of using the previously

mentioned term "*professionals.*" This was an example of a question needing further clarification of the terms used.

On the issue of whether to use free-response questions vs. multiple-choice questions, Gardner found that free-response answers were more difficult to quantify and therefore made it more difficult to report results, although they did allow the respondents the opportunity to provide extra information. However, on the negative side, providing more information takes additional time for the respondent and might lessen the number willing to answer the survey. Adding a "Comments Section" to the survey for additional input from respondents or offering "Other" or "None of the Above" to the answer options in case some aspect of the question was missed, was suggested to avoid this problem. However, Gardner noted that in question #10 of the survey, "*Who, if anyone, reviews the electronic journal selections?*"[6] she did provide several options, including "Department Head or Director," "Systems Librarian," "Electronic Resources Librarian," and "Special Committee," but failed to include other equally important choices, such as "Collection Development" or "Administration."

Gardner also emphasized that with multiple-choice options, all answers must be mutually exclusive unless several responses are allowed; it was advisable to provide definitions of terms for greater clarification. As an example, question #6 asked, "*Have you had any of the following to help you deal with electronic journals over the past year: extra training; a workshop; a seminar; a class; a conference?*"[7] Several of these options were not mutually exclusive, since training can be given at a workshop, conference, class or seminar. These terms are often used interchangeably so the responses given did not add much to the survey.

Another design flaw that emerged from the survey was that even when a question appeared confusing or unanswerable, respondents often forced an answer to fit it or made up an entirely new answer. As an example, in question #14, the survey confused the issue of archiving with perpetual access. Respondents were asked "*Which of the following groups currently archives back issues of your library's e-journals: the library; the publishers; the vendors; a consortia; or not archived?*"[8] This question should have been posed to publishers or vendors, not librarians, especially because of library copyright restrictions. Even so, 15% of the librarians responded to this confusing question, further skewing the results. A better question might have asked, "*Of the e-journals now received, what percent guarantee perpetual access in the event that the title is cancelled, the journal ceases publication, or the aggregator/ publisher no longer handles the journal?*"

Another survey question that Gardner felt produced less accurate results than desired was question #5 which asked, *"Has your job description or classification level been upgraded over the past year because
you are taking on more duties that are related to electronic journals?"*[9]
This question proved to be too general, providing an equally general answer. A better question would have been more specific. Perhaps there
was a salary increase with no upgrade in position, or special recognition
was given for taking on additional responsibilities related to electronic
journals.

Question #4 was another example of a question being too general
when it asked, *"Compared to the amount of staff time previously spent
on print journals, has the amount of staff time spent on electronic journals: Increased a lot; Increased a little; Not increased; Decreased?"*[10]
Rather than asking such a broad question, Gardner believed it would
have been better to specify certain time allotments, like electronic journals "doubled the time spent on print journals."

When asking a question that is designed to measure change, Gardner
suggested that the survey should refer to both the "old" and the "new"
changes to provide the correct context for the question. For example,
question #1 asked, *"In your library, which departments are involved in
one or more aspects (selection, acquisitions, licensing negotiations,
bibliographic control, maintenance, or renewal) of electronic journals:
Acquisitions, Administration, Bibliographic Services, Cataloging, Collection Development, Electronic Resources, Info/Technology Systems,
Reference, Serials, Other?"*[11] Since the survey was trying to measure
what additional departments were now involved in e-journal management, a better question would have asked which departments were previously involved with print journals compared to those now involved
with electronic journals.

The same measurement problem was evident in question #8 that
asked, *"Who selects electronic journals for your library?"*[12] Once
again, several types of librarians were listed, such as "Collection Development Librarian," "Electronic Resources Librarian," "Reference Librarian," and "Serials Librarian." Asking which librarians previously
selected journals as compared to those librarians now selecting electronic journals would have produced a more measurable response.

The workshop concluded with some general suggestions for developing and administering good surveys. Gardner found that Web surveys
proved to be both faster and cheaper than mailing print surveys; however,
they were more difficult to code and it was more difficult to maintain the
anonymity of the respondents. Web surveys were also heavily dependent

upon the Internet sophistication of the respondents. Gardner also recommended that setting up the survey questions in an orderly fashion, with one leading to the next, rather than randomly arranging them, is less confusing to the respondents and is easier to analyze and report the results. Keeping the survey brief also encourages more people to respond.

While not going into much detail about the results of her original serial survey, Gardner did confirm what most serial librarians already suspected–that the time and staff needed to effectively manage electronic serials is much greater than with traditional print journals. For those in the audience who were more interested in learning about the actual survey results, the speaker directed them to her original article, "The Impact of Electronic Journals on Library Staff at ARL Member Institutions: A Survey and a Critique of the Survey Methodology," published in *Serials Review*.[13] Although some of the design flaws in the instrument, along with Gardner's admittedly limited knowledge of serials management, lessened the effectiveness of some of the questions on the survey, her honest critique of these mistakes and the constructive suggestions she offered for avoiding such pitfalls in the future provided a good basic introduction for others who might consider designing their own surveys.

NOTES

1. Susan Gardner, "The Impact of Electronic Journals on Library Staff at ARL Member Institutions: A Survey and Critique of the Survey Methodology," *Serials Review* 27 (2001): 18.
2. Ibid, 18.
3. Ibid, 31.
4. Ibid, 32.
5. Ibid, 32.
6. Ibid, 32.
7. Ibid, 31.
8. Ibid, 32.
9. Ibid, 31.
10. Ibid, 31.
11. Ibid, 31.
12. Ibid, 32.
13. Ibid, 17-32.

CONTRIBUTORS' NOTES

Susan Gardner is Instruction/Reference Librarian at East Carolina University. Susan B. Markley is Head, Periodical Department, Falvey Memorial Library, Villanova University.

APPENDIX

Survey
Electronic Journals Survey

1) In your library, which departments are involved in one or more aspects (selection, acquisitions, licensing negotiations, bibliographic control, maintenance, or renewal) of electronic journals?

Acquisitions ☐

Administration ☐

Bibliographic Services ☐

Cataloging ☐

Collection Development ☐

Electronic Resources ☐

Info Technology/Systems ☐

Reference ☐

Serials ☐

Other (please specify) [＿＿＿＿]

2) What new positions, if any, has your library created in the past two years to help with the acquisitions or maintenance of electronic journals?

3) The literature reports many changes in staff patterns as a result of electronic journals. Compared to the number of staff members who worked with print journals before your library started receiving electronic journals, have the number of staff who work with electronic journals:

Increased a lot ○

Increased a little ○

Not increased ○

Decreased ○

4) Compared to the amount of staff time previously spent on print journals, has the amount of staff time spent on electronic journals:

Increased a lot ○

Increased a little ○

Not increased ○

Decreased ○

Comments:

5) Has your job description or classification level been upgraded over the past year because you are taking on more duties that are related to electronic journals?

Yes ○

No ○

Discussed (no action) ○

Comments:

6) Have you had any of the following to help you deal with electronic journals over the past year:

Extra training ☐

A workshop ☐

A seminar ☐

A class ☐

A conference ☐

Comments:

7) Please indicate how the following technical services departments have changed over the past 18 months:

	Acquisitions	Serials	Collection Development	ILL	Cataloging	Systems
Merged with another Dept.	☐	☐	☐	☐	☐	☐
Downsized an existing section	☐	☐	☐	☐	☐	☐
Expanded an existing section	☐	☐	☐	☐	☐	☐
Abolished an existing section	☐	☐	☐	☐	☐	☐
Created a new section	☐	☐	☐	☐	☐	☐
Created new positions	☐	☐	☐	☐	☐	☐

8) Who selects electronic journals for your library?

Collection Development Librarian ☐
Electronic Resources Librarian ☐
Reference Librarian ☐
Serials Librarian ☐
Systems Librarian ☐
Other (please specify) [_____]

9) Do electronic journals or print journals require a higher number of professionals to become involved in the ordering process:

Electronic journals ○
Print journals ○
Both require the same number of upper-level staff members ○

10) Who, if anyone, reviews the electronic journal selections?

Not reviewed ☐
Dept. Head or Director ☐
Systems Librarian ☐
Electronic Resources Librarian ☐
A special committee ☐
Other (please specify) [_____]

10b) If you answered "special committee," what departments are the members from?

Acquisitions ☐
Electronic Resources ☐
Reference ☐
Systems ☐
Other (please specify) [_____]

11) Do you have a standardized procedure for negotiating license agreements of electronic journals, or is each journal treated as a separate case?

Standardized procedure ○
Every journal is negotiated separately ○
There is some standardization among e-journals with similar access criteria ○

12) Who negotiates license agreements for electronic journals in your library?

Acquisitions ☐
Administrators ☐
Cataloging ☐
Collection Development ☐
Consortium ☐
Electronic Resources Librarian ☐
Reference ☐
Serials ☐
Systems ☐
Other (please specify)
[_____]

APPENDIX (continued)

13) Do you have any special legal consultants who help with the licenses?

Yes ○

No ○

14) Because electronic journals are leased rather than owned, sometimes access to back issues is problematic. Which of the following groups currently archive back issues of your library's e-journals:

The library ☐

Publishers ☐

Vendors ☐

Consortia ☐

Not archived ☐

Other (please specify) [_____]

15) How do you maintain bibliographic control over your electronic journals?

Online catalog has direct links ☐

Mount separate web page for electronic journals ☐

Other (specify) [_____]

15b) What department is responsible for this?

Cataloging ○

Reference ○

Serials ○

Systems ○

Other (specify) [_____]

16) Maintenance of electronic journals is a continuous process due to the constant flux in journal holdings, frequency, access points, links, and content. Who, if anyone, at your library updates electronic journals once they have arrived?

We rely primarily on link maintenance software ○

We rely mostly on user feedback to become aware of changes ○

Catalogers ○

Collection Development Librarians ○

Electronic Resources Librarians ○

Reference Librarians ○

Systems/Information Technology ○

17) How many professional staff are employed by your library?

20-60 ○

61-100 ○

101-140 ○

141-180 ○

Over 180 ○

Do you have any additional comments about the survey?

[_____]

ILS Conversion
and the Prediction Pattern Conundrum:
What Do You Do on Day 1?

Michael Kaplan
Kim Maxwell

Workshop Leaders

Sarah Tusa

Recorder

SUMMARY. The task of setting up predictive serials check-in records after ILS migration can be daunting. However, Michael Kaplan of Ex Libris and Kim Maxwell of MIT Libraries explained the advantages of shared prediction pattern records as initiated by CONSER. OCLC/CONSER implemented the 891 to stand in for holdings. This initiative provides a standardized format that allows libraries to contribute and share predictive patterns in batch, rather than by inputting them one by one. *[Article copies available for a fee from The Haworth Document Delivery Service: 1-800-HAWORTH. E-mail address: <docdelivery@haworthpress.com> Website: <http://www.HaworthPress.com>]*

[Haworth co-indexing entry note]: "ILS Conversion and the Prediction Pattern Conundrum: What Do You Do on Day 1?" Tusa, Sarah. Co-published simultaneously in *The Serials Librarian* (The Haworth Information Press, an imprint of The Haworth Press, Inc.) Vol. 44, No. 3/4, 2003, pp. 171-174; and: *Transforming Serials: The Revolution Continues* (ed: Susan L. Scheiberg, and Shelley Neville) The Haworth Information Press, an imprint of The Haworth Press, Inc., 2003, pp. 171-174. Single or multiple copies of this article are available for a fee from The Haworth Document Delivery Service [1-800-HAWORTH, 9:00 a.m. - 5:00 p.m. (EST). E-mail address: docdelivery@haworthpress.com].

http://www.haworthpress.com/store/product.asp?sku=J123
10.1300/J123v44n34_19

Many serials librarians are likely to recall the laborious process of setting up predictive check-in patterns in an integrated library system (ILS) for the first time. Sadly, the phrase "set it and forget it" does not apply to library automation. ILS conversions have become inevitable for many libraries. For serials librarians, the question of what to do with incoming dailies, weeklies, quarterlies, etc. on the first day of the new ILS truly gives one pause, if not sheer panic. As the first speaker, Michael Kaplan, pointed out, the proprietary nature of most serials modules prohibits the transfer of check-in information from one ILS to another. The solution presented in this workshop is the CONSER Public Pattern Initiative, which began in 1999.

The purpose of the above-named project is to "enable the cooperative creation, sharing, and distribution of pattern and holdings data via the CONSER database and among local systems, and [to] promote full use of the MARC21 MFHD by local systems." As host of CONSER, OCLC launched a two-year pilot project. As of spring 2000, nineteen volunteers were participating. Through June 2001, one thousand records were added manually, yielding three thousand records to date. To accommodate the necessary data, the OCLC 891 field was especially designed for the CONSER Patterns and Holdings Project to "stand in" for the holdings fields as delineated below:

- 891 $9 853 to store captions and publication patterns for basic units
- 891 $9 854/855 for supplements/indexes
- 891 $9 863 to store enumeration and chronology for the first bibliographic unit with that pattern.

Kaplan further points out in his handout that III and VTLS make use of the 891 field data.

Kaplan then posed the largely rhetorical question, "What does the prediction do?" In the case of this CONSER project, prediction entails the following: based on a complicated (or not so complicated) series of codes and in combination with captions, prediction patterns can pre-build a series of check-in records. These check-in records are also the basis of manually or automatically generated claims when issues do not arrive on an expected day plus a predetermined number of days of additional elapsed time. Kaplan's handout provided examples of the form used for inputting data in the predictive pattern fields. With the form provided, it is not necessary to know the codes. The database that contains these predictive patterns is ALEPH500. Similar to the OCLC

Union List, the ALEPH500 pattern database will be created and maintained by customers. It is predicted to grow as customers batch contributions. The MARC record fields used for matching records are the 001, 022, 035, and 245.

Libraries have a number of choices in using ALEPH500. Since the patterns are stored in separate files by contributing institutions, the customer can decide whose patterns s/he prefers, based on institutional preferences. However, Kaplan warned, patterns are derivative and only the first ones created in isolation are "pure." Hence, the incremental numbers of new patterns will require working through all the files.

Kaplan gives examples of some sites that use ALEPH500. Reportedly, one of the mentioned sites laboriously added one record at a time, but then they were convinced to use ALEPH500. Another site was able to cover fifty-five percent of their serials titles with their initial load of these shared patterns. For further testimony, Kaplan quoted Bob Gerrity at Boston College, who indicated that his library was able to load 2,154 new patterns in approximately seven minutes.

Kim Maxwell, Serials Acquisitions Librarian for the MIT Libraries, then reported on her library's experience with the CONSER project. She explained that they did not migrate their patterns during their migration because the data were in proprietary format, they were not always able to accurately predict irregular frequencies, and ultimately, it was not worth the effort to map all their titles to a new system.

They decided to obtain their patterns through Ex Libris because this system could provide the pattern data in MARC format. At the time the MIT Libraries migrated, patterns were available from four institutions, and MIT used all of them. They used OCLC number and subfield a of the ISSN to match records. They chose not to match by title as this method proved too inexact. They loaded records by institution without overlaying records. Maxwell reported that the match rate differed by subject area and that generally the records matched better for journals than for book-like serials.

Maxwell and her staff faced a few challenges in using the downloaded records. The first of the challenges was that her support staff had to learn the MARC format. Another complication was not knowing who created the pattern or when it was modified. The purpose in wanting to know, however, was primarily to be able to ask questions of the contributing library. Maxwell also noted differences in the way each institution had implemented the standard, and it was very difficult at first to understand the way Ex Libris implemented the standard in their system. One of the challenges Maxwell and her staff continue to face is the management of multiple formats for one title. For example, if they have print and microfiche holdings attached to the same record, they must pick only one frequency.

The benefits of using the CONSER patterns cited by Maxwell were several. First, the database was a great learning tool that gave her plenty of examples of records. Furthermore, the conversion required less start-up time since they were editing records rather than having to create pattern records from scratch. Another reported benefit is that their data are now in a standard format that can be shared in a variety of ways, such as with other Ex Libris customers and with CONSER.

CONTRIBUTORS' NOTES

Michael Kaplan is Director of Product Management at Ex Libris, Inc. Kim Maxwell is Serials Acquisitions Librarian for the MIT Libraries. Sarah Tusa is Interim Coordinator of Acquisitions at Lamar University.

Writing for Serialists in the Work Environment

Bob Schatz

Workshop Leader

Jane Thompson

Recorder

SUMMARY. In the workplace we are all called upon frequently to produce written documents that have a variety of purposes. This demands that the effective writer take the time to consider all aspects of the particular project in order to produce an effective piece. "Good writing" is not necessarily effective writing. The measure is if the writing accomplishes its purpose. The keys to success are to: determine your objective for writing, build an outline, think about the audience, follow a logical path, proofread your work, validate the piece against the stated and unstated objectives, and get feedback after the fact. Above all, welcome any opportunities to write for your organization–practice makes a better writer. *[Article copies available for a fee from The Haworth Document Delivery Service: 1-800-HAWORTH. E-mail address: <docdelivery@haworthpress.com> Website: <http:// www.HaworthPress.com>]*

[Haworth co-indexing entry note]: "Writing for Serialists in the Work Environment." Thompson, Jane. Co-published simultaneously in *The Serials Librarian* (The Haworth Information Press, an imprint of The Haworth Press, Inc.) Vol. 44, No. 3/4, 2003, pp. 175-179; and: *Transforming Serials: The Revolution Continues* (ed: Susan L. Scheiberg, and Shelley Neville) The Haworth Information Press, an imprint of The Haworth Press, Inc., 2003, pp. 175-179. Single or multiple copies of this article are available for a fee from The Haworth Document Delivery Service [1-800-HAWORTH, 9:00 a.m. - 5:00 p.m. (EST). E-mail address: docdelivery@haworthpress.com].

Workshop leader Bob Schatz opened the session with a question: Why is it important to write effectively? Effective writing is writing for a purpose, and its effectiveness is measured by the outcome–did the writing accomplish its purpose? Different kinds of writing projects have different purposes: to inform, to describe, to summarize, to evaluate, to confirm, to sell, to record (accuracy is paramount here), and perhaps the most difficult outcome to achieve, to influence. Written pieces can include e-mails, letters, employee evaluations, reports, announcements, newsletters, RFPs, policy statements, and brochures. Even signs are written, so one needs to consider the point of the sign and to make sure the appropriate message is delivered.

Every writing project deserves thought and consideration. The objective must be clearly defined in order not to disappoint the intended audience. Thinking about the reasons to produce the piece will help the writer to arrive at a clear understanding of the objective before beginning to write. After all, the written document will become the permanent archival record.

Whether you are assigned or volunteer to create a piece of writing, you have an opportunity to make yourself stand out as someone who is valuable to the organization in addition to achieving the outcome that is the goal of the writing the work in the first place.

When beginning a writing project, rule number one is never to begin a writing project by writing, but to begin by determining the objective for writing. Determine the destination–where is this piece going to wind up? What is your goal? If you do not do this, you will lose readers along the way because the objective is ill-defined.

There are four kinds of objectives: public, private, personal, and composite. The public objective is the "official" assignment. The assignment helps to delimit the format of the piece; it will designate whether you should create a report, an evaluation, an informational text, etc. You will need to gather information to get to know your audience. Most workplace writing fails because the writer stops his or her analysis at this stage. The writer must think about what else is going on in the corporate environment. It's impossible to consider the content without the added insights that this further analysis provides.

The private objective is where effective writers pay the most attention. This objective requires understanding the needs, goals, or objectives of the people with the most authority and who hold the highest stake in the outcome, and who may or may not have stated their interests (for a variety of reasons). To paraphrase: What is the director really after? Is this part of a campaign to win a promotion? Is this a plea for more money? It's essential to get the background from the person in charge so that you understand what the real goals are. Of course, sometimes the purpose may be more nefarious; for example, the purpose may be to document the failings of a person or a plan. There may be personal agendas that may or may not be stated. You need to ask yourself how you feel about the situation and act accordingly.

The personal objective asks the questions: What do you want out of this? Can you support the stated and unstated objectives? To what can you commit, and/or what compromises are you willing to make? Are you willing to lie about a service? Stretch the truth? Do you understand the objectives? You are not ready to write until you can answer all of these questions.

Finally, the writer must address the composite objective, which will be the result of combining the publicly announced goal of the piece with the background agendas or conditions that may be associated with the assignment, and your personal needs or values.

The next step is to build an outline. PowerPoint is a wonderful tool to aid in outline building. An outline demonstrates the flow of your logic, and allows you to move things around easily to improve the flow of the overall piece. It also allows you to approach the writing in different ways. For example, you can start with the end and work backwards from the conclusions to the starting point to check the logic. You can try different openings, such as the buried lead versus the direct statement. The outline can also help with different formats, such as inserting graphics and experimenting with design.

A writer must always consider his or her audience. Are you writing for one or for many? Which group should get the most attention? Determine the right target by understanding how much background information the intended audience will need, their level of understanding, and their mindset about the subject. Consider whether the audience comprises insiders or outsiders, which will affect how much background is necessary. Consider the level of the audience–is the piece intended for students or for business people? Remember the experience of sitting through a lecture given by a brilliant scholar who was unable to speak to the level of his audience. Consider how the document you are creating will be used; your name will travel with the document and will henceforth be associated with its success or lack thereof.

The actual writing begins with a statement of purpose. Decide whether you want a buried lead or a direct approach. The buried lead sets the scene and evokes sympathy. It can work for people with no background in the subject, or with a hostile audience by recasting facts into visual language that invites people in, gives them a context, and persuades them to consider your point of view. The direct lead, on the other hand, presents the factual environment directly. With word processing, it is possible to make notes to yourself that you delete from the final version. Refer to your outline to maintain the logical flow. Check the flow of the logic within sentences, paragraphs, sections, and the entire piece.

When you have the first draft, reread your work out loud and rewrite as needed. Edit stringently. Always proofread your work. Do not rely on spell checkers; you won't learn to spell any better and the checker won't pick up a correctly spelled word in the wrong context. Have someone else proof your work if time allows. You are looking for someone who can comment on the logical flow, as well as point out typos. Choose someone who is uninvolved in the project to get objective feedback; if you wish to test your ideas, ask someone who has the appropriate background. A proofreader who can spot the political "hot spots" can be useful.

Be committed to rewriting some or all of your work. Do as many rewrites as necessary to achieve the proper objectives. Validate the whole piece against the stated (and unstated) objectives. Did you hit the right targets? If not, rewrite with the objectives in mind, get help, or lower your expectations if you think that you are being asked to do an impossible task.

After the piece has been distributed, seek feedback. Try to find out if the essential audience and the purpose of the piece came together as a result of your writing. Listen for clues that will make you a better writer next time.

Don't "wade through molasses." Power comes from the way you put language together. Use language that you understand and can control. Big words aren't always necessary. Remember the outcomes you wish to occur, and check the logical flow to keep on track. Save the original and make a copy to use as a working draft so you still have the original in case anything happens.

Notice what writing particularly impresses or annoys you. Think about language and grammar. Don't be shy about volunteering for writing assignments; the more you write, the better you will become. Never forget that effective writing is about results. Stay focused on outcomes; if you lose sight of your objective, you may wind up arguing the opposite view.

Schatz then offered many tips for specific formats: compose sensitive e-mails in word processing before sending; resumes should reflect the environment of the desired employment; some reports benefit from a glossy binder presentation; executive summaries are crucial to getting the points across in a long report. Get your outside reader to read for obnoxious messages or tone.

To summarize, to produce good effective writing determine your objective for writing, build an outline, think about the audience, follow a logical path, proofread your work, validate the piece against the stated and unstated objectives, and get feedback after the fact. Welcome any opportunity to write–practice makes a better writer. Effective writing is an achievable goal, produced when the writer approaches the piece *strategically*. Working from an outline is preferable; working from a stated objective is essential.

Audience participation was enthusiastic. Topics discussed included obnoxious or irritating cover letters for job applications, the value of objective readers of your work, and the challenges of writing procedures for different audiences (sometimes two or more versions of the same information can be used with different audiences). Sidebars can be both positive and negative contributions to a work; make sure they are relevant to the content, not over-used, and match the facts in the main text. A comment about the over-use of graphics and the importance of making certain that visuals add something to the content drew much agreement from the audience.

Schatz added that it's important to stay in control of what you are using. Stay within yourself–you will be caught if you attempt to "fake it." Also, he cautioned that one should remember the Web sites that had so many graphics that they took forever to load, and lost their audience.

Skills will improve with use and you will be able to expand your scope through experience. So slow down, think about what you are doing, and keep writing. There was generous applause at the conclusion of this practical workshop.

CONTRIBUTORS' NOTES

Bob Schatz is Director of Sales and Marketing for Franklin Book Company. Jane Thompson is the Journals Collection Development Librarian at the University of Cincinnati Health Sciences Library.

Maneuvering Your Serials Troops Through the Mine Fields of Change

Rene J. Erlandson

Workshop Leader

Sandra Barstow

Recorder

SUMMARY. This workshop allowed participants to assess their current means of dealing with change. It provided methods for planning the process of change, suggestions for handling the psychological aspects of organizational change, and opportunities for sharing positive and negative experiences related to change. *[Article copies available for a fee from The Haworth Document Delivery Service: 1-800-HAWORTH. E-mail address: <docdelivery@haworthpress.com> Website: <http://www.HaworthPress.com>]*

INTRODUCTION

Erlandson began the workshop by having the participants introduce themselves and state the types of change they were facing in their orga-

[Haworth co-indexing entry note]: "Maneuvering Your Serials Troops Through the Mine Fields of Change." Barstow, Sandra. Co-published simultaneously in *The Serials Librarian* (The Haworth Information Press, an imprint of The Haworth Press, Inc.) Vol. 44, No. 3/4, 2003, pp. 181-187; and: *Transforming Serials: The Revolution Continues* (ed: Susan L. Scheiberg, and Shelley Neville) The Haworth Information Press, an imprint of The Haworth Press, Inc., 2003, pp. 181-187. Single or multiple copies of this article are available for a fee from The Haworth Document Delivery Service [1-800-HAWORTH, 9:00 a.m. - 5:00 p.m. (EST). E-mail address: docdelivery@haworthpress.com].

nizations. Common responses included system changes, integrated library system migrations, reorganizations, space renovations, new buildings, electronic journals, new unit head in the department, weeding projects, cancellations, retirements of experienced librarians, employee turnover, and reclassification projects. Everyone in the room had experienced some kind of change in the work setting, and many felt they could have handled the change more effectively.

FOUR TOUCHSTONES

Erlandson discussed four touchstones for successful implementation of change: communication, flexibility, laughter, and the ability to relax. She stated that communication is the key to successful implementation of change. Good communication builds a positive environment for change. Even if change is not imminent, the manager needs to build trust by fostering openness. Employees need to feel comfortable coming to the manager with their questions, concerns, and ideas. Maintaining open communication channels increases understanding, builds relationships, fosters cooperation and trust, and thus creates a positive environment for change.

Flexibility involves asking people to turn away from principles and procedures with which they are comfortable, so that they can accept new approaches. The staff may feel that implementing a new strategy is risky. It is necessary to create a flexible environment, encouraging people to ask questions and offer suggestions. Managers must be open to staff input. One should go into change realizing that everything will not go according to plan.

Laughter is an essential component of successful implementation of change. Finding humor in situations relieves tension, decreases stress, improves morale, and helps people relate to one another. Asking oneself "Am I going to care about this in ten years?" may help put the situation in perspective. It is important to use humor, not sarcasm, in reacting to situations.

The ability to relax will also help diffuse tense situations. Several techniques for relaxing were provided, such as taking a deep breath and exhaling slowly; repeating a calming phrase while breathing slowly; changing gears to work on something different; and detaching oneself from the situation.

SKILLS ASSESSMENT

Erlandson distributed a questionnaire, "Assessing Your Change Management Skills,"[1] which allowed the participants to evaluate how they dealt with change in the workplace. For each of 32 statements, participants assigned a numerical rating from 1 to 4, indicating the frequency with which they implemented the statement. The numbers were added to reach a total score indicating the degree to which the participant was able to manage the demands of change. Erlandson cautioned that there was not a positive or negative connotation associated with a particular score. For example, if a person's score indicated that they embraced change, she suggested that he or she should be careful not to implement change just for the sake of change, since this approach may cause undue stress on staff. The exercise was intended as a heads-up for the participants so they would be aware of how they currently approach change.

PLANNING FOR CHANGE

In the next part of the workshop, Erlandson provided a framework for change by discussing the steps in developing a change plan. She identified nine steps:

- Clarify the cause
- Define the change
- Create a timeframe
- Identify groups/individuals affected by the change
- Build consensus and support
- Prepare for change (training)
- Implement change
- Celebrate
- Analyze

The first steps in the process of planning for change are to recognize the need for a change and to define the change. Erlandson suggested collecting evidence to support the need and then getting together a group to brainstorm the problem, define the change and its expected outcome, and put it in writing. This approach assists the change team in articulating the change and impending process as the idea is presented to others outside of the initial brainstorming group.

In developing a timeline for the project, Erlandson suggested determining the specific date by which the change needs to be implemented. Work back from this deadline to create a timeframe, including time for meetings, briefing sessions, training sessions, and the actual implementation process. The analysis step should also be included in the schedule, as should time to celebrate the completion of the project. The schedule should be flexible enough to allow for setbacks and failure to meet intermediate time goals.

Erlandson emphasized the importance of looking outside the core management group to determine who might be affected by the change. Meeting with these people early in the process will help refine the change and will be useful in building support. Some frequently asked questions about workplace change include:

- How will this change affect me?
- How will the impending change affect my position?
- Am I going to lose my job?
- Will this change affect my job description?
- Why are we doing this?
- Who is going to train me?
- Who decided we need this change?
- What is wrong with the way we used to do this?
- If I am spending time doing this, who is going to do my "regular" work?
- Does this mean I am going to have *more* work to do?
- If I am doing more work, will I be paid more?
- If no, then what's in it for me?
- When is the change going to be implemented?
- Am I doing something wrong?
- What are we trying to achieve with this change?
- Why are we changing when so-and-so isn't?

Erlandson suggested some ways of dealing with resistance. A good way to deal with a naysayer who never agrees with anything is to bring that person into the change management group. As a participant, this person will see that there is a need for the change and may become less resistant, even if the manager never achieves 100% buy-in for the change from the naysayer.

Erlandson stressed the importance of providing both training and documentation prior to implementing the change. Documentation allows trainees to have something to take back to their work area for future reference. It is helpful to know the current level of expertise of the staff and to develop training sessions for people who do not know the basics and other sessions for people who are more advanced. She suggested providing overview sessions as well as hands-on sessions where trainees walk through the new workflow and get a view of the change.

Erlandson's advice for this part of the project was "Just bite the bullet and do it!" If the change project has been well planned and there is time for setbacks built into the schedule, there is no need to wait for conditions to be perfect. It is important to keep everyone informed about how the implementation is progressing.

It is important to acknowledge everyone's hard work by having some kind of celebration fairly close to the end of the project. Erlandson noted that a lot of managers leave out this step, but it is a good way to close the project and recognize the effort expended by everyone involved in implementing the change.

Another step that might be overlooked is the analysis phase. Erlandson suggested keeping the change management team in place for three to six months after the change, to evaluate the process and to try to determine if the change has had the desired outcome. The analysis should be put in writing, so the manager can look at it later to see what elements of the process worked well (or did not).

EXPERIENCING CHANGE

Following the formal presentation, Erlandson asked the audience to talk about successful changes in which they had participated. This discussion was quite lively. At one point in the discussion, Erlandson commented that when implementing a major change such as a systems migration, there are a lot of unknowns, and managers need to be willing to tell staff "we don't know." It is better to admit ignorance and promise to get an answer, than to make an unfounded statement or to say nothing at all. These types of response can breed the feeling that information is being withheld.

Two participants described their experiences with reorganization. In the successful implementation, there was a lot of information provided to the people who were affected. A reorganization where only the top administrators were involved in designing the change led to resistance from the staff. The lack of two-way communication meant that it took the administration several months to realize the flaws in the change. Erlandson commented that resistance is often a knee-jerk reaction to change, especially when the people making the change fail to consider the possible emotional reactions of the people affected.

DEALING WITH RESISTANCE

Erlandson provided some ways of successfully dealing with resistance. From the manager's standpoint, it is helpful to depersonalize the situation, respect the opposing viewpoint while not losing sight of the goal, stay relaxed, and try to find humor in the situation. From the resistor's perspective, presenting potential solutions as well as complaints is helpful, as is a focus on the specific problems rather than just appearing to resist the plan altogether. If the plan needs to be adjusted based on comments and suggestions from staff, it is important for the manager to let everyone know right away, thus avoiding people being blind-sided by the change in the plan. This approach also demonstrates the manager's flexibility and responsiveness to people's valid concerns.

BUILDING AN ORGANIZATION THAT EMBRACES CHANGE

Erlandson concluded the workshop with some thoughts on the evolution of libraries into learning organizations–institutions where change is expected, accepted, and embraced. Library staff need to realize and understand that their jobs will evolve and change as the mission of the library changes, in order to best meet the needs of patrons.

Hiring people who are open to change is very helpful in creating a learning environment within libraries. In the screening process, the manager should emphasize the fact that change and flexibility are important aspects of each position. The expectation for employees to embrace change should also be written into employees' job descriptions. Managers can develop the change management skills of existing staff by designing jobs that provide a variety of duties. Cross training is also useful to give employees a sense of how their jobs fit into the overall process. The library is an evolving organization, and developing an environment that is open to change makes the evolution go more smoothly.

CONCLUSION

The workshop was entertaining and informative, and the participants seemed fully engaged throughout the session. Although the session ended on time, the participants were still talking with each other about the content as they left, and several people stayed to discuss their specific issues with Erlandson after the close of the session.

NOTES

1. Questions were adapted from Heller, Robert and Tim Hindle, *Essential Manager's Manual*. New York, NY: DK Pub., 1998.

CONTRIBUTORS' NOTES

Rene J. Erlandson is Senior Cataloger, Illinois Newspaper Project, University of Illinois at Urbana-Champaign. Sandra Barstow is Assistant Director for Administrative and Technical Services, University of Wyoming Libraries

Teaching Electronic Journals: Finding, Using, and Citing Them

Stewart Brower
Janice M. Krueger

Workshop Leaders

Jill Emery

Recorder

SUMMARY. Today's library users are Web savvy but not always Web educated. As more and more of a library's print journal collection becomes part of the library's electronic collection, we must take on the roles of guiding and teaching students how to navigate and learn from their interactions with electronic journals. The Teaching Electronic Journals workshop discussed the opportunities we have to educate our users about electronic journals and how to use and cite them effectively. *[Article copies available for a fee from The Haworth Document Delivery Service: 1-800-HAWORTH. E-mail address: <docdelivery@haworthpress.com> Website: <http://www. HaworthPress.com>]*

As library collections continue to shift from being print-based to becoming available electronically, the educational needs of our users are also shifting. Stewart Brower opened the workshop by explaining that

---

[Haworth co-indexing entry note]: "Teaching Electronic Journals: Finding, Using, and Citing Them." Emery, Jill. Co-published simultaneously in *The Serials Librarian* (The Haworth Information Press, an imprint of The Haworth Press, Inc.) Vol. 44, No. 3/4, 2003, pp. 189-194; and: *Transforming Serials: The Revolution Continues* (ed: Susan L. Scheiberg, and Shelley Neville) The Haworth Information Press, an imprint of The Haworth Press, Inc., 2003, pp. 189-194. Single or multiple copies of this article are available for a fee from The Haworth Document Delivery Service [1-800-HAWORTH, 9:00 a.m. - 5:00 p.m. (EST). E-mail address: docdelivery@haworthpress.com].

students are interested to know why they cannot access some titles from home, what the costs are for these resources, why these resources aren't freely available to everyone, how they can find out what the library owns, and why some things are only available in one format. Talking with students and faculty at the University at Buffalo Health Sciences Library, Brower also learned that people do care what is going on behind the scenes at the library and like to be informed as to the collection development decisions being made, how these resources are acquired, and the reasons why access may vary from one electronic resource to another. From these questions and others that arose in instructional sessions or at the reference desk, Brower developed them into teaching objectives. Some of the objectives that Brower developed for his electronic journals classes became:

- Students will learn the best methods for locating UBHSL electronic journal subscriptions.
- Students will learn to look for the common elements that electronic journals share regardless of their format, including table of contents information, archives, and instructions to authors.
- Students will learn the difference between specific electronic formats for journal articles and compare their strengths and weaknesses.

In order to meet these objectives, Brower has developed a common outline that he uses when teaching electronic journal classes. First, he starts with teaching how to access the resources. In this section he describes who the producers are and explains the differences between society publishers, for-profit publishers, what an aggregator is and how it is compiled, and the importance of using abstracting and indexing resources. Second, he focuses on access technology, IP access, passwords, and proxy servers and the impact each has on differing resources. Third, he describes the online public access catalog (OPAC) and how electronic journals can be found by searching the OPAC. Fourth, he talks about online lists of journals; lastly, he mentions other services that may be available such as scientific search engines, etc.

From teaching access, Brower moves on to teaching features of the electronic journals or electronic journal collections. He starts with table of contents information and then moves into current issue information. He talks about archives and why there may not be archives with some electronic journals or why the archives may not be very deep. From here, he describes the search forms and some commonalities to look for across various providers. Brower then mentions current awareness and the e-mailing of table of contents information and how these functions can help students keep up with the advancements of research areas and stay on top of the latest information available to them. Lastly, Brower covers the instructions to authors because many of his students will be attempting to publish their research at some point and are interested to know where this information is found. In the last section of his outline, Brower explains the difference between HTML files and PDF files and why electronic journal content is created in one format or in both formats, and the relative advantages and disadvantages.

Once the objectives for the class have been set and presented to the class on hand, Brower emphasized that timing is key. He suggests keeping class time limited to forty minutes to insure enough time to cover the electronic journals to be presented but not enough time to overwhelm the audience. He also strongly suggested giving up some of the control of the class by allowing the students to guide the discussions and state what they feel is most important to them to learn. Once the class has identified the resources of greatest importance, Brower suggests focusing on the common elements that exist with these journals in differing databases or platforms.

For the format of the class, Brower suggests keeping the assessments of any given resource simple and tuned to the points the class has deemed important. One technique he often applies is to have the class to work in pairs or small groups and proposes the methodology of "think–pair–share" in which the students consider a problem separately, come together as a pair or in a group to work through the problem, and then share their results with the larger audience. Lastly, Brower reminded the workshop attendees to remember to build in time for assessment of the teaching process, or at least provide an evaluation form for feedback. He has found this feedback helpful for refining the teaching methods he employs and for understanding the major problems or concerns of the students he is teaching. In summation, Brower strongly encouraged serials librarians to be the ones to teach workshops on electronic journals.

At this point Brower opened the discussion for questions. He was asked which specific journal collections he focuses on when teaching hands-on classes. Brower identified that Elsevier's ScienceDirect and Journals@Ovid were both collections he taught on a regular basis. Someone else asked if he ever covered ILL for timely retrieval of journal articles. Brower responded that he didn't at this time but was planning to incorporate the ILL process in his classes.

Janice Krueger began her section of the workshop by reviewing the different style manuals that are employed by students on her campus. She identified these as APA, Chicago, MLA, and Turabian. For most of her presentation, Krueger focused on APA and MLA, since the majority of her students generally use one or the other when writing papers.

First, she outlined how citations for print resources are formatted in both APA and MLA styles. Next, Krueger discussed some of the issues raised during the early stages of full-text access, such as not always having an easily identified author, understanding the difference between the producer and publisher, and lastly, not always having a discernable date of publication. From here, she moved to the problem of understanding from where citation information is derived–does one identify just the journal title, the database, or both? Is there a specific designator for journal articles? In response to the last question, one audience member stated that the DOI (digital object identifier) was indeed a unique identifier for journal articles but not always readily available from the publisher/producer of the article.

As an exemplification of how difficult the process could be, Krueger displayed a screen shot for an electronic journal collection that displayed one article. She then walked the audience through citing the article in both APA style and in MLA style.

In APA style the citation would be:

> Schmoldt, Inga et al. (1998). On variational dynamics in redshift space. *Astronomical Journal*, 115(6) 121-126. Retrieved 18 April 2002 from *http://www.journals.uchicago.edu/AJ/journalissues/v.115n6/980018/ 980018.html.*

The MLA style citation would read:

> Schmoldt, Inga et al. "On Variational Dynamics in Redshift Space." *Astronomical Journal* 115.6 (1998). 18 April 2002 *http://www. journals.uchicago.edu/AJ/journal issues/v.115n6/980018/980018.html.*

At this point, an audience member asked why she did not use the "export bibliographic information" button located on the right hand of the screen shot. Krueger responded that she had not used this functionality in this collection and did not know if it could export directly into MLA or APA style.

Krueger then gave an example of an article located in an aggregator database and again, walked the audience through citing the article in both APA and MLA style.

In APA style the citation would be:

> Schuhmann, P.W., & Easley, J.E., Jr. (1998, December). Stock dynamics and recreational fishing welfare estimation: Implications for natural resource damage assessment. *American Journal of Agricultural Economics 80*, 1032-1038. Retrieved December 20,2000, from Expanded Academic Asap database.

And in MLA style:

> Schuhmann, P.W., & Easley, J.E., Jr. "Stock Dynamics and Recreational Fishing Welfare Estimation." *American Journal of Agricultural Economics* 80 (1998): 1032-1038. *Expanded Academic Asap*. Infotrac. Univ. of the Pacific Lib., Stockton, CA. 20 Dec. 2000 *http://infotrac.galegroup.com/itWeb/uop_demo*.

One audience member asked what was the point of providing this level of granularity within the citation. Krueger responded that it helped professors when they were grading the papers to know exactly where the article had been found. The audience member retorted that it was up to the faculty to do that type of work and he felt providing just a general citation of the article was enough. Another audience member pointed out that not all electronic journals are exact replicas of print journals and sometimes there were discrepancies between the print and electronic version. Therefore, this audience member felt that one needed to cite the electronic version specifically. Discussion ensued.

The use of citation software such as ISI's EndNote then arose. Krueger stated that she tried using this software but had found it difficult to use and many in the audience agreed with her assessment. Another member of the audience pointed out that many database providers are building citation exportation functions into their design and this helps with students trying to cite resources. In some instances, this functionality is sophisticated enough to export into the different styles such as APA or MLA. The workshop ended with the hope that citation software that is both easy to use and that covers the major style manuals would be developed soon in order to make this task easier for all of us.

In summation, this workshop was extremely well presented and provided the grounds for many discussions with the audience. A large audience attended this workshop and the audience appeared to be pleased with the content that was delivered. The focus on the end-user of electronic journals was an especially refreshing point of view and it is hoped this type of programming grows in the future.

CONTRIBUTORS' NOTES

Stewart Brower is Coordinator, Information Management Education, University at Buffalo Health Sciences Library. Janice M. Krueger is the Electronic Resources and Serials Librarian, University of the Pacific. Jill Emery is the Director, Electronic Resources Program, University of Houston Libraries

Thinking and Working
Outside the (Library) Box:
From Revolutionary Idea
to Strategic Alliance

Carol MacAdam
Dana Walker
D. Ellen Bonner
Merrill Smith
Sharon Sullivan

Workshop Leaders

Anne Mitchell

Recorder

SUMMARY. This discussion-intensive workshop featured a panel of five librarians who have worked both in libraries and in the commercial environment sharing their diverse experiences. The panelists provided brief overviews of their careers to date, then spoke in greater depth about what they look for in a job, what has motivated them to move from libraries to the commercial sector or vice versa, and what they have learned in the process. *[Article copies available for a fee from The Haworth Document Delivery Service:*

[Haworth co-indexing entry note]: "Thinking and Working Outside the (Library) Box: From Revolutionary Idea to Strategic Alliance." Mitchell, Anne. Co-published simultaneously in *The Serials Librarian* (The Haworth Information Press, an imprint of The Haworth Press, Inc.) Vol. 44, No. 3/4, 2003, pp. 195-200; and: *Transforming Serials: The Revolution Continues* (ed: Susan L. Scheiberg, and Shelley Neville) The Haworth Information Press, an imprint of The Haworth Press, Inc., 2003, pp. 195-200. Single or multiple copies of this article are available for a fee from The Haworth Document Delivery Service [1-800-HAWORTH, 9:00 a.m. - 5:00 p.m. (EST). E-mail address: docdelivery@haworthpress.com].

http://www.haworthpress.com/store/product.asp?sku=J123
10.1300/J123v44n34_23

1-800-HAWORTH. E-mail address: <docdelivery@haworthpress.com> Website: <http://www.HaworthPress.com>]

The panel represented a wide range of functional specialties and work experiences. Carol MacAdam, Associate Director for Library Relations for JSTOR, first went to work for a vendor when her serials position in a large academic library began to feel too routine. This foray into the for-profit sector was largely a positive experience, but MacAdam discovered she was not entirely comfortable with the emphasis on the bottom line. Her role at JSTOR combines the entrepreneurial perspective of a business with the opportunity to advocate for libraries. Dana Walker, now the Electronic Resources Coordinator for the University of Georgia Libraries, has moved between vendors and libraries several times during her career, seeking variety and challenge. Originally employed in academic library acquisitions, Walker initially wanted to explore the vendor side of acquisitions and found that she enjoyed working in a faster-paced environment while still providing useful services to libraries. D. Ellen Bonner is the Technical Services Coordinator at Rensselaer Polytechnic Institute. Her cataloging experience and specialization in fine arts led to positions with museum libraries, specialized academic collections, and an indexing and abstracting service. After a period of providing behind-the-scenes library support for a book vendor, Bonner is back in an academic library setting where she feels the most interesting problems in the field of librarianship are currently being explored. Merrill Smith spent much of her career as the Dean of Learning Resources for a community college system. The wide variety of services under the umbrella of "learning resources" sustained her interest for many years, but eventually she sought a change of scene and went to work for a book vendor. Smith returned briefly to the community college setting when she tired of the constant travel required of her sales position, but is now back in the vendor sphere as an Account Services Manager for EBSCO Information Services. Sharon Sullivan's experience is largely on the vendor side, beginning in the area of approvals and cataloging for a book vendor. Sullivan has worked for other companies as well as a small academic library since that time, and is currently Regional Sales Manager for Swets Blackwell.

Based on a show of hands, the workshop attendees primarily consisted of academic librarians in a cataloging or management capacity. Vendor representatives as well as public, government, special, and self-employed librarians were also in attendance. Several audience members were willing to share their own experiences, which ranged from a private consultant with two decades of academic library cataloging experience to a former vendor employee who discovered an affinity for library public services during library school. Because most of the audience was already familiar with the traditional library environment, questions for the panelists focused on their experiences in the commercial sector.

MacAdam opened the discussion by asking her fellow panelists what originally prompted them to leave the traditional library setting, and what considerations might induce them to return. Most of the panelists began their careers in academic libraries, where professional roles are somewhat predictable and the pace of change is generally less than exhilarating. The commercial sector offered a faster pace and a new perspective on library needs and services. Walker enjoyed the challenge of working outside her personal "comfort zone," and other panelists appreciated the more results-oriented atmosphere and greater individual accountability in the private sector. By contrast, library employment tends to be less taxing and more secure, but the relatively sedate pace of libraries has its own advantages. Bonner pointed out that libraries are better equipped than many for-profit businesses to nurture experimentation and creativity because the economic consequences of failure are less immediate. Furthermore, people who work best in a contemplative environment or who thrive on direct interaction with the public may prefer libraries to the faster-paced, behind-the-scenes work on the vendor side.

The discussion turned to the logistics of vendor employment, including geographic location and opportunities for at-home or part-time work. In the panelists' experience, field-based positions like outside sales are generally more geographically flexible than inside positions, which in most cases require proximity to the company's facilities. Smith was able to remain geographically situated when she changed jobs, whereas other panelists intentionally pursued a change of location. In general, vendors may have more flexibility than libraries to accommodate at-home and freelance employment, but Sullivan stressed that the level of flexibility in any particular position is contingent on the company, the nature of the position, and the employee. Some positions require interaction with on-site staff to an extent that makes working from home impossible, and effective at-home work requires a degree of self-imposed structure that may not be appropriate for everyone. Companies may be more inclined to make this concession for employees who have worked for them previously. Part-time positions are not the norm at most companies, and the opportunities that do exist primarily go to people with whom the company is already familiar, such as retirees who are coming back to work on a limited basis. Not surprisingly, prospective employees with strong experience and a desirable skill set will be in the best position to negotiate an arrangement that is to their liking.

There was considerable interest in the relationship between vendors and publishers, which is essentially invisible to librarians. According to several panelists, there is movement of personnel between publishers and the publisher side of vendor operations comparable to what takes place between vendors and libraries, but the jump between libraries and publishers is much less common. Even within a vendor, the publisher liaisons tend to work in a different part of the organization from the library liaisons; the two sides meet to exchange status reports and other information pertaining to specific projects. A number of factors account for this division. There are very few degreed librarians in the publishing industry, which makes it difficult for people in publishing to switch to the library side, and it can be similarly difficult to move into publishing without an "in." Smith pointed out that in many cases publishers overlook the existence of libraries entirely, because they consider vendors or individual end users, rather than libraries, to be their customers. This has especially been the case with trade publishers, although electronic resources are beginning to change the relationship somewhat.

Sullivan asked the audience to describe what advantages they felt librarians in vendor positions brought to libraries. Audience members emphasized that they prefer to work with "insiders" when they interact with vendors. A vendor representative with firsthand library knowledge makes a common language possible; librarians appreciate that they don't have to explain every aspect of their operations, and like the feeling of working with colleagues rather than salespeople. The panelists indicated that as librarians, they brought certain strengths with them to the commercial environment, particularly the analytical approach to problem solving that catalogers and public services librarians are known for. Many vendors also value the MLS because the professional degree lends credibility to their library-side operations. Library customers like knowing that their contact at the vendor understands their needs, particularly in areas like cataloging that require high levels of technical skill and training.

Making the change from a library to a vendor, or vice versa, comes with a certain amount of culture shock. One panelist was surprised to discover that library colleagues expected her to entertain them on a lavish expense account after she went to work for a vendor; others were frustrated by the perception they were "former librarians" and felt pressured to justify their new positions. Bonner found that she was expected to implement the decisions and priorities of upper management without further discussion, a decision-making style that is particularly foreign to academic libraries. At the same time, she encountered a greater willingness on the part of commercial enterprises to commit systems support and other resources to a project than is typically the case in libraries. All the panelists agreed that the fast-paced, production-intensive attitude of the private sector was quite unlike what they were accustomed to in libraries, and those panelists who have returned to academia have had to readjust to the slower pace of change. They brought back with them an ability to take chaos in stride and make decisions on the fly, as well as a better understanding of the vendor's perspective.

When asked whether there is a gap between the services vendors could provide for libraries and what libraries are prepared to adopt, Sullivan pointed out that the cultural incongruity between libraries and their corporate business partners makes that question difficult to answer. At first glance, the culture of innovation seems much more vigorous in the corporate setting than in the traditional library; the corporate milieu tends to attract energetic, stress-tolerant employees who are not fazed by rapid change, and economic pressures discourage businesses from clinging to what Bonner referred to as "legacy methodology" in the way that libraries are famous for. Libraries, on the other hand, have much more freedom to pursue interesting ideas without immediate consideration of the bottom line, but vendors may be reluctant to take libraries up on suggestions that do not seem economically viable. Several panelists registered frustration at how many libraries lack a clear understanding of the actual cost of their operations, and make decisions without considering the lifecycle of a procedure or its total cost to the organization. Sullivan offered the example of shelf-ready approvals–libraries often resist shelf-ready approvals on the grounds that pre-processed items can't be returned, but the savings realized by returning a small number of unwanted titles is dramatically offset by the cost of cataloging and processing the remaining majority of approval materials in-house.

Getting down to brass tacks, an audience member inquired about where to find position announcements for vendors and publishers. Positions may be announced by formal channels familiar to librarians, including discussion lists and professional publications, as well as informal channels like word of mouth and direct recruitment. Most of the panelists reported finding their first vendor position through an advertisement, but relied more on informal networking for later positions. Although companies don't always require them, Sullivan recommended tailoring a resume to emphasize the qualities and experience most pertinent to the job in question. Bonner added that the first person to evaluate the resume of a prospective employee might be a human resources officer unfamiliar with the intricacies of library work, so skills should be spelled out as explicitly as possible. As the discussion turned to salary, the panelists agreed that much depends on the company, the position, and the individual. Many sales jobs include a commission or bonus, whereas inside positions are more likely to have a regular salary. The private sector has a reputation for greater negotiating breadth than libraries are known for. Negotiating skills are not necessarily something that librarians learn or are inherently good at, but at this stage in their careers the panelists all indicated that they are confident negotiators.

An audience member asked the presenters to imagine the ideal work environment. "Retirement!" joked one panelist, while another expressed longing for the elusive committee-free academic library. However, this workshop demonstrated that a rewarding career is far from imaginary. Driven by a sense that stasis is more dangerous than change, these five librarians have fearlessly pursued opportunities for creativity and challenge both within and outside libraries. The underlying theme in each of their stories is not that vendors have more fun, but rather that with self-awareness, confidence and a healthy sense of adventure, anyone can build a unique and satisfying career.

CONTRIBUTORS' NOTES

Carol MacAdam is Associate Director for Library Relations, JSTOR. Dana Walker is Electronic Resources Coordinator, University of Georgia Libraries. D. Ellen Bonner is Technical Services Coordinator, Rensselaer Polytechnic Institute. Merrill Smith is Account Services Manager, EBSCO Information Services. Sharon Sullivan is Regional Sales Manager, Swets Blackwell Inc. Anne Mitchell is Metadata Coordinator, University of Houston Libraries.

Success in Searching for Serials:
What Is the MAGIC Solution?

Mary Jo Zeter
Allen Thunell

Workshop Leaders

Jean Maguire

Recorder

SUMMARY. Workshop leaders Zeter and Thunell have observed the difficulty with which some library patrons identify and locate journals. They used this session to explore questions about how libraries today offer access to serials and how information about serials is presented to the public. They noted some characteristics of typical student researchers and discussed the cause of increased user demand for serials. They demonstrated the two electronic serials "pathways" used at Michigan State University (MSU), Erasmus and MAGIC, and described their respective advantages and disadvantages. Zeter and Thunell ended with recommendations for serials searching improvements and suggestions of issues for future study. *[Article copies available for a fee from The Haworth Document Delivery Service: 1-800-HAWORTH. E-mail address: <docdelivery@haworthpress.com> Website: <http://www.HaworthPress.com>]*

[Haworth co-indexing entry note]: "Success in Searching for Serials: What Is the MAGIC Solution?" Maguire, Jean. Co-published simultaneously in *The Serials Librarian* (The Haworth Information Press, an imprint of The Haworth Press, Inc.) Vol. 44, No. 3/4, 2003, pp. 201-207; and: *Transforming Serials: The Revolution Continues* (ed: Susan L. Scheiberg, and Shelley Neville) The Haworth Information Press, an imprint of The Haworth Press, Inc., 2003, pp. 201-207. Single or multiple copies of this article are available for a fee from The Haworth Document Delivery Service [1-800-HAWORTH, 9:00 a.m. - 5:00 p.m. (EST). E-mail address: docdelivery@haworthpress.com].

http://www.haworthpress.com/store/product.asp?sku=J123
10.1300/J123v44n34_24

The process of identifying and locating journals is one of the most difficult tasks for library users, according to workshop leaders Mary Jo Zeter and Allen Thunell of Michigan State University (MSU). This observation prompted them to ask questions about how libraries today offer access to serials and how information about serials is presented to the public. Zeter began exploring these questions in the workshop by noting some characteristics of the typical undergraduate student researcher and the increased user demand for serials. She and Thunell then described the advantages and disadvantages of the two "pathways" offered by MSU Libraries for serials access, Erasmus and MAGIC. Thunell concluded the workshop by suggesting ways to improve serials searching and by citing issues for future study.

PATRON CHARACTERISTICS

Zeter discussed "serials illiteracy," expectations of quick and convenient access to information, and an Internet-searching frame of reference as common characteristics of the typical undergraduate library patron. She cited a study by Barker in which only twenty-five percent of the participants were able to understand journal article citations, indicating the pervasiveness of "serials illiteracy."[1] Students' expectations of speed and convenience are based on their experience with new technologies and are manifested by a strong preference for electronic formats and by impatience with lengthy screen displays and the research process in general. The research experience of many students consists primarily of Internet searching, and Web browsers are often the only research technology that students have used prior to attending college.

The good news, according to Zeter, is that students are more likely to ask for journals today. She and Thunell believe the increased demand for journal access is caused by the proliferation of electronic indexes of journal articles. These indexes in turn have led to a shift from keyword searching to title searching in OPACs (online public access catalogs) as patrons try to locate the journal titles they have turned up in their index searches. The growing predominance of title searches has been reported by Wallace, who found that title searches in her institution's OPAC increased from twenty-four percent of searches to forty-eight percent between 1992 and 1996.[2] At MSU Libraries, management information system reports consistently show a title-search rate of thirty-eight to forty-two percent of all searches in the OPAC. Zeter showed a report from one recent ten-day period in which forty-five percent of searches were performed in the title index. A review of title search logs confirms that a large proportion of them are for journal titles. Zeter and Thunell then examined the effectiveness of Erasmus and MAGIC, the two serials "pathways" that MSU presents to patrons.

ERASMUS

Thunell led the workshop participants in what he called "a journey through Erasmus." Erasmus is not a catalog but a locally created subject-based browsing list of electronic resources.[3] It includes databases, research guides, new resources, trial resources, and electronic journals, newspapers, and books.

The first page of Erasmus features databases, but users may select the "Electronic Journals" option from the top of the screen. The Electronic Journals page offers users several ways to search for the e-journals. For example, users can view journals arranged by subject (subjects are assigned to the e-journals by library selectors, and Erasmus gives users the option of e-mailing the subject specialist in any given area) or arranged alphabetically by title. Alternatively, users may enter a search for a specific title.

Beside each e-journal listed in Erasmus, there is a link to an "About" page, which serves three purposes: to display coverage information, which can often change; to provide access information, which is especially important to assist remote users and to demonstrate compliance with licensing requirements; and to serve as a one-stop place for journal URL maintenance. Access to the journal is provided by a "Connect to [journal title]" link.

Thunell reviewed the limitations of Erasmus for the participants. First among them are searching issues. Erasmus does not contain records for all electronic journals. MARC-based, vendor-supplied record collections like those for ProQuest titles cannot be loaded into Erasmus because it is not MARC compatible. Another searching limitation is that no standard cross-references are included. In addition, the title search capability is limited because the user must enter the exact title.

Thunell also believes the access restriction information and terms like "IP" may be confusing for users. They may not know what the information means or what it is for. Another source of confusion cited by Thunell is the frequent duplicate listing of journals that are available from multiple vendors. Erasmus is also getting more difficult to use because the number of titles and subject categories has grown to the point where the browsing list is too big. As Thunell noted, a list that is too long defeats the purpose of a subject browse. Lastly, Erasmus is expensive to maintain in terms of human and other resources.

Thunell went on to highlight the ways in which Erasmus aids patrons in attaining a successful search. Erasmus still provides the simplest form of subject browsing, a capability which has special appeal for faculty since they can use it to keep up to date in their respective fields. Finding known titles in Erasmus is also a simple task. Even if users don't know the exact spelling of a title, they can locate it by using the subject or alphabetical title list. Another significant advantage of Erasmus is that it does not require the user to learn search strategies in order to use it.

MAGIC

MAGIC is MSU's Web OPAC, which is a part of their Innovative Interfaces integrated system.[4] Zeter began her demonstration of MAGIC by reviewing its strengths relative to Erasmus. Perhaps its greatest advantage over Erasmus is the inclusion of all formats, not just electronic media. It also delivers all the benefits of cataloging–multiple controlled access points, title changes, cross references, and added entries for journal title abbreviations used in citation databases. Like many other OPACs, MAGIC also displays index screens, which allow users to view nearby terms. A related advantage is the automatic search redirect capability which offers an alternative keyword search in the case of "no direct hits" searches. According to MSU's system reports, patrons elect to redirect nearly half of their "no direct hits" searches.

Zeter went on to discuss issues related specifically to serials access via MAGIC. Although MAGIC includes more journal titles than Erasmus, it still does not include all of the Libraries' e-journal titles. For example, if MSU receives free online access with a print subscription, only the record for the print version is in MAGIC, with a link added for access to the electronic version. As in Erasmus, the various access methods and restrictions for e-journals can frustrate and bewilder users. Similarly, multiple manifestations of many journal titles can confuse patrons.

MSU has been working on reducing the complexity of displays in MAGIC. The Database Advisory Committee (DBAC), which is charged with making recommendations related to the quality of the MAGIC database, asked library staff for input that would help to improve the OPAC displays of holdings and location information. Among other changes, old terminology was replaced by language that was more clear and jargon-free, location information was consolidated in one place, and an effort was made to streamline the appearance throughout.

Zeter said questions remain as to how successfully patrons navigate among print and electronic versions of the same journal title in the OPAC. Do they understand the differences in content and coverage? What do patrons make of multiple electronic versions?

To help workshop participants explore these questions, Zeter took them through a search in MAGIC for online access to the most recent issue of the same journal that had been located in the Erasmus search, *Hispanic American Historical Review* (HAHR). When users enter a search for the title, limited to periodicals only, the system returns three results–one record for the print version and two records for online versions. The term "Online" beside the second and third titles on the initial retrieval screen makes it clear that they are electronic resources, but the terms "JSTOR" and "Project Muse," which also appear, may be meaningless and confusing to users.

If users select the second of the three titles–the JSTOR title–they are taken to the full bibliographic record, where they can click on the link "Connect to online resource." In doing so, they may well expect to be taken directly to the journal, but are taken instead to an intermediary "About" page, the same one seen in the Erasmus search. Only when users arrive at this screen are they likely to realize that the JSTOR version does not include the most recent issues. However, if users persist and return to their initial list of results, they can access the issue they need by two routes. They can either select the third record, which is for the Project Muse version, or select the first one, which brings them to a list of all items related to HAHR (including the print and electronic versions of the journal itself). In the case of the latter option, the MSU Libraries have tried to ease the way for users in an otherwise confusing search by placing two links near the top of the record for the print version of HAHR that offer users the option to "Connect to recent issues online" or "Connect to older issues online." In this way, users have all the information they need in one place.

RECOMMENDATIONS

Thunell began his summation of the workshop by asking two questions: How many resources can MSU give to each of its two serials pathways and how much longer will the two exist? Erasmus is good for simple searches and MAGIC has a powerful search engine. Thunell expects that they will probably coexist for a long time.

Thunell urged the audience to work–both within the library community and with vendors–to improve public catalog displays. Improvement would include reducing screen clutter, adopting national CONSER holdings standards in order to be more consistent in public displays, and giving users the natural language they seem to want. His question to catalogers is, "If you were a patron, how would you interpret this display?" He suspects that immersion in serials jargon makes it difficult for catalogers to think about the public's perception. For that matter, he asks, what *is* the public's perception of the information that is displayed? There is a need for more up-to-date data in this area.

Thunell stressed the importance of continuing to improve searching pathways and setting goals for that improvement. Librarians should be able to offer users simple answers and direct pathways when they ask, "Do we have this issue or not?"

Zeter and Thunell's conclusions also touched on controversial topics. They believe separate records for electronic and print versions of serials provide more complete and accurate information for patrons than single records. Thunell alluded to disagreement among librarians on this issue. Indeed some disagreement was expressed by workshop participants who favored the single-record approach. Thunell responded by saying that choosing between single and separate records is a local decision, and that the most important principle is that serials records should provide accurate descriptions, not "bibliographic stews." Additionally, he said, some systems make the use of a single record complicated. In Thunell's opinion, catalogers often act too much like archivists. He argued that what users need is current information, which would make electronic versions primary, not print.

Thunell noted that patrons will need better bibliographic literacy training for systems like Erasmus and MAGIC to be truly effective. This is a problem he believes should be addressed nationally through education at the K-12 level.

Zeter and Thunell also recommended further study on ways to assist remote users. Thunell said we need to ask how we can compete with other Web information sources and Internet search engines. Even though librarians hear this question again and again, Thunell warned that they must avoid complacency and be more ready to tell people how libraries can help them. Librarians must know their patrons in order to help them be successful searchers. While he views MARC as an excellent metadata format, Thunell wonders how well librarians will use it. He suggests that it depends on how well they know their patrons. Thunell concluded by saying, "We do what we do well; we just need to do it better."

NOTES

1. Barker, Joseph W. "Now Which Buttons Do I Press to Make These Articles Appear on the Screen? Electronic Journals at the University of California at Berkeley," *Serials Review* 25, no. 3 (1999): 49-54.

2. Wallace, Patricia M. "Periodical Title Searching in Online Catalogs. Two Transaction Log Studies at the University of Colorado at Boulder," *Serials Review* 23, no. 3 (1997): 27-35.

3. "Michigan State University Libraries–Databases." http://er.lib.msu.edu (2 Aug. 2002).

4. "MSU Libraries–Online Catalog." http://magic.lib.msu.edu (2 Aug. 2002).

CONTRIBUTORS' NOTES

Mary Jo Zeter is Latin American and Caribbean Studies Bibliographer. Allen Thunell is Bibliographic Enhancement Team Manager, Michigan State University. Jean Maguire is Technical Services and Serials Librarian, New England Historic Genealogical Society.

E-Journals and Citation Patterns: Is It All Worth It?

Kimberly Parker
Kathleen Bauer

Workshop Leaders

Paula Sullenger

Recorder

SUMMARY. For many decades librarians have attempted to measure use of serial collections and the advent of electronic journals has opened up new avenues for measuring use. However, many vendor-supplied usage statistics are unsatisfactory. Two Yale University librarians tried another approach and conducted a citation analysis to compare usage before and after the arrival of electronic journals. They wanted to answer a basic question: Did the purchase of electronic journals not previously held in print affect citation patterns of Yale authors? *[Article copies available for a fee from The Haworth Document Delivery Service: 1-800-HAWORTH. E-mail address: <docdelivery@haworthpress.com> Website: <http://www.HaworthPress.com>]*

Kimberly Parker, Electronic Publishing and Collections Librarian at Yale University, began the presentation with a brief review of elec-

[Haworth co-indexing entry note]: "E-Journals and Citation Patterns: Is It All Worth It?" Sullenger, Paula. Co-published simultaneously in *The Serials Librarian* (The Haworth Information Press, an imprint of The Haworth Press, Inc.) Vol. 44, No. 3/4, 2003, pp. 209-213; and: *Transforming Serials: The Revolution Continues* (ed: Susan L. Scheiberg, and Shelley Neville) The Haworth Information Press, an imprint of The Haworth Press, Inc., 2003, pp. 209-213. Single or multiple copies of this article are available for a fee from The Haworth Document Delivery Service [1-800-HAWORTH, 9:00 a.m. - 5:00 p.m. (EST). E-mail address: docdelivery@haworthpress.com].

http://www.haworthpress.com/store/product.asp?sku=J123
10.1300/J123v44n34_25

tronic journals at Yale. Like most other university libraries, Yale's electronic journal collection began with a few titles in the mid-1990s. Yale purchased its first "big deal" package in 1996. This was the first package that included journals they did not own in print. Yale has added many single electronic journals and several more "big deals" over the last five years, and in 2002, Yale added its first foreign script package.

Yale librarians wanted to know what kind of use these packages are getting instead of just adding titles blindly. They were dissatisfied with the limited (or non-existent) usage reports available in the late 1990s. Parker pointed out that librarians must take some of the blame for the lack of consistent statistics available; we have not been consistent in articulating what we want from the publishers. Fortunately, there are some groups now working on usage reporting standards. Even great statistics still leave librarians with a problem–knowing the use of electronic journals does not get us very far in how the use of our serials has changed. Change in use will affect future buying and cancellation decisions. Yale has been fairly well funded and has been able to delay electronic-only vs. print-only decisions. Right now Yale can afford both, but soon will have to make the decision that other libraries currently face. Parker and Bauer want to know if it is possible to differentiate use from one version to another.

The presenters considered comparing reshelving statistics before and after electronic journals appeared in concert with vendor-supplied data of online usage statistics. They wanted to see if the print plus online combinations are used more than print only. However, this data was too difficult to obtain and interpret. They considered and discarded other approaches and finally settled on using citation analysis.

The presenters decided that the information they could obtain from citation analysis would be useful even with the known drawbacks. For example, the delay in publication after the actual use skews some usage, and not all legitimate uses result in citations. However, citations are "impartial" and can result from someone using either the print or electronic version. They wanted to answer a basic question: Did the purchase of electronic journals not previously held in print affect citation patterns of Yale authors?

Kathleen Bauer, Nursing Librarian at the Yale School of Medicine, explained the methodology they used in the study. They wanted to compare pre-electronic journal usage patterns with usage after electronic journals became prevalent. They began by retrieving Yale authors from the Social Sciences Citation Index (SSCI) within the Web of Science database. They used two years, 1991 and 2001, to represent the pre- and post-electronic journal eras. Using "address=Yale" as the search query, they retrieved 658 unique articles for 1991 and 1112 unique articles for 2001. As there were too many citations to review, they used a random number generator to pick three letters of the alphabet, C, L, and W, to narrow the search. Using the previous search query in conjunction with "author's last name begins with C, L, or W," they retrieved 193 unique articles for 1991 and 358 unique articles for 2001.

The presenters exported the resulting records into Endnote 5, which put the cited references into a notes field. They then extracted these references and put them into a text file and imported them into Microsoft Access. For each cited reference, the Access file has a field for the author, journal, volume, year, and page number. The presenters found some citations they could not use, such as book citations and "in press" citations that the Yale authors probably did not obtain from library sources.

When the presenters analyzed the data, they were struck by the differences in the age of the citations referenced in the two study years. Although the presenters felt that citation age is probably not something to concentrate on in the future, the results are interesting. The 193 articles retrieved for 1991 cited 4,697 references. The oldest 1991 reference cited had been written 348 years earlier. The mean age of the 1991 references was 11.7 years, with a median age of 7 years and a standard deviation of 16.8 years. The 358 articles retrieved for 2001 cited 9,520 references. The oldest 2001 reference cited had been written 193 years earlier. The mean age of the 2001 references was 10 years, with a median age of 8 years and a standard deviation of 8.8 years.

Bauer noted that most citation studies show the greatest use in the most recent ten years of publication and then a steady decline in use for older materials. The 2001 data followed that pattern, as did the 1991 data except for the oldest material, which they defined as fifty-one years or older. This was disturbing for her as a medical librarian since major research on current hot topics such as smallpox and anthrax was conducted decades ago and not much has been published recently. Researchers relying only on material found in online resources with their relatively short backfiles could miss some important information.

The main focus of this study, of course, was electronic journal usage. This study concentrates on costly "big deal" packages, although the presenters realize usage of the online journals they receive as "free with print" is just as important for a clear picture of online journal use. Bauer said that for this preliminary study, they wanted to focus on electronic journals that were fairly stable. They settled on three electronic journal packages to use as a subset: Blackwell Science, Academic Press's IDEAL, and the Wiley Interscience packages, chosen for their stability and the fact that many of their titles had been available for at least five years. This gave the presenters a total of 709 journals that were available online at the time of the study to compare to the citations referenced in the sample drawn earlier.

In 1991, of the 709 journals available, only 40 had been cited with 128 total cited references for an average of 3.2 citations per journal. In 2001, of the 709 journals available, 78 had been cited with 407 total cited references for an average of 5.2 citations per journal. The vast majority of journals had no citations at all.

Parker and Bauer noted that the number of citations increased greatly from 1991 to 2001. The number of journals cited nearly doubled from 40 to 78. The number of citations to those journals, though, more than tripled from 128 to 407. They cannot explain this, but believe that the larger number of journals available cannot explain this growth.

Looking again at the age of citations, the average citation for the electronic journal subset in 1991 was 7.8 years old, with a median of 6 years. The average citation for the electronic journal subset in 2001 was 8.5 years old, with a median of 7 years. These citations are slightly "younger" than the citations for all the journals cited as a whole earlier. The 1991 average and mean were 7 and 11.7, while the 2001 average and mean were 8 and 10.5 years. The presenters wonder if this difference could be the result of just having younger journals represented in this subset.

The presenters next looked at the breakdown of citations by subscription type. In 1991, of the 128 cited references, 115 references (89.8%) came from journals to which Yale held a print only subscription, the only kind of subscription available then. The remaining 13 citations (10.2%) came from journals that Yale did not own. In 2001, of the 407 cited references, 176 references (43.2%) came from journals to which Yale held a print only subscription. Eighteen references (4.4%) came from journals to which Yale held an electronic-only subscription, and a further 189 references (46.4%) came from journals to which Yale held a print plus online subscription. The remaining 24 citations (5.9%) came from journals that Yale did not own in any form.

The citations from journals not owned by Yale fell from 10.2% to 5.9%. However, the 2001 citations from journals held in electronic only form (those received as part of "big deal" packages) represent only 4.4% of the citations. The 2001 electronic only and not owned at all references together total 10.3%, which is virtually the same as the 1991 percentage of 10.2%.

Parker and Bauer feel their study told them many interesting things, but they need more data. They would like to compare their electronic journal subset with journals with no electronic subscription. They tried to do so in this study, but so much is available electronically now that it was too hard to search out print only journals. They would also like to compare the electronic journal subset with journals for which the print component was cancelled. They were disturbed by the lack of citation to nineteenth- and early-twentieth-century information. They would like to see new education initiatives highlighting the importance of older journals.

The audience was interested in this new use of citation analysis and had many questions and suggestions for the presenters. A couple of people suggested other means of obtaining the original citation data. Regarding the SSCI data, people wondered if coverage increases by the database could account for the huge increase in the number of citations from 1991 to 2001. SSCI indexing changes for secondary authors could have had an impact on the number of citations. This increase may also be due to changes in how a particular discipline is covered in the journals studied. Members of the audience thought more than two years needed to be examined.

Someone pointed out that this method does not measure use by students and clinicians at all. David Goodman from Princeton noted that his institution is considering measuring citations from senior theses to obtain some student data. Another person noted that other institutions are reporting more hits on their non-subscribed titles than Yale found, though Goodman felt the Yale data was consistent with that of large institutions. The presenters agreed that these are drawbacks, and cautioned that no study should be used in isolation for cancellation decisions and this was not intended for use in canceling individual titles.

CONTRIBUTORS' NOTES

Kimberly Parker is Electronic Publishing and Collections Librarian at Yale University. Kathleen Bauer is Nursing Librarian at the Yale School of Medicine. Paula Sullenger is Serials Acquisitions Librarian at Auburn University.

Cataloging Serials Reproductions:
Annoying Applications–Reprint Serials

Keiko Okuhara

Workshop Leader

Kevin M. Randall

Recorder

SUMMARY. Keiko Okuhara, Japanese Catalog Librarian at the University of Pittsburgh, presented guidelines and detailed instruction on the cataloging of microform reproductions and paper-based reprints. She used citations to the standard cataloging tools and used sample records to illustrate her points. The final portion of her presentation dealt with matters affecting the future direction of reproduction cataloging, such as the forthcoming revision to AACR2 and developments relating to multiple versions. *[Article copies available for a fee from The Haworth Document Delivery Service: 1-800-HAWORTH. E-mail address: <docdelivery@haworthpress.com> Website: <http://www.HaworthPress.com>]*

INTRODUCTION

Keiko Okuhara is Japanese Catalog Librarian in the East Asian Library at the University of Pittsburgh. She prefaced her presentation by

[Haworth co-indexing entry note]: "Cataloging Serials Reproductions: Annoying Applications–Reprint Serials." Randall, Kevin M. Co-published simultaneously in *The Serials Librarian* (The Haworth Information Press, an imprint of The Haworth Press, Inc.) Vol. 44, No. 3/4, 2003, pp. 215-222; and: *Transforming Serials: The Revolution Continues* (ed: Susan L. Scheiberg, and Shelley Neville) The Haworth Information Press, an imprint of The Haworth Press, Inc., 2003, pp. 215-222. Single or multiple copies of this article are available for a fee from The Haworth Document Delivery Service [1-800-HAWORTH, 9:00 a.m. - 5:00 p.m. (EST). E-mail address: docdelivery@haworthpress.com].

saying that she feels her "destiny is to be a cataloger of reproductions because of my Japanese background. Another factor is 'war,' since during the Pacific War, Tokyo–where a lot of intellectual and artistic works were housed–was attacked. In order to restore missing information, reproductions or reprints were used for the dissemination of information. So I really cannot send these annoying applications to the back shelf but I need to face these materials and become friends with them. My choice enabled me to pick up serials reprint cataloging."

DEFINITIONS

"What is a reproduction?" To answer the question Okuhara quoted from footnote 1 in chapter 11 of the *Library of Congress Rule Interpretations* (LCRI): "A reproduction is a manifestation that replicates an item. . . . Reproduction is generally a mechanical rather than an intellectual process." Drawing extensively from information in *Anglo-American Cataloging Rules,* 2nd ed. (AACR2), the *CONSER Cataloging Manual* (CCM), and LCRI, she elaborated on two formats of reproductions: microforms and reprints.

MICROFORMS

Examples of specific formats given in AACR2 rule 11.0A1 are microfilms, microfiches, microopaques, and aperture cards. There are three types of microform publications to consider: original (or micropublication–first issued in microform), reproduction (content existed previously in another physical format), and microform sets (compilations of bibliographically unrelated titles). Okuhara pointed out the difference between microform sets and multiple versions, the latter of which are defined in CCM module 32 as "Publications that are identical in content but different in physical format."

REPRINTS

From the AACR2 glossary, Okuhara defined a reprint as "an item made from the original type image" which "may reproduce the original exactly" or have minor changes, or "a new edition with substantially unchanged text." It may also be a facsimile reproduction, which is "a reproduction simulating the physical appearance of the original in addition to reproducing its content exactly." CCM module 17.7.1 describes three types of serial reprints: a serial reprinted by the same publisher, a serial issued by a reprint publisher, and bibliographically unrelated serials reprinted together.

CATALOGING

Microforms

Guidelines for cataloging microforms can be found in CCM module 32. First one must determine whether the microform is an original or a reproduction. In the case of a microform set, the set itself will usually be considered an original publication, because it exists as a collection only in microform; the individual titles included will be considered reproductions.

Then, one must determine whether the microform is a serial. For an original microform, this determination is made by consulting LCRI 12.0A. For a reproduction microform, one follows the treatment used for the original hard copy. One should treat a microform set as a monograph if it contains bibliographically separate titles and the set itself is finite, but it should be treated as a serial if the set is a continuing publication.

An original microform is cataloged based on AACR2 chapter 11. The chief source of information is the title frame; eye-readable data may be substituted if the title frame is lacking or does not contain sufficient information. A reproduction microform is cataloged based on LCRI chapter 11, which states in part: "Transcribe the bibliographic data appropriate to the original work being reproduced." The sources of information are from the original work. The *CONSER Editing Guide* (CEG) strongly encourages the creation of CONSER records for preservation master microforms.

Information about the format is given in the form of a bracketed general material designation in subfield $h of field 245 and a specific material designation in subfield $a of field 300 (for an original microform) or in subfield $a of field 533 (for a reproduction microform). Records for preservation masters have three 007 fields: one each for service copy, preservation master, and printing master ("c," "a," and "b," respectively, in subfield $i). For a commercial microform, only one 007 field would be used, for service copy.

For a reproduction microform, field 533 gives the type of reproduction (subfield $a), dates of publication and/or sequential designations of the reproduced issues (subfield $m; required for preservation masters, optional in other cases), place of reproduction (subfield $b), agency of reproduction (subfield $c), date of reproduction (subfield $d), physical description of reproduction (subfield $e), series statement of reproduction (subfield $f), and note about reproduction (subfield $n; when multiple titles are filmed together, a "Filmed with" note would go here). Field 776 is used to link the records for the original and the reproduction, when a record exists for the original. If a series statement is given in field 533, the series added entry would be given in field 830.

National Library of Canada uses AACR2 chapter 11, not the LCRI, to catalog microforms. Field 533 is not used for reproductions. Instead, the specific material designation would go into subfield $a of field 300, and details about the original would go into field 534. CONSER participants are not to modify the NLC records, but should instead create new records following LCRI chapter 11.

Okuhara illustrated many points in her discussion with sample records. She suggested CEG appendix M as a good "cheat sheet" for cataloging microforms.

Reprints

In cataloging reprints, three issues need to be examined: the publisher, the number of serials included, and the number of issues included. Guidance can be found in CCM module 17.7.3 and LCRI 12.0.

A single record approach can be taken if the reprint is published by the same publisher as the original. Generally no note regarding the reprint is made in the bibliographic record. However, if the reprinted issues have a different or additional title, a note and added entry may be provided in field 246, with the text "Some issues reprinted with title:" in subfield $i. If the reprint is published by a different publisher, create a new record for the reprint. If the number of issues of the serial is small, or if multiple bibliographically unrelated serials are published together, the reprint can be cataloged as a monograph. If reprinted issues are acquired to fill in gaps in the library's holdings, the single record approach can be taken.

Reprints pose special problems because they usually have more than one source that can be considered the chief source of information. Areas of the description use different sources; LCRI 12.0B1 gives the prescribed sources of information, and CCM module 17.7.4 gives further instruction. The title and statement of responsibility, the edition statement, and the designation are taken from the earliest reprinted issue. The publisher statement is taken from the reprint title page. The physical description is based on the reprint, and if the reprinted serial is complete, the number of physical volumes, instead of bibliographic volumes, is recorded for the extent of item. A series statement is recorded only if the reprint itself is in a series. No "Description based on" note or source of title note is given, because of the variety of sources of information. Known data that would be included in the description of the original but do not appear on the reprint may be supplied in brackets.

Information about the original publication is given in field 580. Angle brackets may be used around the dates of publication of the original if the first reprinted issue is not in hand. If the reprint carries a different title, a separate note may be given along with an added entry in field 246, with the text "Reprint title page title:" in subfield $i. Field 775 can be used to link to the record for the original, if one exists. In the fixed field, Form of item (008/23) code "r" is used for regular print reprints. The Dates (008/07-14) and Publication status (008/06) values pertain to the original.

Okuhara used sample records to illustrate several points in her discussion. She recommended CEG Appendix L as a good cheat sheet for regular-print reprints.

FUTURE TRENDS

To address the theme of the conference, "Transforming Serials: The Revolution Continues," Okuhara talked about some new directions that may affect reproductions.

In the forthcoming revisions to AACR2, the scope of chapter 12 has been expanded to cover all kinds of continuing resources (including serials and integrating resources) in all media. There will be new terminology and new definitions based on the new concepts in the rules. For example, some new terms are "bibliographic resource," "continuing resource," "integrating resource"; the term "serial" has a new definition. The chapter will be applied to handle the continuing aspect of all integrating resources, both finite and continuing.

The revised AACR2 will include the concept of major and minor changes in title proper. If a change is considered minor, a new record is not created; in case of doubt, the change is to be considered minor. One example of a major change is the addition, deletion, or change of any word other than an article; there are some exceptions to this that constitute some of the minor changes.

The Format Variation Working Group of the Joint Steering Committee for Revision of Anglo-American Cataloguing Rules was formed to incorporate terminology from IFLA's "Functional Requirements for Bibliographic Records" into AACR, and to devise system functional requirements for managing separate records for related manifestations at the global level and consolidating them for display at the local level. At the ALA Midwinter 2002 meeting of MARBI, the Working Group expressed its concern that not all situations involving multiple versions are scalable.

AACR2 rule 0.24 deals with multiple versions. The rule has two major functions. First, it helps the cataloger determine how to describe an item that has multiple characteristics, for example an item falling into more than one chapter of AACR2. Second, it is the only place that raises the question of when to create a new record for an item similar to another item that has already been cataloged. The report of the ALCTS CC:DA Task Force on Rule 0.24 describes the progress of the rule revision.

The paper "Functional Analysis of the MARC 21 Bibliographic and Holdings Formats: Displays for Multiple Versions from MARC 21 and FRBR" discusses the issue of displaying records for multiple manifestations of the same work. Several debates on the matter are happening currently. Okuhara referred to Edgar A. Jones's description of the FRBR model to define some terms: "A *manifestation* is the totality of *items* that are identical both in their intellectual/artistic content and in their bibliographic and physical format." The "item" is more commonly known as the "piece in hand," and "manifestation" more commonly known as "version." The "totality of bibliographically identical *items* constitutes a *manifestation*," and "the totality of textually, graphically, etc., identical *manifestations* constitutes an *expression* . . . an *expression* is the same 'text' . . ."[1] Okuhara then showed an example of a hierarchical display for multiple expressions and manifestations of *The English Patient* (the novel by Michael Ondaatje, the motion picture in both film and disc formats, and the published screenplay by Anthony Minghella).

In concluding her discussion of future trends, Okuhara referred to the matter of CONSER application of LCRI 1.11A for a microform-like approach to the description of electronic versions. CONSER had decided in 2001 not to apply the rule interpretation, but as of the May 2002 meeting of its Operations Committee it is reconsidering that decision.

NOTE

1. Edgar A. Jones, "Multiple Versions Revisited," *The Serials Librarian* 32, no. 1/2 (1997): 183.

RESOURCES CITED

Anglo-American Cataloguing Rules. 2nd ed., 1998 revision. Chicago: American Library Association, 1998. Updated with amendments 1999 and 2001.

Association for Library Collections and Technical Services, Committee on Cataloging: Description and Access. *Guidelines for Bibliographic Description of Reproductions.* Chicago: American Library Association, 1995.

Association for Library Collections and Technical Services, Committee on Cataloging: Description and Access, Task Force on Rule 0.24. [Home page]. http://www.ala.org/alcts/organization/ccs/ccda/tf-024a.html (8 Aug. 2002).

CONSER Editing Guide. 1994 ed. Washington, D.C.: Library of Congress, Serial Record Division, 1994. Updated through update 13 (spring 2001).

CONSER Operations Committee Annual Meeting summary, May 1-3, 2002. http://www.loc.gov/acq/conser/conop2002.html (8 Aug. 2002).

Delsey, Tom. "Functional Analysis of the MARC 21 Bibliographic and Holdings Formats." Jan. 4, 2002, revised Mar. 21, 2002. http://www.loc.gov/marc/marc-functional-analysis/home.html (8 Aug. 2002).

Graham, Crystal. "Guidelines for Bibliographic Records for Preservation Microform Masters." Sept. 1990. http://www.arl.org/preserv/guide.html (8 Aug. 2002).

Hirons, Jean L., ed. *CONSER Cataloging Manual.* Washington, D.C.: Library of Congress, Cataloging Distribution Service, 1993. Updated through update 11 (fall 2000).

International Federation of Library Associations and Institutions, Study Group on the Functional Requirements for Bibliographic Records. "Functional Requirements for Bibliographic Records, Final Report." Sept. 1997. http://www.ifla.org/VII/s13/frbr/frbr.htm (8 Aug. 2002).

Joint Steering Committee for Revision of Anglo-American Cataloguing Rules. "Current activities." http://www.nlc-bnc.ca/jsc/current.html (8 Aug. 2002).

Jones, Edgar A. "Multiple Versions Revisited." *The Serials Librarian* 32, no. 1/2 (1997): 177-198.

Library of Congress. "Bibliographic Control of Web Resources: A Library of Congress Action Plan." Revised July 25, 2001. http://lcweb.loc.gov/catdir/bibcontrol/draftplan.html (8 Aug. 2002).

Library of Congress. *Library of Congress Rule Interpretations.* 2nd ed. (1989). Washington, D.C.: Cataloging Distribution Service, Library of Congress, 1990. Updated through 2002, issue 1.

Library of Congress, Network Development and MARC Standards Office. "Functional Analysis of the MARC 21 Bibliographic and Holdings Formats: Displays for Multiple Versions from MARC 21 and FRBR." Updated as of June 27, 2002.

http://www.loc.gov/marc/marc-functional-analysis/multiple-versions.html (8 Aug. 2002).

MARBI Discussion Paper 2002-DP04, "Addition of Imprint and Physical Description fields to the MARC 21 Holdings Format." Dec. 18, 2001. http://lcweb.loc.gov/marc/marbi/2002/2002-dp04.html (8 Aug. 2002).

MARBI Discussion Paper 2002-DP08, "Dealing with FRBR Expressions in MARC 21." May 30, 2002. http://www.loc.gov/marc/marbi/2002/2002-dp08.html (8 Aug. 2002).

MARBI Meeting minutes, ALA Midwinter Meeting, Jan. 19-21, 2002. http://lcweb.loc.gov/marc/marbi/minutes/mw-02.html (8 Aug. 2002).

CONTRIBUTORS' NOTES

Keiko Okuhara is Japanese Catalog Librarian, East Asian Library, Hillman Library, University of Pittsburgh. Kevin M. Randall is Head of Serials Cataloging, Northwestern University Library.

Revolutionary Relationships: Catalogers' Liaison Role as Metadata Experts in the Creation of the K-State Digital Library

Char Simser

Workshop Leader

Miriam Childs

Recorder

SUMMARY. The Kansas State Digital Libraries Program gave Kansas State catalogers the opportunity to play an integral role in the university's digital initiative. The project enabled catalogers to display their expertise in organizing information and expertise in metadata. Catalogers were asked to provide descriptive data for the materials that were digitized for the Digital Libraries Program. Involvement in digital projects brings catalogers out of the library and into working relationships with faculty, administrators, and staff on campus. These new relationships could bring about organizational change as involvement in digital initiatives continues. *[Article copies available for a fee from The Haworth Document Delivery Service: 1-800-HAWORTH. E-mail address: <docdelivery@haworthpress.com> Website: <http://www.HaworthPress.com>]*

[Haworth co-indexing entry note]: "Revolutionary Relationships: Catalogers' Liaison Role as Metadata Experts in the Creation of the K-State Digital Library." Childs, Miriam. Co-published simultaneously in *The Serials Librarian* (The Haworth Information Press, an imprint of The Haworth Press, Inc.) Vol. 44, No. 3/4, 2003, pp. 223-228; and: *Transforming Serials: The Revolution Continues* (ed: Susan L. Scheiberg, and Shelley Neville) The Haworth Information Press, an imprint of The Haworth Press, Inc., 2003, pp. 223-228. Single or multiple copies of this article are available for a fee from The Haworth Document Delivery Service [1-800-HAWORTH, 9:00 a.m. - 5:00 p.m. (EST). E-mail address: docdelivery@haworthpress.com].

http://www.haworthpress.com/store/product.asp?sku=J123
10.1300/J123v44n34_27

INTRODUCTION

This workshop presented a view of catalogers as metadata experts and how catalogers' skills are applicable in a digital world. The catalogers at Kansas State University Library had previous experience with electronic materials before becoming involved with the Digital Libraries Program when Kansas State acquired and cataloged over 3,000 electronic journals. Additionally, some monographs included URLs on imported records, and URLs were added to K-State publications. K-State recently purchased netLibrary e-books as well.

Cataloging is located within the technical services area at Kansas State, and as with cataloging departments at most institutions, it includes a mix of professional and non-professional staff. Original catalogers serve as team leaders and have supervisory duties; their duties also include committee and team work outside the department, and for some, professional development activities. As with other cataloging departments, the staff handles authority database cleanup and serials cataloging. The K-State Digital library initiative added something new to the traditional duties of the K-State catalogers.

K-STATE DIGITAL LIBRARIES TASK FORCE

The Digital Libraries Task Force was formed in the fall of 2000. Composed of librarians, administrators, teaching faculty, and university computing staff, its main charge was to establish standards and organizational requirements for selecting and managing the content, technologies and access for the Digital Library. The KSU Digital Library would be a university-wide digital library, containing more types of information than found in a typical "library." The content for the digital library was spread across campus in different departments and in individual databases. These isolated information sources were to be consolidated, allowing users to access all of the content from one place, very much like an information portal. With this in mind, the Task Force began working on a prototype of the digital library.

The Task Force first needed to identify a search engine for the data, select a method for organizing the data, and choose the collections to include in the prototype. The Task Force selected Endeavor's Oracle-based program EnCompass as the search engine and database organizer. Software for encoding video was added. For the initial digitization, the Task Force selected materials from the K-State Agricultural Extension, which publishes a wide variety of materials; the library catalog; video and audio materials; the index to the *K-State Collegian*, the university newspaper; the Information Support Services for Agriculture (ISSA) citation database; and the Wildflower collection, a Web resource compiled by one of the science librarians at K-State.

BUILDING THE DIGITAL LIBRARY

With the content identified, the next step was to identify which materials to include in the prototype and to make them available for searching. Two working groups, a collections working group and a training/oversight working group, were put in charge of the process.

The training/oversight group developed a set of required elements for the document type descriptions (DTDs) to ensure consistency across all collections; they decided on title, format, and place of publication. The DTDs would make up a record for a particular item and would then be entered into Oracle using Dublin Core metadata tags. The training group also was in charge of general training for the project, managing the project, and managing future proposals relating to the project.

The collections working groups consisted of content creators, technical support, and a cataloger. The group recognized the catalogers' expertise in organizing information with their familiarity with metadata. Specifically, the cataloger's role in the working group was to provide input to the content creators on additional document description elements such as style of entry, title identification, subjects, and keywords. Each collections working group met to identify specific items to add to the prototype and define its own set of DTDs. The catalogers helped to define elements beyond the ones required by the training/oversight group. The catalogers' level of involvement in each collections working group varied.

The Web project managers of the Research & Extension department were already using Dublin Core metadata tags for electronic publications, and they needed little to no cataloging assistance in setting up the DTDs for the database. They used what was already on their Web publications for entry into the database.

The ISSA citation database was originally developed in Microsoft Access. Prior to the formation of the Task Force, it was converted to MARC using Data Magician. Catalogers were heavily involved in this conversion, which was a sort of precursor to the Digital Libraries Program. ISSA staff had been using consistent headings, which was helpful for setting up DTDs. The cataloger worked closely with the ISSA collection group to define its Dublin Core tags. Additionally, due to an agreement between the China Agricultural Library in Beijing and Kansas State University Library, a collection of Chinese agricultural documents was made available in PDF format. The cataloger defined the tags for this collection so that the Chinese DTD documents could contain links to the PDF files and the original Word documents.

The video working group was unfamiliar with describing content. A lecture series by Donna Shalala and tractor safety videos were chosen as content for the prototype. The cataloger spent a good deal of time with this group, providing an overview of required elements from a master DTD and then helping to define elements beyond the basics. Those who digitized the videos provided descriptive information for the cataloger, who then entered the DTDs into the database.

With the *Collegian* index collection group, there was a Microsoft Access database consisting of an in-house subject thesaurus with consistent entry. Unfortunately, the Access database couldn't be mapped into Dublin Core by the implementation date, so this collection was not included in the prototype.

The Digital Library prototype debuted in May 2001 and has received a very positive reception. The creation process raised some questions. For instance, for data with multiple formats, such as print and video, should there be separate records in the database? How would links between the different formats affect the DTD fields? Who will have permission to access materials in the digital library, and how would EnCompass provide rights management? Where should the materials be archived, on a library server or a campus server? These issues continue to be discussed.

TOWARD THE FUTURE

Kansas State has a development partnership with Endeavor, Cornell University, University of Pennsylvania, and the Getty Museum. From June 2001 through February 2002, the Task Force met to test some possible new technologies. The search engine needed to be improved, and it had a limited ability to work with data in multiple formats. The Agricultural Extension received a grant to digitize weather data for Kansas back to the 1920s and data documenting grain elevator explosions. The College of Veterinary Medicine is interested in digitizing surgical videos for use as a teaching tool, and the Apparel, Textile, and Design Department wants to contribute its historical costume collection. Digital Library 2.0 was installed in April of 2002, but at the time of the conference was not customized for K-State. Its search engine is much improved over the prototype. Rights management issues are holding up progress, so in the meantime the new Digital Library is being tested and configured. The new Library will incorporate commercial content such as A & I databases and electronic journals. It will employ OpenURL standards for searching: authentication allows users access to the databases which they have permission to use. To ensure that catalogers continue to be involved in digital projects, the cataloger position description at K-State has been updated to include Digital Library duties, and a Digital Library department has been formed.

CATALOGING ROLE CHANGE

Catalogers involved in the K-State Digital Libraries Project learned most of all about the power of cooperating with several departments across campus. Catalogers collaborated with faculty, computing staff, and others to successfully implement university-wide projects. Commitment from both the library and the university is essential for the success of any digitization project.

Taking part in digital initiatives could mean that catalogers end up with more prominent roles within the university community. Catalogers would work with faculty and administrators that, in a traditional role, they would probably never meet. The "outside world" will eventually recognize catalogers' expertise at organizing information and will see how this skill is desirable in the digital age. Catalogers have increasingly become familiar with new technologies, and taking part in initiatives will highlight that knowledge. Involvement in digital initiatives could bring about a change in how technical services departments are organized if librarians have wider university roles. As digital opportunities arise, catalogers could spend less time on cataloging acquired materials. There may also be a change in the way electronic resources are currently cataloged. Ultimately, digital initiatives will take the cataloger out of Technical Services and increase involvement with the rest of the campus, which could be beneficial for the library as a whole.

CONCLUSION

Projects like the K-State Digital Libraries Program demonstrate that now is an exciting time for catalogers, full of possibilities. Catalogers have skills that can be very useful in many arenas, not simply within a library. However, the reality is that the work catalogers normally do never ends, so backlogs can and do develop when catalogers are involved with a project like the Digital Libraries Program. Staffing needs increase, but there could be support to increase staff when catalogers contribute to a popular university-wide initiative. The success of the Digital Libraries Program hints at the possibilities that await catalogers, and it could cause revolutionary organizational changes both within and outside of the library.

CONTRIBUTORS' NOTES

Char Simser is Chair of Technical Services at Kansas State University. Miriam Childs is Serials Librarian at the University of New Orleans

Cataloging for Consortium Catalogs

Paul Moeller
Wendy Baia

Workshop Leaders

Jennifer O'Connell

Recorder

SUMMARY. This session describes the University of Colorado at Boulder's participation in Prospector: The Colorado Unified Catalog. Issues with cataloging serials within a consortium catalog, including latest vs. successive entry cataloging, single vs. separate record treatment of electronic journals, and holdings are discussed. Specifically, the issues of title changes and handling of supplements are discussed. The presenters offer recommendations based on their experience. *[Article copies available for a fee from The Haworth Document Delivery Service: 1-800-HAWORTH. E-mail address: <docdelivery@haworthpress.com> Website: <http://www.HaworthPress. com>]*

At the beginning of the session, Paul Moeller, serials cataloger and Wendy Baia, head, Serials Cataloging and assistant head, Cataloging Department at the University of Colorado at Boulder, queried the audience to see how many different consortia were represented. There were

---

[Haworth co-indexing entry note]: "Cataloging for Consortium Catalogs." O'Connell, Jennifer. Co-published simultaneously in *The Serials Librarian* (The Haworth Information Press, an imprint of The Haworth Press, Inc.) Vol. 44, No. 3/4, 2003, pp. 229-235; and: *Transforming Serials: The Revolution Continues* (ed: Susan L. Scheiberg, and Shelley Neville) The Haworth Information Press, an imprint of The Haworth Press, Inc., 2003, pp. 229-235. Single or multiple copies of this article are available for a fee from The Haworth Document Delivery Service [1-800-HAWORTH, 9:00 a.m. - 5:00 p.m. (EST). E-mail address: docdelivery@haworthpress.com].

http://www.haworthpress.com/store/product.asp?sku=J123
10.1300/J123v44n34_28

attendees representing 36 different consortia (both sessions combined), many of whom attended because they were in the process of working on shared cataloging.

The workshop's purpose was "sharing consortium cataloging knowledge, experiences, problems, solutions and recommendations." Two major questions were posed: Relating to the concept of the consortium master record, does one size fit all? Second, has membership in a consortium catalog changed the way we catalog serials?

Moeller began by describing the development of Prospector: The Colorado Unified Catalog. Based on the "master record" concept, using Innovative Interfaces (III) INN-Reach software, the purpose was for users to view records, including holdings, from all member institutions and initiate interlibrary loan (ILL) requests. During the development stages, a Cataloging/Reference Task Force was established to make bibliographic and display decisions. Later, a focus group met to discuss the serials cataloging issues including single vs. separate record approach, successive vs. latest entry, and holdings. The group discovered that there were variations in practices among the Prospector Libraries.

Moeller went on to describe the process of merging the records from the member libraries. Prospector matched by OCLC number, ISBN, and ISSN together with title word matching, and chose the record with the highest encoding level in order to pick the most complete record. The Prospector software automatically excludes local fields. It has the capability to suppress records from display in the consortium catalog; however, Moeller recommends doing this only in unusual cases. Prospector's member libraries appointed cataloging liaisons that facilitate maintenance. However, Baia noted that no one has ever contacted her library's Prospector cataloging liaison in that capacity.

Today, Prospector is composed of 15 libraries from Colorado and will soon include the University of Wyoming. Another advantage of the unified catalog is that it facilitates checking holdings for four of the member libraries that have a joint storage facility, PASCAL. Only one copy of a serial can be stored at PASCAL among the four member libraries. Members can check holdings in the unified catalog to avoid sending duplicates.

Moeller provided an overview of the interesting features of several consortia. The CIC Virtual Electronic Library does not provide a central catalog but allows searching of all member library catalogs individually or as a group. VIVA, The Virtual Library of Virginia, does not have a consortium catalog, but has documentation providing guidelines for best cataloging practices for the electronic resources it purchases.

OhioLINK, which was a leader in the development of a central catalog to facilitate the sharing of resources, has become a purchaser of e-resources. CDL, the California Digital Library, employs centralized cataloging of the e-resources purchased by the consortium. Moeller stressed the importance of documentation, pointing out that the CDL has done an especially good job of documenting their cataloging policies. He also recommends that those developing documentation for consortium cataloging practices follow CONSER standards. He noted that national standards undergo revision and decisions will sometimes have to be made before everything is settled in the standards.

Moeller made the following recommendations for the cataloging of e-resources:

- Make a decision whether the catalog will follow single vs. separate record approach.
- Follow accepted cataloging standards as appropriate for your institution.
- Normalize the use of the 856 field.
- Decide the best place to put URLs.
- Document the decisions that are made and reassess these decisions periodically.
- Appoint maintenance contacts.
- Train catalogers to consider the impact of their decisions in a shared cataloging environment.
- When making decisions, you need to consider what the consortium's system can do.

Several issues were raised specifically regarding the decision between single vs. separate records. Though the single record approach has several benefits, including the need to do fewer original e-journal records, these same benefits can be questioned. One may ask whether separate records do a better job of describing the resource. Although it is supported by Public Services as easier for the patron to understand, the single record approach results in longer displays and could be confusing. Separate records may be easier to maintain. Adding e-access to print records can be time consuming. Also, it may be easier for patrons to look directly for electronic versions, if that is what they are interested in. Despite these issues, Moeller and Baia recommend the use of the single record approach, if appropriate. They also recommend shelving accompanying materials with the main piece when possible as this helps to facilitate patron access, ILL, and reserves.

Another major issue is holdings. Moeller recommends that you choose a standard, including level of detail and style of display, MARC or non-MARC, and whether to use level 3 or 4 of ANSI/NISO Z39.71-1999. Be consistent within the catalog. If you choose to do non-standard holdings, add them in a uniform manner. Consider the impact upon the consortium catalog when making a change. Consistency facilitates ILL and makes the catalog more comprehensible to the user. Moeller also recommends adding e-journal holdings when manageable.

According to Baia, title changes are "one of the greatest challenges in cataloging serials for consortium catalogs." Issues of successive vs. latest entry cataloging generated heated discussions during Prospector planning. Only CU and one other library were using latest entry for current cataloging, although most other libraries had older latest entry records. In the summer of 1999, the Cataloging/Reference Task Force decided that Prospector members could no longer contribute current latest entry cataloging to Prospector. Although CU serials cataloging changed their title change practices according to the new guidelines, Baia cautioned the CU serials catalogers to check Prospector before doing any questionable title changes. Her study of Prospector serials records showed that many libraries were treating some "title changes" as 246 variant title. Baia said it would defeat the purpose of the master record concept if CU created a new successive record when all other library holdings were attached to a record with one or more 246s to account for title variations.

Baia analyzed records for title changes in the CU catalog, Prospector, Orbis and OhioLINK. Baia cited *Barron's* as an example of varying title change practices. OCLC has 26 records for various successive and latest entry records for *Barron's*, CU has one record, Prospector has six, Orbis has eight, and OhioLINK has 11 serial records including both successive and latest entry.

From her research on title changes, Baia concludes that in all consortium catalogs viewed "there are a variety of title change treatments, holdings that don't match the master record's publication history and a proliferation of records." If staff members who check in serials find a record that seems to match the title, often title changes get missed. A record in a library may have open holdings and be attached to a master record in the shared catalog with closed holdings. While a master record may cover the full run of the serial including all title variations, the local records for the libraries attached to this master record may have cataloged the same title as successive and have their holdings split on successive records. Microform holdings were often added to print records regardless of the publication history in the 362. Finally, Baia found that the proliferation of records and variations in the handling of title changes in consortium catalogs might make it difficult to find a specific volume.

Baia had several recommendations for handling title changes. Catalogers should understand the match points used for other library's holdings being added to the master record. For questionable title changes, catalogers should check their consortium catalog to see how the title changes have been handled. Public Services staff should understand that records exist in a variety of ways in the consortium catalog and that multiple records may need to be consulted to cover title variations.

The second major issue discussed by Baia was the issue of supplements. There are several options for supplement treatment. They can be checked in with the serial either by including a 525 note stating "includes supplements" or by adding notes and added entries for the distinctive supplement titles. Supplements can be cataloged as separate serials with their own numbering or as monographs. They can also be ignored altogether although this is not recommended. Baia stressed the importance of having notes and appropriate title added entries for supplements in the master record so that others can locate them.

Third, with consortium catalog master records, access points and special subject headings, such as NLM, which are searchable in the local catalogs may not be searchable in the consortium catalog if they do not exist in the master record. Likewise, notes and updated information in one catalog may not be present in the master record

According to Baia, the conclusions are that the master record model has some of the same problems that OCLC has, but without the benefit of a program like CONSER. Due to variations within local catalogs, holdings can be dispersed among different records. Multiple records could actually be beneficial if some records have access points that the other records do not. Baia stated that the ideal of one record for each serial publication currently exists more in theory than reality. Different local needs often require different local treatment decisions, thus different records. Duplicate records could be prevented if member libraries had the ability to move their holdings to another master record. However, this is often not possible. Baia concluded that "the goal of user friendly search results and updated comprehensive records won't be attained without cataloger awareness of the results of their cataloging in the consortium catalog and a dependable method of consortium catalog maintenance."

The following recommendations were made:

- Before making complex and non-obvious cataloging treatment decisions, check the consortium catalog for other libraries' treatment.
- Code library-specific notes with fields that don't display in the consortium catalog.
- Use cataloger's judgment to balance local user needs with efficient searching and comprehension in the consortium catalog.
- Train staff and patrons to be sophisticated searchers to avoid confusion and obtain the most comprehensive results.
- Establish best practice recommendations to promote uniformity of practice.
- Library representatives to consortium oversight groups should maintain good communication with staff in their libraries.

Moeller asked the discussion question, "In what ways does your consortium catalog fail to meet the needs of its users?" The audience felt that some of the things crucial to the success of the consortium catalog included response time, successful ILL requests due to accurate holdings, and education on the use of the catalog.

Members of the audience stressed the importance of communication with other libraries within the consortium. Working with other libraries to resolve issues should be common practice. Creating catalogs with the understanding that all catalogers will not agree is important. Members of the audience also stressed the importance of establishing "best practices" and following national guidelines when possible. Agreeing on single vs. separate records is an important part of the process.

Overall, the general feeling of the audience was that they were dealing with some of the same issues in their shared catalogs. While discussing the issue of single vs. separate records, one of the issues raised was the use of aggregator records, such as those from EBSCO or Wiley. The audience felt that these might be hard to keep on one record at this time, but this is likely to be easier in the future with new technological developments with system vendors. Another point that was raised cited Michael Gorman's concept that "one record is simple to browse, but complex at the record level, while separate records are complex to browse, and simple at the record level." One of the main concerns was display. This is often dependent on the capabilities of the ILS system. Baia stated, "Serials are complex, we would like to simplify them, but they are complex by nature."

CONTRIBUTORS' NOTES

Paul Moeller is Serials Cataloger, University of Colorado at Boulder. Wendy Baia is Head, Serials Cataloging/Assistant Head, Cataloging Department, University of Colorado at Boulder. Jennifer O'Connell is Database Librarian, EBSCO Subscription Services.

What to Do When Disaster Strikes:
The California State University, Northridge, Experience

Susan E. Parker
Don Jaeger

Workshop Leaders

Kristen Kern

Recorder

SUMMARY. The catastrophic earthquake disaster that hit the California State University, Northridge campus in 1994 offers lessons in preparing for and responding to an event of this magnitude. The workshop leaders emphasized the importance of thorough planning for disasters before they occur, working cooperatively with risk management agencies such as FEMA when they do, and understanding the vital role that remediation companies, back volume vendors, binders and others play in recovering from a disaster. Susan E. Parker from CSU, Northridge, and Don Jaeger, Alfred Jaeger, Inc., presented the university library and back volume vendor perspectives on the disaster's consequences and recovery effort, particularly in relation to the replacement of bound periodical back

[Haworth co-indexing entry note]: "What to Do When Disaster Strikes: The California State University, Northridge, Experience." Kern, Kristen. Co-published simultaneously in *The Serials Librarian* (The Haworth Information Press, an imprint of The Haworth Press, Inc.) Vol. 44, No. 3/4, 2003, pp. 237-242; and: *Transforming Serials: The Revolution Continues* (ed: Susan L. Scheiberg, and Shelley Neville) The Haworth Information Press, an imprint of The Haworth Press, Inc., 2003, pp. 237-242. Single or multiple copies of this article are available for a fee from The Haworth Document Delivery Service [1-800-HAWORTH, 9:00 a.m. - 5:00 p.m. (EST). E-mail address: docdelivery@haworthpress.com].

http://www.haworthpress.com/store/product.asp?sku=J123
10.1300/J123v44n34_29

volumes lost in a storage area mold outbreak. Jaeger described the appraisal methods used for valuing collections. *[Article copies available for a fee from The Haworth Document Delivery Service: 1-800-HAWORTH. E-mail address: <docdelivery@haworthpress.com> Website: <http://www.HaworthPress.com>]*

Susan E. Parker, Associate Dean of the University Library at California State University, Northridge, began the workshop by presenting the library's perspective on the destructive 1994 earthquake and its consequences for the campus, located twenty-five miles north of Los Angeles. Parker noted that in 2002 the university is just completing the rebuilding of the campus. The Delmar T. Oviatt Library, originally constructed in 1973, was enlarged with East and West Wings in 1991. At that time, an innovative automated storage and retrieval system (AS/RS) was installed by HK Systems in the lower two levels of the East Wing. The storage area has the capacity to house one million books, bound periodicals, and manuscripts in 13,300 bins constructed in five different sizes. There is a public catalog interface to access items identified by unique barcodes that can be retrieved in ten minutes by a robotic crane from the bins.

The 6.8 magnitude earthquake hit the Northridge campus on January 14, 1994, at 4:30 a.m., the epicenter of which was less than a mile from campus. As a result of the immense damage to university buildings and infrastructure, the Federal Emergency Management Agency (FEMA) became the insurance agent for the disaster recovery effort. FEMA in turn hired an engineering firm, DMJM/JGM to act as an intermediary between the agency and the university. The firm hired contractors and arranged the bids for construction projects, which were then reimbursed by FEMA. The university term had just begun and was only delayed two weeks due to the immediate assembling of tents, trailers and other temporary structures to accommodate academic and administrative activities.

The core of the library was relatively undamaged, although asbestos remediation was necessary. Temporary library services resumed in four months. The structural viability of the newer library wings, however, was studied over a three-year period, and when irreparable structural damage was discovered they were razed down to the ceiling of the storage area. Rebuilding of the wings was funded by FEMA and scheduled to begin in early 1998.

In the fall of 1997 and again in January 1998, because a temporary roof to cover the storage structure was not in place, water from unexpected rainfall leaked into the library storage area and caused a major mold outbreak. Administration declared an occupational safety emergency, an action that protects the library. After consulting the campus Environmental and Occupational Health and Safety office, the area was closed down and Clayton Environmental Consultants were hired to perform tests for types of mold, mold growth and damage, and the moisture content in books. At this point, DMJM/JGM hired BMS/Cat to begin mold remediation immediately. Following the required bidding process another firm, Marcor, was awarded the remediation contract. Marcor was trained and continued to operate the AS/RS system. A protocol of standards, procedures and definitions (what is wet? clean?) was developed with both remediation companies. A separate inventory database was constructed to track items that were freeze-dried or withdrawn from the collection. As appropriate, salvaged materials were given a light chemical wiping and dusting. Five thousand unsalvageable books were discarded, of which over four thousand were bound periodical back volumes up to 1990. As of 2002 work continues on the archival material placed in the storage area.

The library was able to use the catalog to identify lost material as part of the damage assessment process. It was important to the library to replace the lost items; using a single source to provide this service was desirable. Alfred Jaeger, Inc. was asked to submit a proposal and provide a cost estimate for replacing the unsalvageable volumes.

Parker concluded her remarks with a brief discussion of the pivotal role of risk management agencies in responding to a disaster of this magnitude. The California State University, Northridge, disaster is the largest yet to have impacted a campus in the United States. FEMA, the engineering firm DMJM/JGM and the Campus Risk Management office provided consultation and reimbursement that were essential for recovering from the devastating, long-term effects of the 1994 earthquake. Parker commented that documenting the institution's condition after the earthquake began immediately and that a digital archive is now being built.

Don Jaeger, president of Alfred Jaeger, Inc., then presented the back volume vendor perspective on responding to a library disaster. Alfred Jaeger, Inc. had worked with California State University, Northridge, previously, and Jaeger echoed Parker's advice that engaging one vendor to assist in replacing lost material saves time and energy. Jaeger further pointed out that the company has access to resources worldwide that would expedite replacing volumes. After the library contacted the company, Jaeger prepared the replacement value appraisal that FEMA requested.

At this juncture, Jaeger explained the three types of appraisals and their uses. Fair market value appraisals are used for tax and donation purposes. A third party may be employed to establish the value of items and those valued over $5,000 require completed forms. For insurance and disaster recovery, the replacement value method is used. This is the amount required today to pay for the replacement of older material. Every item, including those not replaced, is valued in this appraisal. The third method of appraising a collection is the cumulative sum. This kind of evaluation is used for assessing material that has not been appraised for a long time. For this method, a benchmark per volume value is established. This appraisal is useful for particular collections such as the biomedical literature whose pricing index has risen from $62.00 to $318.00 over a period of twenty years.

After Jaeger provided the replacement value quote to FEMA, communication between all parties involved began. The logistics of delivery for the replacement volumes, which required FEMA approval, and procedures for FEMA's payment were finalized. Jaeger commenced the process of replacing the damaged material first from the company's own inventory, and then from secondary sources. Volumes acquired from other vendors were consolidated and cleaned if necessary. Additional resources for volumes included publishers and reprint companies. In the case of California State University, Northridge, it was not necessary to replace other media such as microfilm or compact discs. If no replacement was found in hard copy for a volume, the library was financially compensated. The mold outbreak disaster resulting from construction damage led to a repeat of the volume replacement process, with the difference that in this instance an insurance company, not FEMA, was involved.

Jaeger offered advice based on his experience as a back volume vendor responding to library disasters. He emphasized the importance of having an updated disaster plan in which critical staff members are identified and duties defined. Cooperation and communication in the face of disaster are essential since every situation is different. He also recommended evaluating a library's collection at least every five to ten years to maintain a credible replacement cost figure. Jaeger closed his presentation on a positive note, reminding the audience that in the event of a disaster, help is out there from remediators, back volume vendors, binders, and others concerned with a library's operation.

A third speaker, representing Marcor, Inc., the industrial remediation company employed to undertake the clean up of the library, was scheduled to speak but did not appear.

During the discussion period, several interesting points emerged. The automated storage and retrieval system, originally built for storing automobile parts, sustained very little damage from the earthquake. Parker remarked that it is better to install this system when a building project is underway rather than later. Other institutions using this system for library storage include Eastern Michigan University and University of Nevada, Las Vegas.

Regarding the risk management agencies, Parker noted that having FEMA on campus helped to expedite invoice payment, as did having one person from the engineering consulting firm be responsible for arranging FEMA payments. Parker also recommended becoming acquainted with your institution's risk management officer. She reflected that visits by then-President Clinton and Vice President Gore probably generated visibility and priority attention for campus recovery operations.

Clear communication between all the partners–the remediation agency, staff, vendors, insurers and funding agencies, consultants, and risk management officers–involved in the recovery effort is important for the success of the process. In addition, both speakers urged being as prepared as possible for an emergency. Parker stated that while the library had a good disaster plan before the earthquake, it is better now. Recommended activities included practicing response procedures, such as evacuation plans, monthly; reading the disaster plan; agreeing on salvage priorities; adding violence and terrorism to the list of threats in the disaster plan; ensuring that digital data is secure and backed up providing staff wallet cards with basic emergency response procedures and indispensable phone numbers; informing staff of the names of disaster response team members; and writing up protocols for dealing with damaged, wet, mold infested books for staff to use in responding to an emergency.

Two key messages emerged from this workshop. First, if disaster strikes a library, there is help available from vendors, funding agencies, consultants and others for recovery, even though the time it takes may last longer than anticipated. Second, being as prepared as possible for an emergency is crucial and it behooved us as an audience to make good use of the California State University, Northridge, experience in preparing our own institutions for potential emergencies.

SELECTED RESOURCES

Alire, Camila, ed. *Disaster Planning and Recovery Handbook*. New York: Neal-Schuman, 2000.

California Preservation Clearinghouse. *http://cpc.stanford.edu* (9 Aug. 2002)

Kahn, Miriam B. *Disaster Response and Planning for Libraries*. Chicago: American Library Association, 1998.

Northeast Document Conservation Center, Andover, MA. 17 July, 2002. *http://www.nedcc.org* (9 Aug. 2002)

Nyberg, Sandra. *Invasion of the Giant Spore.* SOLINET Preservation Program Leaflet No. 5, November 1, 1987.

Price, Lois Alcott. *Managing a Mold Invasion: Guidelines for a Disaster Response.* Philadelphia, PA: Conservation Center for Art and Historic Artifacts, 1996. CCAHA Technical Series, No. 1. *http://www.ccaha.org/*(9 Aug. 2002)

Stanford University Libraries. Preservation Department. CoOL: Conservation On Line. *http://palimpsest.stanford.edu* (9 Aug. 2002)

Wellheiser, Johanna and Jude Scott. *An Ounce of Prevention: Integrated Disaster Planning for Archives, Libraries, and Record Centres.* 2nd Ed. Lanham, MD and London: Scarecrow Press, 2002.

CONTRIBUTORS' NOTES

Susan E. Parker is Associate Dean of the University Library at California State University, Northridge. Don Jaeger is President of Alfred Jaeger, Inc. Kristen Kern is Preservation/Catalog Librarian at the Branford Price Millar Library, Portland State University.

Transforming AACR2:
Using the Revised Rules
in Chapters 9 and 12
Part 1

Jean Hirons
Leslie Hawkins

Workshop Leaders

Bridget Clark

Recorder

SUMMARY. "Transforming the *AACR2*" was presented to an overflow-ing room of serialists and catalogers. Les Hawkins and Jean Hirons, both from the Library of Congress, explained the upcoming revisions in Chapters 9 and 12 of the *Anglo-American Cataloguing Rules* (AACR2). *[Article copies available for a fee from The Haworth Document Delivery Service: 1-800-HAWORTH. E-mail address: <docdelivery@haworthpress.com> Website: <http://www.HaworthPress.com>]*

The workshop began with the outline for the general time frame of the upcoming publications defining the specific changes. The AACR2

[Haworth co-indexing entry note]: "Transforming AACR2: Using the Revised Rules in Chapters 9 and 12, Part 1." Clark, Bridget. Co-published simultaneously in *The Serials Librarian* (The Haworth Information Press, an imprint of The Haworth Press, Inc.) Vol. 44, No. 3/4, 2003, pp. 243-248; and: *Transforming Serials: The Revolution Continues* (ed: Susan L. Scheiberg, and Shelley Neville) The Haworth Information Press, an imprint of The Haworth Press, Inc., 2003, pp. 243-248. Single or multiple copies of this article are available for a fee from The Haworth Document Delivery Service [1-800-HAWORTH, 9:00 a.m. - 5:00 p.m. (EST). E-mail address: docdelivery@haworthpress.com].

amendments are due in fall 2002, with the implementation for Library of Congress beginning on December 1, 2002. The *Library of Congress Rule Interpretations* (LCRI) will be published during the summer of 2002. The *CONSER Editing Guide* (CEG) will be issued by the end of the 2002 calendar year, and the *CONSER Cataloging Manual* (CCM) should be ready by fall 2002.

The timeframe for MARC 21 revisions (leader (Code 1) and 260) are not to be implemented before 2003. The 022, 222, 310, 321, and the 362 fields may be implemented for book materials/integrating resources (code m) format in 2002.

Conceptual categories are outlined for a better understanding of the different levels of definitions used under the term "bibliographic resources." Bibliographic resources refer to an expression or manifestation of a work or an item that forms the basis for bibliographic description or, simply, what is being catalogued. A bibliographic resource can be tangible or intangible. The basic concept behind the revision of the term is to allow for a clearer description of the resource in hand.

The conceptual categories are labeled in three levels. The first level is bibliographic resources. Under bibliographic resources comes the second level of finite and continuing resources. The third level consists of two branching terms stemming from the second level. These are monographs and finite integrating resources from the finite level. Serials and continuing integrated resources are found below the continuing resources level (see Figure 1).

With this structure in mind, one can see that bibliographic resources can be separated in terminology by merely defining it as finite or continuing. These two terms make up the second level under the heading bibliographic resources.

The first term, finite resources, has no formal definition, but can be seen as the opposite of continuing. Finite resources are deemed as anything that has a predetermined conclusion, and should be completed within a finite number of parts or iterations. Finite resources encompass monographs and finite integrating resources. Conversely, continuing resources are materials that are issued over time with no predetermined conclusion. Continuing resources encompass serials and continuing integrating resources.

The third level of the structure is designed to help define how and in what format the finite or continuing resource of the bibliographic resource is issued. The third level subdivides under finite and continuing resources. Under the finite resources stem the monographs and finite in-

FIGURE 1. Bibliographic Resources

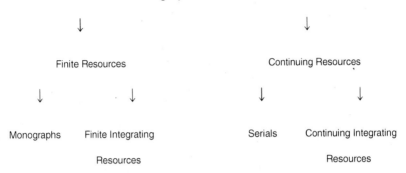

tegrating resources. Serials and continuing integrating resources fall under the continuing resources section.

The monograph can be defined as a bibliographic resource that is complete in one part or intended to be completed in a finite number of parts. On the opposite end of the spectrum are serials, which are defined as a continuing resource issued in a succession of discrete parts, usually bearing numbering, that has no predetermined conclusion.

Integrating resources are defined as bibliographic resources that are added to or changed by means of updates that do not remain discrete and are united into the whole. Integrating resources can also be finite or continuing. There are three major types of integrating resources.

First is the loose-leaf resource that requires updating. This is a bibliographic resource that consists of a base volume(s) updated by separate pages, which are inserted, replaced, removed, and/or substituted. Next, there is the database that requires updating. This is a collection of logically interrelated data stored together in one or more computerized files that are usually created and managed by a database management system. Third is the Web site that requires maintenance or has to be updated. This category includes materials that do not fit into one of the other types of continuing resource categories.

Continuing integrating resources are issued over time in a series of iterations with no predetermined conclusion. Hence, most integrating resources are continuous. The opposite is true with a finite integrating resource. These are issued over time with a predetermined conclusion. They are intended for completion within a finite number of iterations or repeated issues.

Other changes to chapter 9 of the *AACR2* are as follows. Chapter 9, now titled "Computer Files," will become "Electronic Resources." This change is effected to help encompass the wide spectrum of formats now available for cataloging. The sources of information have been broadened to include the entire resource being catalogued.

The major changes in chapter 12 also entail title changes. The chapter title will change from "Serials" to "Continuing Resources." It will now cover rules for serials and integrated resources. The new rules will now include provisions for specific examples of electronic resources. The rules will also be more complete for the cataloger. Rules will include former RIs/CONSER practice, and there will be more recognition of cataloging from complete works. It is important to note that CONSER will not make retroactive changes. There will be no going back to change records that exist in the old format.

Chapter 12 will cover rules for all continuing resources, whether they are successive or integrating in nature. It will also cover rules in the publications of limited-duration events, reprints of serials and finite integrating resources. Publications of limited duration events are resources that exhibit the characteristics of serials, such as successive issues, numbering, and frequency, but whose duration is limited. This will enhance the functionality that is similarly used with serials that have content or scope that is not predetermined. Regular reports of a limited-term project, annual reports of a commission that will exist only for a limited time, newsletters from a non-recurring event, and working papers from a single conference are prime examples of limited duration events.

What is the difference between cataloging a serial, a monograph, and an integrating resource? The newly revised LCRI 1.0 will enhance the criteria for determining the scope of this question. It will provide guidelines by which a decision can be based. It will also include types of electronic resources to be treated as serials or integrating resources. The emphasis will focus on the application of numbered issues or discrete parts being issued.

The scope for cataloging as a serial will include sources that are online resources having material added as discrete, numbered issues or as articles that remain discrete, or an online resource with only the current issue available as an issue and content of back issues available as separate articles. Also cataloged as a serial will be any CD-ROMs that contain issues of one or more than one serial issued on a regular or irregular basis. This includes any CD-ROMs that may be replaced or discarded.

Integrating resources include online resources that consist of articles from more than one journal, such as databases of articles (e.g., ProQuest) and online resources that are updated over time. This will include resources that were serials in print form. Abstracting and indexing services and directories are prime examples of this scope.

The 12.0B section, "Sources of Information," will be broken out into three separate rules: 12.0B1 will be the basis of description, 12.0B2 will be the chief source of information and 12.0B3 will be the prescribed sources of information.

According to rule 12.0B1, the "basis of description" for serials will be the first or earliest issue rather than a source associated with the whole serial or with a range of more than one issue or part. This includes reprints and reproductions, along with electronic serials. There will be no change for print serials; the first or earliest is still the basis of description. This section of the revised AACR2 will look quite different; it will make the rules more explicit.

Section 12.0B2, Chief Source of Information: Serials, will also be considerably different. For printed serials, the source will continue to be the title page or title page substitute. CD-ROMs and online (and other non-print) have been added to this section. For CD-ROMs, the preferred chief source of information is the physical carrier or its label. The revised chapter 9 includes carrier/labels as one possibility, while chapter 12 says to "prefer" them. For online serials, the preferred chief source is a source associated with the first issue or part. For other non-print serials, the revised AACR2 will refer to the sub rule .0B in the relevant chapter. The source of title proper for online serials should be the most complete presentation of title (AACR2 9.0B1) in conjunction with the first or earliest available issue (AACR2 12.0B1). Prescribed sources of information (12.0B3) are not new and deal with bracketing. For non-print serials, one will be referred to the appropriate sub rule .0B.

The "basis of description" for integrated resources is the same as the current iteration. It will be cataloging "what you see." The following areas are based on the current iteration: title and statement of responsibility; edition; publication; distribution, etc. (excluding dates); physical description (does not include remote access e-resources); and series. The areas for basis of description of integrated resources based on *first and/or last* iterations are the dates of publication, distribution, etc. Finally, areas based on all iterations and any other source are note and standard number and terms of availability.

The chief source of information for integrated resources (12.0B2) that are printed resources (loose-leaf) should come from the title page or the title page substitute. If the integrated resource is non-print, the revised AACR2 states that one should follow the directions of relevant chapter (chapter 9 for electronic resources).

Rules for changes in the serials will greatly benefit the cataloger. The descriptive rules will now include more provisions for how to handle minor changes that occur over time and will allow the cataloger more flexibility. For example, successive entry cataloging for serials will require a new record when there is a major change. For integrating resources the same record will be used, but will reflect changes in the appropriate fields, according to the principles of integrating entry.

There is currently no provision in the new Chapter 12 for e-serials that do not retain their earlier titles. LCRI 12.0B1 states that, in such cases, the description will be based on the latest title and that earlier titles should be treated as a note. If the title changes subsequently and the earlier title is retained a new record must be created (revert to successive entry).

Another addition will be new and revised definitions in the AACR2 glossary. This will enable the cataloger to access more enhanced explanations for materials/resources being catalogued. The revision will bring the cataloging terminology more up to date.

In summary, the revised AACR2 will allow for more "serial-like" cataloging. The entry convention of latest or "integrated entry" will be applied to integrating resources when changes are made to a record. For the first time, rules have been included for loose-leaf materials, Web sites and databases that are updated over time.

The workshop was very successful. At the conclusion of the workshop, the presenters were asked many specific questions. Jean and Leslie accomplished a daring feat by explaining and defining sections of the upcoming changes in the AACR2.

CONTRIBUTORS' NOTES

Jean Hirons is CONSER Coordination at the Library of Congress, Serials Records Division. Les Hawkins is CONSER Specialist, Library of Congress, Serials Records Division. Bridget Clark is Library Assistant, Longwood University Library.

Transforming AACR2:
Using the Revised Rules
in Chapters 9 and 12
Part 2

Jean Hirons
Leslie Hawkins

Workshop Leaders

Suzanne Thomas

Recorder

SUMMARY. During Part 2 of the workshop, Les Hawkins and Jean Hirons gave presentations about the changes to the AACR2 rules for the description of serials and for the concept of major/minor changes. The objective of the developing new rules is a desire for fewer new records and fewer new ISSNs. Harmonizing the rules for AACR, ISSN and ISBD was another objective. *[Article copies available for a fee from The Haworth Document Delivery Service: 1-800-HAWORTH. E-mail address: <docdelivery@haworthpress.com> Website: <http://www.HaworthPress.com>]*

[Haworth co-indexing entry note]: "Transforming AACR2: Using the Revised Rules in Chapters 9 and 12, Part 2." Thomas, Suzanne. Co-published simultaneously in *The Serials Librarian* (The Haworth Information Press, an imprint of The Haworth Press, Inc.) Vol. 44, No. 3/4, 2003, pp. 249-253; and: *Transforming Serials: The Revolution Continues* (ed: Susan L. Scheiberg, and Shelley Neville) The Haworth Information Press, an imprint of The Haworth Press, Inc., 2003, pp. 249-253. Single or multiple copies of this article are available for a fee from The Haworth Document Delivery Service [1-800-HAWORTH, 9:00 a.m. - 5:00 p.m. (EST). E-mail address: docdelivery@haworthpress.com].

http://www.haworthpress.com/store/product.asp?sku=J123
10.1300/J123v44n34_31

DESCRIPTIVE CATALOGING RULES

The second part of the workshop on Transforming AACR2 began with Les Hawkins' presentation. The workshop provided very detailed and thorough coverage of changes in AACR2 for the description of serials. Changes in the descriptive cataloging rules include the transcription of the title, the recording of other title information, punctuation, numbering, physical description, and notes.

Introductory words no longer have to be transcribed as part of the title proper, according to AACR2 1.1B1. Titles such as *Welcome to NASA quest* would be transcribed simply as *NASA quest*. However, words in a title that are grammatically linked are considered a part of the title: *Political pulse's education beat* is transcribed as *Political pulse's education beat* and has a title added entry for just *Education beat*.

The rule for selecting full form versus acronym or initialism has been changed to be consistent with practices with ISSN. No longer is there an exception to choose the acronym over full form when the acronym is the only form of the title presented in other locations in the serial. Catalogers should always choose the full form.

Changes in the edition statement can now be a reason for a new bibliographic record if the change indicates a change in subject matter or physical format. This is currently in LCRI 21.3B but will later be added to the rules in order to harmonize with ISBD-(CR).

The rules for numeric/alphabetic and chronological designations have some sensible changes. To begin with, the area is now simply referred to as "numbering." Punctuation in the transcription of dates and numbering can now be edited rather than being transcribed as they appear on the piece. Hyphens can be changed to slashes and dates can be repeated as necessary. There is a new provision to supply a date when there is no designation and if it is more appropriate than supplying [no.1]. Most importantly, numbering that begins again with the same form of designation no longer requires creation of a new bibliographic record. The cataloger can now supply: *[new ser.]*.

Publisher statements will no longer have cataloger-supplied abbreviations of names, for example, *The Bureau*. Transcribing the full name of corporate bodies will aid online searching and display of publisher information in online catalogs. The comma following the publisher when there is no date information is no longer supplied. When the date information is incomplete, the information is surrounded by square brackets instead of leaving off the final bracket.

The rules for physical description now provide the option to use conventional terminology such as CD-ROM and DVD. However, a change in format still requires a new record according to the CONSER standard.

In addition to the description based on note, a new "latest issue consulted" note will be provided in records to reflect the scope of issues covered by the description. The description based on and source of title notes can be combined, as they both refer to the same issue. However, the latest issue consulted note will be given as a separate note because it refers to a different issue.

The presentation ended with examples of bibliographic records before and after the rule changes. Because of the amount of material still to be covered, questions were held until after the following presentation.

MAJOR AND MINOR CHANGES

Jean Hirons covered the concept of major and minor changes in the new rules and rule interpretations and how they would impact serials cataloging. The intent of the new rules is to harmonize AACR, ISSN and ISBD-(CR) as well as reduce the number of new records and new ISSN.

The new concepts introduced are major changes and minor changes, which are covered in the rules 21.2A1 and 21.2A2. The terminology *title change* will no longer be used any time a new record is made, because the concept of major changes encompasses more than title changes. A major change for serial will result in a new bibliographic record and represents a new entity.

The following are considered major changes: the main entry changes, a translated serial undergoes change in the original title, change in a corporate body used as uniform title qualifier, major change in title proper, change in physical format, and major change in edition statement.

Major changes in the title proper are the addition, deletion, change, or reordering of any of the first five words (minus the initial article), unless the change is among the minor change exceptions. After the first five words, a change that results in a change of meaning of the title proper or scope of the serial would also be a major change. If the name of the corporate body is a part of the title proper and the body changes its name, this is considered a major change.

The exceptions in the minor change rules overrule the major changes when they apply. Minor changes are reflected in notes and added title entries and are sometimes just ignored when truly minor. The new exceptions for minor changes focus on corporate bodies, words indicating type of resource, and words in a list.

As long as the same body is represented, the name of the corporate body can be added, deleted or change its representation even within the first five words of the title, and be considered minor. For example, *CONSER annual report* could become *Annual report of CONSER* and it would be considered a minor change because it was just a change in position.

A word describing the type of resource can be added or deleted. For example, *Parents magazine* becoming *Parents* would not be a major change and would be reflected in a title added entry. However, words indicating frequency are excluded from this type of minor change.

Words in lists can change as long as the meaning of the title or topic covered is not changed. The order can change or items can be added or deleted. As long as the overall scope remains the same, it is a minor change not a major change requiring a new bibliographic record. According to the LCRI for this rule, a list must consist of three or more topics.

What is considered a minor change in the representation of words has expanded to include full forms, acronyms and initialisms. For example *Television monthly* changing to *TV monthly* would now be considered a minor change.

A change in the edition statement can be major or minor, depending on whether the scope of the edition statement has changed. For example, a change from *Doctors' edition* to *Physicians' edition* would be minor, but a change from *North American edition* to *North and Central American edition* would be major and require a new bibliographic record. If in doubt whether a change is major or minor, consider it to be minor.

The workshop finished with examples of changes and the audience participated in determining if the changes were major or minor. There were not clear and consistent results; in fact, resolution of some examples was still under discussion at the Library of Congress.

DISCUSSION

The presentations stimulated many questions from the audience. The new concepts of major and minor changes were welcomed. The relationship of minor change exceptions to major changes elicited several questions based on the examples. The example of *Organic chemistry review* changing to *Organic chemistry* was a minor change but the next change to *Review of organic chemistry* would be a major change. The point of the example was to compare to the title proper not added title entries for minor changes. Because organic chemistry is not a corporate name, the change in the order of the first five words was considered a major change. (However, after the conference, there was further discussion at the Library of Congress and a rule interpretation was being developed for the circumstances of this example.)

Other issues were raised during the question and answer session. One issue was the impact of the minor change rules on libraries that shelved periodicals by main entry. The current title on the piece may be a minor change and not match the title in the main entry. The minor changes would also impact checking in current issues when titles did not match the title proper.

The impact of minor changes in OPAC displays would make records longer and more confusing to interpret, which may be better than having multiple records for the same entity with only minor changes in titles.

Another question was whether the Library of Congress would recatalog titles for the new rules. The answer was no, but specific titles that came up in discussion indicated that there may be exceptions.

CONCLUSION

The back-to-back presentations provided critical information to serialists facing the new cataloging rules. There was considerable information to absorb. Having handouts of the slides was a good aid to take notes on this very detailed information presented in a relatively brief amount of time. The practicality of learning how to work with the new rules will take some time and experience.

CONTRIBUTORS' NOTES

Jean Hiron is CONSER Coordination at the Library of Congress, Serials Records Division. Les Hawkins is CONSER Specialist, Library of Congress, Serials Records Division. Bridget Clark is Library Assistant, Longwood University Library. Suzanne L. Thomas is English Language Cataloger, University Library System, University of Pittsburgh.

How I Learned to Stop Worrying
and Give Up Journal Check-In

Rick Anderson
Steven D. Zink

Workshop Leaders

Susan Davis

Recorder

SUMMARY. This workshop addressed the experiences at the University of Nevada, Reno, as they discontinued check-in for print journals. The presenters reviewed the circumstances that led to this decision, such as the reduced number of print subscriptions and the increasing number of electronic journals in the collection. The Libraries also stopped binding the majority of their journals, and claiming is based more on shelf reviews than check-in records. Nearly a year after implementing this decision, the presenters deem it a success. *[Article copies available for a fee from The Haworth Document Delivery Service: 1-800-HAWORTH. E-mail address: <docdelivery@haworthpress.com> Website: <http://www.HaworthPress.com>]*

[Haworth co-indexing entry note]: "How I Learned to Stop Worrying and Give Up Journal Check-In." Davis, Susan. Co-published simultaneously in *The Serials Librarian* (The Haworth Information Press, an imprint of The Haworth Press, Inc.) Vol. 44, No. 3/4, 2003, pp. 255-260; and: *Transforming Serials: The Revolution Continues* (ed: Susan L. Scheiberg, and Shelley Neville) The Haworth Information Press, an imprint of The Haworth Press, Inc., 2003, pp. 255-260. Single or multiple copies of this article are available for a fee from The Haworth Document Delivery Service [1-800-HAWORTH, 9:00 a.m. - 5:00 p.m. (EST). E-mail address: docdelivery@haworthpress.com].

http://www.haworthpress.com/store/product.asp?sku=J123
10.1300/J123v44n34_32

INTRODUCTION

Presenters Rick Anderson (Director, Resource Acquisition) and Steven D. Zink (Vice-President of Information Technology and Dean of University Libraries) from the University of Nevada, Reno, addressed this intriguing topic that they subtitled, ". . . or, How to Horrify Your Staff without Really Trying."

Zink gave the audience some general background on the University of Nevada, Reno. It was the first institution of higher education in Nevada, established in 1887 as a land grant institution. It is currently the fastest growing campus within the nation's fastest growing higher education system. The university has about 14,000 students.

REALITY CHECK

Zink noted that the Libraries are an integral part of the information resources and technology structure on campus, with direct reporting lines to the university president. This structure allows an emphasis on a broader view of information resources and supporting technologies. The Libraries have identified several "realities" that impact how they operate. These are:

- The "Wild Wild Web" is the preferred information source for their users.
- They want to leverage the ubiquitous information retrieval experience of their users.
- They acknowledge the "principle of least effort" and mass attention deficit in user behavior.
- Libraries have placed an over-emphasis on access and availability.
- Content is not king, rather content over the Web is king.

In concluding his portion of the workshop, Zink described librarianship as a "profession in paralysis" that is trying to maintain some control over an increasingly miniscule part of the information landscape. Questioning of print practices in a rapidly changing electronic environment is necessary in order to position staff resources where they are most effective in meeting the realities of twenty-first century user behavior.

WHY CHECK IN?

Rick Anderson then spoke in more detail about the decision to give up some print journal check-in. First, he identified the benefits of check-in, such as status of the current issue, publication patterns, title changes/mergers/splits, and bindery and claiming mechanisms. However, he cautioned, these functions are important mostly when the journal collection is primarily print and the institution is focused on managing information that few patrons use or care about. Anderson then described the problem at the university–they no longer have a primarily print collection and diminished staff resources do not allow for the management of what they consider irrelevant information. As a matter of fact, only 20 percent of their journal collection is print (2,700 print subscriptions) compared to the 13,000-14,000 online journals to which they have access.

MAKING THE SWITCH

Flipping the switch, so to speak, to divert staff attention to electronic publications is not so easy. Print issues are really a push technology; incoming mail deliveries bring materials that subtly cry out for your attention because they physically hang around until dealt with. Online information is easy to ignore because it just sits out on a server somewhere waiting for you to do something with it. There are no stacks of unprocessed issues cluttering up the work area. Staff have become fairly comfortable in the print environment; job security is an issue when radical changes are proposed.

Shortly after he was hired, Anderson was approached by Zink with the suggestion of eliminating print check-in. The idea percolated for several months before Anderson decided to look into it. The Libraries conducted a use study of their current issues, and discovered that the average issue received less than one use. They concluded that their print journals were the least used part of their collection, so why check in the least used part of the collection? Another factor was budgetary. The Libraries have a fairly flush materials budget, but relatively few staff. Anderson has a staff of only 2.5 FTE, and he needed to prioritize the best use of staff resources. There were workflow problems before he had arrived at Nevada, and there were too few staff to deal with print and electronic journals. Experience told him that about 80 percent of issues are received on time and that only a small number of claims actually result in supply of the issue. Even if an issue is checked in, there is no guarantee it is on the shelf and available to use. All of these factors and observations led Anderson and his department to propose they discontinue the check-in of print issues as well as binding.

IMPLEMENTATION

This proposal was accepted and implemented in August 2001. In actual practice, the Libraries have not completely discontinued check-in and binding. Instead they have selected a limited number of high-cost, high-use, or graphics-intensive titles to check in and bind. They also enhanced their document delivery service and offered it for free.

So how does the serials unit process incoming print issues? At one time they maintained a printed list of all their subscriptions. Incoming issues were compared against this list; matches were property stamped and tattle-taped. Now the procedure has been further simplified to checking incoming issues against a smaller list of titles. Only these matches are tattle-taped. All issues are sent out to be shelved, and it is when the shelvers do not find a match that the issues are returned to a library assistant for investigation. Claiming is usually done based on shelf observations. Since most journals are not bound, they worry more about large gaps in service than single missing issues. However, they do track a few high-use, high-cost journals.

Binding only occurs with a very few high-use, graphics-intense titles. The Libraries do keep back issues of other journals. However, they use plastic pamphlet boxes to house these back issues in the stacks. Item records are created and the boxes are labeled with the journal's call number. Anderson reported that their overall binding costs had been reduced from $20,000 to $4,000 for the boxing. Holdings are recorded with open-ended statements.

SUCCESS!

So far the Libraries at the University of Nevada, Reno, have been very satisfied with the results of this decision. Their patrons have no idea that issues are not checked in somewhere. Current issues are out on the shelves faster and they do not disappear for several weeks to go to an outside binder. Reshelving to boxes has had very little impact on the workload. And lastly and most importantly, they have achieved significant improvements in the management of online journals.

DISCUSSION

A lively question and answer period followed the presentations. In response to a question about why the unbound back issues weren't simply discarded, Anderson explained that there were political reasons for keeping the issues. He responded that his staff are now spending more time checking and verifying access to high/use, high/cost online journals. When the library staff was asked to comment, only one reference librarian responded that they missed the check-in boxes in their ILS. The department uses three to four students, totaling about forty hours per week of help. The University did not inform their subscription vendor about their change in practice. They felt that their decision had no impact on the vendor's dealings with the publisher. The Libraries still expected their subscriptions to be fulfilled.

CONCLUSION

It was readily apparent that there was a lot of interest in this topic, both from the attendance numbers and the questions posed. Even though the topic was controversial, Anderson congratulated the audience on being very open-minded. Both presenters did note that eliminating print journal check-in is not necessarily the best decision for every library. Individual and institutional circumstances must be carefully reviewed before such a change is warranted. This reporter sensed that attendees were keen to learn the "why" behind the decision and to see the practical impact on day-to-day work. Many libraries are facing similar challenges as those at Nevada. Increasing amounts of the material budget are spent on electronic information; print processing is still labor-intensive; staffing is not being increased to handle the very complex and time-consuming tasks related to the acquisition and management of electronic subscriptions and access. With limited resources tough choices become necessary. Based on the situation at Nevada, Zink and Anderson feel they have made the best decision in order to best serve their patrons.

CONTRIBUTORS' NOTES

Rick Anderson is Director, Resource Acquisition, and Steven D. Zink is Vice-President of Information Technology and Dean of University Libraries, both at the University of Nevada, Reno. Susan Davis is Head, Periodicals at the University of Buffalo (SUNY).

Use Studies:
Tools for Understanding Changing Patterns of Serials Use

Philenese Slaughter

Workshop Leader

Elna L. Saxton

Recorder

SUMMARY. Historical data for serials use continue to be needed for cancellation decisions or justification of serials expenditures. An ongoing use study at Austin Peay State University has evolved from a cumbersome manual record to a sophisticated Access and Excel reporting tool for collection management decisions. A recent cancellation project made full use of the data; future enhancements include cost analyses, tracking inflation rates, and linking data for title changes. *[Article copies available for a fee from The Haworth Document Delivery Service: 1-800-HAWORTH. E-mail address: <docdelivery@haworthpress.com> Website: <http://www.HaworthPress.com>]*

Usage studies of serial publications continue to be a widely used serials management tool. The number of research articles and reports found

[Haworth co-indexing entry note]: "Use Studies: Tools for Understanding Changing Patterns of Serials Use." Saxton, Elna L. Co-published simultaneously in *The Serials Librarian* (The Haworth Information Press, an imprint of The Haworth Press, Inc.) Vol. 44, No. 3/4, 2003, pp. 261-264; and: *Transforming Serials: The Revolution Continues* (ed: Susan L. Scheiberg, and Shelley Neville) The Haworth Information Press, an imprint of The Haworth Press, Inc., 2003, pp. 261-264. Single or multiple copies of this article are available for a fee from The Haworth Document Delivery Service [1-800-HAWORTH, 9:00 a.m. - 5:00 p.m. (EST). E-mail address: docdelivery@haworthpress.com].

in the professional literature are indicative of the ongoing validity of this tool. A search of *Library Literature* readily uncovers seventeen citations for this topic in the past three years. In the current environment of increasingly tight budgets in higher education, usage data and reports for serials are typically focused on cancellation decisions.

At Austin Peay State University in Clarksville, Tennessee, Philenese Slaughter, Technical Services Coordinator, inherited a wealth of usage data, which, unfortunately, were all in manual format. These data, consisting of sheets of paper listing periodical titles with various colors of hatch marks representing reshelving in different time periods, were cumbersome to maintain, inaccurate due to staff resistance to daily compilation, and difficult to tally. When requests for data were received from individual departments, it took months to gather and cumulate.

Microsoft Access and Excel were used to develop the database for moving usage data to a computerized platform. From July through December of 2000, six years of data were manually transferred to the new database. This database provides for easy collecting of reshelving statistics–no flipping pages to find the title, no multi-colored pens required to indicate semester dates. Students search by title prior to reshelving, and a count for each reshelved issue is automatically entered. Students appreciate the ease of use of this computerized method, which had an immediate impact on the speed of reshelving. The former delays and backlogs associated with reshelving were completely eliminated. Data are kept per semester, and four tables are available for reports: department, title, use, and "dead or alive."

Serials subscriptions at Austin Peay had been protected since 1994, at the expense of monographs, reference, and electronic resources. At 95% of the collections budget, serials had completely overtaken other resources, in 2001/2002 no monographs or reference materials were purchased. Now, Austin Peay Library is seeking to regain a balance in the collections budget, requiring a 35-45% serials cancellation project for 2003. Austin Peay State University, with almost 5,000 FTE, is the only liberal arts university in the Tennessee Board of Regents system, and the Library had 2,250 current subscriptions prior to this cancellation project. The periodical collection is shelved on one floor, is non-circulating, and titles are organized in alphabetical order. Bound volumes, microfilm, and current issues are interfiled.

Facing a deadline for cancellation decisions, twenty-seven departments needed comprehensive data and more sophisticated reports than were possible in the past. More tables were added to the database: fiscal year, standing order charges, vendor, and core titles. If the department did not provide core titles needed for accreditation, *Magazines for Libraries* was used. In less than six months, lists of current serial subscriptions for each department at Austin Peay were prepared. These lists included titles and memberships, last year's cost, and subscription format. No usage statistics were provided at the outset because previously departments had criticized the validity of the usage data. By providing reshelving data only upon request, the library was in effect requiring the department to validate the usefulness of this tool. Not all departments requested the data, and it followed that their decisions did not necessarily pinpoint the low-use titles. Even without budget restraints, many libraries choose to conduct a review of their collection. Over time, subscriptions often continue to exist for programs that have long been eliminated, or that were selected for faculty that are no longer on staff. Usage data are key for decision-making, and they must be accurate.

At the individual department meetings, three budget scenarios were presented listing cuts at 35, 40, or 45%. These three levels clearly showed the incremental increase required by a deeper cancellation. Faculty were to indicate at which level each cancellation should be made. A firm deadline for response was given. For departments who did not make the necessary cuts, the library director and the serials librarian made the decisions based on usage data and the departmental curricula. After the cancellation decisions were made, the library posted the proposed titles on the library Website. This allowed an overall review, particularly important with cross-disciplinary titles.

With approximately thirty in attendance at this session, lively discussion ensued following the presentation. Varying experiences with alternative methods of conducting usage surveys included hand-held scanners and an item record for recording circulation statistics on the OPAC, a barcoded list, or a barcoded shelf label. Usually it is only the current collection that is monitored for usage data; these data can nevertheless affect the decision to weed the back-run of bound volumes if a title is cancelled.

Electronic resources can be used to fill in the gaps to access to serial literature that a large-scale cancellation project creates. Some libraries track the use of electronic resources, but it is typically true that while reshelving data are undercounting use, use data for electronics do the opposite by overcounting use. Changes in the library environment will impact the use of print journals–the move to cost recovery printing in the library may affect the print collection. Some libraries have experienced that as more electronic journals were made available, the use of both print and electronic resources increased. Perhaps the electronic version did not have the most current articles, or browsing electronically inspired the use to turn to the print version. Across the board, however, use of print is decreasing.

Future enhancements to the database at Austin Peay include cost analyses, tracking inflation rates, and linking data for title changes. Data will be made available by year, or cumulated, in addition to the current practice of by semester. The reports, made possible by a combination of Access and Excel databases, are limited only by the number of tables chosen for inclusion. What started as a simple use study is rapidly evolving into a complex collection management tool. The presentation slides for this workshop are available at *http://library.apsu.edu/ library/slaughterp/UseStudies.ppt.*

CONTRIBUTORS' NOTES

Philenese Slaughter is Technical Services Coordinator at Austin Peay State University. Elna L. Saxton is Head, Periodicals and Microforms Department, University of Cincinnati.

Just in Time vs. Just in Case:
Examining the Benefits
of Subsidized Unmediated Ordering (SUMO)
vs. Journal Subscription

Louis Houle
Chris Beckett

Workshop Leaders

Chuck Costakos

Recorder

SUMMARY. In this session, there were two presentations covering the same subject from different points of view. The main conclusions are that document supply is a viable alternative to journal subscription and inter-library lending for an academic library; document supply is generally used sparingly to supplement existing collections; and document supply is not a threat to journal subscriptions. The two studies–one for a particular university, the other analyzing summary data for multiple publishers and two document supply services–reinforce each other's conclusions. *[Article copies available for a fee from The Haworth Document Delivery Service: 1-800-HAWORTH. E-mail address: <docdelivery@haworthpress.com> Website: <http://www.HaworthPress.com>]*

[Haworth co-indexing entry note]: "Just in Time vs. Just in Case: Examining the Benefits of Subsidized Unmediated Ordering (SUMO) vs. Journal Subscription." Costakos, Chuck. Co-published simultaneously in *The Serials Librarian* (The Haworth Information Press, an imprint of The Haworth Press, Inc.) Vol. 44, No. 3/4, 2003, pp. 265-269; and: *Transforming Serials: The Revolution Continues* (ed: Susan L. Scheiberg, and Shelley Neville) The Haworth Information Press, an imprint of The Haworth Press, Inc., 2003, pp. 265-269. Single or multiple copies of this article are available for a fee from The Haworth Document Delivery Service [1-800-HAWORTH, 9:00 a.m. - 5:00 p.m. (EST). E-mail address: docdelivery@haworthpress.com].

http://www.haworthpress.com/store/product.asp?sku=J123
10.1300/J123v44n34_34

Louis Houle of McGill University demonstrated that with proper management, document delivery can be a viable alternative both to journal subscription *and* to interlibrary loan for obtaining documents for the library's clients, when one considers all the costs involved in each method as well as the speed of service provided. He summarized the results of a study at McGill University, comparing document delivery via the Canada Institute for Scientific and Technical Information (CISTI) to the subscription costs for the journals involved and to the costs of traditional interlibrary loan (ILL). This was a particularly interesting case study because the borrowing requests were directly from library users unmediated by librarians.[1]

Without question, one of the top problems facing librarians today is meeting their users' needs for journal articles at a manageable cost. In his presentation, Houle succinctly stated the problem: steeply rising subscription prices for journals, growing demand by users for Internet-like speed in providing full text search results, stagnant acquisitions budgets within the library, and the high cost and slow speed of interlibrary lending (ILL). In the face of their budget problems, libraries have transferred money from monographs to serials, and they are spending more money but acquiring fewer serials titles, according to annual statistics from the Association for Research Libraries (ARL).[2]

Moreover, the 9%-per-year rise in journal subscription prices (since 1986) is particularly problematic for Canadian institutions owing to the concomitant drop in purchasing power of the Canadian dollar.[3]

ILL has been the traditional method for libraries to provide their users with more journal articles (and other content) than the library can subscribe to. For libraries overall, ILL has been on the rise for many years. The ARL member libraries have increased their interlibrary borrowing 97% from 1991 to 2000, according to Houle. The total cost of ILL, including processing within the library, is rather high. According to a recent ARL study, the total cost (including borrowing and lending) is nearly US $28. The same study showed that the average turnaround time for a transaction is nearly 16 days, with an average fill rate of 85%.[4]

These factors led McGill to try an alternative: subsidizing library user ordering of document copies directly from a document supplier instead of buying subscriptions or funding ILL, all without mediation by library staff. Using CISTI as the document supplier, McGill turned users loose to request whatever documents they needed. Over a five year period, the fill rate of these requests was 93%. Even more remarkable, the average turnaround time was *15 hours*, compared to the 16 *days* for

ILL that was noted above. The cost of providing this document supply service was funded by cutting journal subscriptions.

The articles requested were distributed widely among the journals. For the most recent period reported (2001-2002), only one article was requested from 35% of the 5,109 titles involved, and only 5 or less articles from 71% of the titles.

From January 2000 through March 2001, users ordered nearly 32,000 articles from 5,100 journals. The cost of document copies was lower than the subscription price in all but 28 of those titles. Here is a key finding: The total cost of all the documents supplied was less than 9% of the total cost if the library had subscribed to all those journals. Although it is clearly important to block users from ordering copies of articles from the journals the library already subscribes to,[5] employing a document supply service can be a cost effective and timely alternative to either journal ownership or interlibrary loan.

Chris Beckett of Ingenta summarized results of the recent (September 2001) study by the Ingenta Institute answering the question, Is document delivery a threat to publisher's subscription income? The answer: Nope!

First, Beckett cited earlier studies of the topic. In 1975, the British Library published an extensive study showing that the journals from which the most copies were requested were the well established journals, widely held by libraries and widely circulated. Requests were concentrated in a few journals. Demand for the least-held journals was low.[6] The British Library Document Supply Centre (BLDSC) and Blackwell Science commissioned research in 1996 that showed interlibrary loan is *not* used as a substitute for journal subscriptions. The majority of use is from institutions who have only an occasional need to consult the journal.[7] Finally, a study by the International Council for Scientific and Technical Information (ICSTI) in 1996 concluded "publishers need not worry that institutions are using document supply as a realistic alternative to subscribing to journals. None of the organisations surveyed came anywhere near the breakeven point at which it would be more economical to subscribe to a journal rather than use document supply for the few requests for articles made."[8]

In 2001, the Ingenta Institute updated that work with a new study. They worked with 15 publishers of 28 journals and surveyed copying of those journals via two major document suppliers, BLDSC and CISTI. (Six of the journals reviewed were also included in the earlier ICSTI report.) Requests for copies in 2000 were matched to subscriber lists for that year. During that period, 12,637 copy requests were made to

BLDSC, an average of 451 per title; 4,751 copy requests were made to CISTI, an average of 217 per title.

The study results showed that 15% of the requests were from institutions that already subscribed to the journal requested. Interestingly, the lowest overlap (8%) was with medical journals, with higher overlaps in physical sciences (22%) and in social sciences (25%). The ICSTI report also showed substantial overlap of requesters and subscribers. In addition, the Ingenta study found that non-subscribers and subscribers requested about the same number of copies from each title on the average, also consistent with the earlier ICSTI study.

The articles requested are not just the recent ones; only 20-50% of the articles were published in the last three years (this varies by discipline).

Another interesting question dealt with in the study is whether availability of electronic journals has had an impact. In the UK, the National Electronic Site Licensing Initiative was established to promote the widespread delivery and use of electronic journals in the UK higher education and research community. There were six journal titles studied both in the 1996 ICSTI report and in the current one from Ingenta. Demand for those six via the British Library's document supply service in the UK grew 15% from 1996 to 2000, while the document supply demand for those *not* licensed grew 26%. In other words, where titles are widely available electronically, as they are in this program in the UK, the rate of growth of document supply demand is being reduced.

Only 13% of the non-subscribers requested more than 10 copies from any title. Therefore, the study concludes, the vast majority of organizations use document supply to meet very occasional needs, and furthermore, there is a real need from a large number of institutions for information provided in this way. The key result is that there is no discernable effect of document supply on journal subscriptions.[9]

NOTES

1. For most of the study, users were blocked from ordering copies of journals held by the library. As part of the study, however, the block was removed for two eight-month periods between 1999 and 2001. The users were not told that the block was removed. During these periods, 42% of the titles and 41% of the articles requested were held by the McGill University libraries, demonstrating convincingly the need for such blocking.

2. Association of Research Libraries (2002). *ARL Statistics*. Retrieved August 2002 from the Association of Research Libraries Web site: http://www.arl.org/stats/arlstat/.

3. Holmes, David (May 2000). *Commentary on the 1998-1999 CARL Statistics: An Introduction and Retrospective Overview*. Retrieved August 2002 from Canadian Associa-

tion of Research Libraries/Association des bibliothèques de recherche du Canada Web site: http://www.uottawa.ca/library/carl/projects/stats/Commentary_Overview.htm.

4. Jackson, M. (1998), *Measuring the Performance of Interlibrary Loan Operations in North American Research and College Libraries,* Association of Research Libraries, Washington, DC. This article reports the results of a 1996 study showing the total average cost to be US $27.83. It compares these results to those of an earlier study in 1992 in which the average total cost of ILL was US $29.55 per transaction.

5. See note 1 above.

6. Line, M. B., and D. N. Wood (1975), *The effects of large-scale photocopying service on journal sales,* Journal of Documentation, 31(4), 234-275.

7. Woodward, A. N. (1978), *Factors Affecting the Renewal of Periodical Subscriptions,* Aslib (London).

8. ICSTI (2002). *A comparative study of access to journals through subscriptions and document delivery.* Retrieved August 2002 from the International Council for Scientific and Technical Information (ICSTI) Web site: http://www.icsti.org/comparative.html.

9. Ingenta Institute (2001). *Assumptions vs. Reality: User behaviour in sourcing scholarly information.* Ingenta Institute (Bath, UK)

CONTRIBUTORS' NOTES

Louis Houle is Serials Subscription Librarian at McGill University. Chris Beckett is Vice President, Global Library Services, with Ingenta. Chuck Costakos is Director, Product Management at the OCLC Online Computer Library Center, Inc

Print Journals:
Off Site? Out of Site? Out of Mind?

Amy K. Weiss
John P. Abbott

Workshop Leaders

Joseph C. Harmon

Recorder

SUMMARY. With paper journals seemingly decreasing in importance, libraries need to consider issues of space allocation and storage of journal volumes. Space solutions may include shelving in open, closed, and/or compact shelving, mass storage in off-site, or onsite, facilities, or even discarding the paper and relying on electronic access. Any solution involving the current paper collections will have a serious impact on technical services. This workshop explores these issues in light of the experiences of Appalachian State University, which is in the planning stages of a new library. *[Article copies available for a fee from The Haworth Document Delivery Service: 1-800-HAWORTH. E-mail address: <docdelivery@haworthpress.com> Website: <http://www.HaworthPress.com>]*

[Haworth co-indexing entry note]: "Print Journals: Off Site? Out of Site? Out of Mind?" Harmon, Joseph C. Co-published simultaneously in *The Serials Librarian* (The Haworth Information Press, an imprint of The Haworth Press, Inc.) Vol. 44, No. 3/4, 2003, pp. 271-278; and: *Transforming Serials: The Revolution Continues* (ed: Susan L. Scheiberg, and Shelley Neville) The Haworth Information Press, an imprint of The Haworth Press, Inc., 2003, pp. 271-278. Single or multiple copies of this article are available for a fee from The Haworth Document Delivery Service [1-800-HAWORTH, 9:00 a.m. - 5:00 p.m. (EST). E-mail address: docdelivery@haworthpress.com].

http://www.haworthpress.com/store/product.asp?sku=J123
10.1300/J123v44n34_35

WHY WE ARE HERE:
THE CURRENT SITUATION AT APPALACHIAN STATE

John Abbott began the workshop with a description of the current university library and the early planning, and politics, surrounding the new library. Appalachian State University was founded as a teachers' college and normal school in 1899. It is now a Carnegie Comprehensive Institution of 12,500 students, with some 900 graduate students, many of whom are among the 800 distance-learning students, and was recently named by *Time Magazine* as "Masters-Level College of the Year." It is part of a consortium with two other University of North Carolina (UNC) system schools–UNC-Asheville and Western Carolina University. The libraries share a common catalog and document delivery system.

The library at Appalachian State, constructed in the late 1960s and enlarged in 1980, is currently full, and the journal stacks are "beyond full." It is expected that the new library will open in 2005 or 2006. Initial funding proposals called for a building of 300,000 gross square feet, but current plans are for about 215,000 gross square foot, with about 150,000 assignable square feet (usable space for collections and people).

THE PLANNING PROCESS

User Survey

In 2001 a survey was taken to ascertain what student, faculty, and alumni wanted in the new library. Students wanted group and quiet study areas, more books, networked computers, scanners, and fax machines, better copiers, full software suites, expanded media holdings, and e-journals. Faculty wanted open stacks, wired carrels, more electronic classrooms, and more print journals. Recent alumni wanted access to more Internet materials. All asked for more online databases, better lighting, and a snack/coffee bar.

Early Thinking

The University administration encouraged the library staff to think creatively, and a generous budget was provided for visits to other institutions with recently completed, new libraries. Many felt that the new library paradigm should push electronic access as far as it would go; some went so far as to advocate tossing the paper and relying on e-access. Funding and politics quickly stifled that idea. There was talk about the library's role as the university's "information commons" and there were debates on the future role of print journals, back-file retention, and the need for remote storage.

Recall that on the user survey, only the faculty listed print journals as a priority. However, the library staff is reasonably confident that most paper print journals and government documents will be history within a decade. To this end several visits were made to institutions with storage facilities. Of particular interest was the on-site facility at Sonoma State University. The Jean and Charles Schulz Information Center stores 750,000 items in floor-to-ceiling bins. The automated retrieval system (see *http://libweb.sonoma.edu/about/schulz/retsys.html*) can deliver the requested item in about 5 minutes. Other storage facilities visited, such as Harvard and Duke, tended to be large remote facilities with considerably longer turn-around times.

Reality

The cost of a Sonoma-like facility ($2-3 million) was high, but in the realm of the possible. Unfortunately, a rumor that the library was planning on using such an innovative system ignited a firestorm of protest among some of the faculty. Forward thinking librarians discovered just how traditionally minded, and politically powerful, many of the teaching faculty can be. Abbott reports that they ultimately adopted "moderately-inaccessible on-site storage, commonly known as compact shelving." This shelving will contain the entire (current and bound) paper journal and government documents collections. It will be on the ground floor, and there will be no room for a reading room or for the display of new periodicals.

While this solution is less innovative than the original plans, and may cause problems in the short term, Abbott feels that not building a storage facility is good for the long-term for a medium-sized academic library. If his predictions of the stability of the electronic medium and the demise of the paper journal prove correct, he expects that, eventually, the paper collection will be discarded, and the compact shelving used for books.

Abbott ended his portion of the workshop with the view that small and medium libraries should not attempt to emulate the large research libraries. "A small library's bailiwick," he said, "is service, not collections. If it isn't used, weed it and borrow it when it is needed." Additionally, Abbott proposed that to assure the on-going construction and operation of research universities' huge storage facilities, small and medium-sized libraries contribute a small amount (perhaps $0.10) per volume for each volume withdrawn from the smaller library's collections. These funds would be collected by the cataloging utility as part of the symbol removal and the funds transferred, as either endowment or liquid assets, to the large in-state or regional academic library that agrees to aggressively store and make available low-use books and journals.

TECHNICAL SERVICES ISSUES

Amy Weiss then talked in general about technical services issues involved in planning and maintaining any storage facility, remote or on-site. She also discussed issues regarding the weeding of journal collections and arrangement of materials in compact shelving. She emphasized the importance of intellectual access for materials that are not physically accessible to users.

For those interested in off-site storage, Amy recommended Nitecki and Kendrick's book "Library off-site shelving" (2001). Nitecki and Kendrick state that large, off-site facilities lead to what they refer to as "the paradox of off-site" which is as follows:

For such sites we take the least used of our collection, and then we

- Inventory them
- Ensure online bibliographic access
- Develop a convenient way to request the material, usually through the online catalog or the Web
- Pull collections from stacks and deliver to a centralized pick-up point
- Provide free copying and faxing
- Implement sophisticated inventory control and operational procedures
- Provide better security
- Provide a superior preservation environment, relative to the open stack libraries on campus[1]

In other words, a library may expend significant resources to preserve and provide access to little-used collections.

Weiss recommended looking at the University of California's Southern Regional Library Facility (SRLF) as an example of what goes into the creation and maintenance of a large, off-site facility (see *http://www.srlf.ucla.edu/*). The SRLF will store only one copy of each item, and requires that the library that submits an item for storage supply a catalog record for that item.

If the library is unable to build a large-scale facility, the issues for technical services remain the same: users need to know what the library has, where it is located, and how users can access it. If these conditions are not met, materials should be discarded. Weiss shared a picture of Appalachian's "storage of shame"–items stored in boxes in a closet, with no effective means of retrieval.

ARRANGEMENT IN STORAGE

There are several possible ways of arranging stored items. An arrangement paralleling the main collection requires minimal cataloging maintenance, usually just a location change. However, adding items to the storage facility may require periodical shifting. An arrangement similar to the "old" collection is possible when you have materials in an obsolete classification scheme, such as Cutter or Dewey, while the library's main collection is arranged by Library of Congress classification. This old collection can be stored as is. Accession numbers will work for large or small facilities, but it takes an up front commitment of staff time to keep the numbers in order.

WEEDING

Appalachian State expects to perform major weeding of the journal collection, prior to the move to the new library. Discarding journals has a major impact on technical services. Areas of involvement will include gifts, transfers, and discarding and recycling materials.

If the journal is of no value to your library but you feel the need to offer it as a gift to other libraries, keep in mind:

- The need to publicize the journals available as gifts.
- The need to store the materials while they are waiting to be sent to the other libraries.
- The need to pack and ship the items, and possibly absorb the cost of shipping the materials.

The library should avoid the "National Geographic syndrome"; i.e., don't offer something as a gift just because it seems too nice to throw away.

Transferring items within the library requires location changes in the catalog. It may also involve updating holdings. Discarding and recycling also requires changes in the catalog, and will require physical work, especially if bindings need to be removed prior to recycling.

ALPHABETICAL ARRANGEMENT VS. CLASSIFICATION OF JOURNALS

At the time of the workshop, Appalachian State was debating the pros and cons of keeping the paper journals in alphabetical (title) order versus classifying the collection. The issues surrounding this decision include the fact that the journals will be going into compact shelving in the new library, and the probability that the journal collection will be steadily decreasing in size as more materials become available electronically.

Alphabetical Order: Pros and Cons

There is a perception of ease of access; i.e., if you know the title, you can find it without consulting the catalog. There is also a perception that less shifting is required than in a classified collection, though there does not appear to be any actual proof that this is the case.

However, bound titles may differ from the journal's real title, and unless the user has read and understood the binding title note in the catalog, they may not be able to locate their journal. Journals may get out of order, as the workers shelving books may or may not understand the ALA filing rules. Title changes will be dispersed throughout the stacks, which may confuse users.

Classified Collection: Pros and Cons

Classification offers ease of subject access, which could be very useful, when someone asks for "all the journals" on a given topic. At present the only way the Appalachian staff can accommodate such a request is to provide a list based on the fund code. Title changes stay together–continuations stay with the preceding title in a classified collection. Classification aids in browsing the journal collection. Teaching faculty at Appalachian have talked of the importance of serendipitous browsing in the stacks. However, compact shelving may nullify this advantage.

That said, classified collections require lots of shifting, which is even more onerous in compact shelving than in regular stacks. Finally, there is the question of whether retrospective conversion is worth the effort; if the journal collection is shrinking; it could be, given the advantages listed above. As the collection shrinks, it could more easily be integrated into the main stacks. On the other hand, it would be easier to wait and classify a smaller collection in the future.

WORKFLOW: PRINT VS. ELECTRONIC JOURNALS

Staffing, workflow, and tasks may differ in the move away from print journals toward electronic journal collections. For example, traditional check-in may well vanish; University of Nevada, Reno, has already discontinued it. However, accurately notifying patrons of capricious and ephemeral online holdings will require more work than paper check-in ever did. A lower budget for local binding and less complex tasks for the binding assistants will be balanced against the need to trust vendors to archive and update their files as needed. Less time will be spent shelving journals and more time will be spent online, but low-level employees will need to be retrained to perform online maintenance.

Appalachian's current journal statistics are based on the number of times a journal is re-shelved. For online journals librarians are dependent on vendor statistics, which vary in quality and usefulness. Libraries must demand better statistics or develop local work-arounds. As for cataloging, in the immediate future, there will be more access to parts of journals through aggregators than access to true full content, with the result that more time will be spent creating brief records or editing templates for use by vendors such as Ebsco or Serials Solutions.

As for government documents, similar issues exist for documents collections as for periodical collections. The government is committed to electronic access of government information. Currently, documents assistants spend a lot of time checking-in, stamping, labeling, and pulling runs for binding. The switch to electronic access suggests that more time will be spent on database maintenance, URL checking, and discarding print materials.

Weiss concluded her presentation with these words: "Whether you're building a new facility or keeping a current library up-to-date, determining the role and importance of print journals for your library will be an important aspect of serials librarianship in the coming decade."

DISCUSSION

The post-workshop discussion centered on the future of the paper journals. The presenters indicated that they had not yet developed a timetable for weeding the collection, and that faculty are involved in weeding decisions.

Much of the discussion revolved around the question of the reliability of online journals. Many faculty continue to demand paper. Some online versions of articles lack graphics (often a copyright issue for the vendor). Some of the participants said that they had become disillusioned with the reliability of the online versions and were purchasing paper back-files of previously cancelled journals. There was certainly no groundswell of sentiment among the participants that libraries could discard their paper file any time soon.

REFERENCES

1. Nitecki, Danuta A., and Curtis L. Kendrick (eds.). *Library Off-site Shelving: Guide for High-density Facilities.* Englewood, CO: Libraries Unlimited, 2001., pp. 2-3.

CONTRIBUTORS' NOTES

Amy K. Weiss is Coordinator of Cataloging, Appalachian State University. John P. Abbott is Coordinator of Collection Development, Appalachian State University. Joseph C. Harmon is Reference and Instruction Librarian, IUPUI University Library.

Don't Tread on Me:
The Art of Supervising Student Assistants

Jeff Slagell

Workshop Leader

Jeanne M. Langendorfer

Recorder

SUMMARY. The presenter provided a commonsense, practical approach to supervising students, based on respect for the student employee, the need to see that the necessary work gets done well, and the belief that coaching and mentoring will grow excellent student employees. The presentation was organized so that basic areas of managing student employees were covered as well as overarching themes of consistency, training, supervision and *[Article copies available for a fee from The Haworth Document Delivery Service: 1-800-HAWORTH. E-mail address: <docdelivery@haworthpress.com> Website: <http://www.HaworthPress.com>]*

Jeff Slagell, a NASIG 2001 Horizon Award winner, said he has supervised over 200 student employees, at one time managing 60 Federal Work Study students, while working in libraries in both staff and professional positions. He has worked in circulation, stacks maintenance, monograph acquisitions, serials, and interlibrary loan.

[Haworth co-indexing entry note]: "Don't Tread on Me: The Art of Supervising Student Assistants." Langendorfer, Jeanne M. Co-published simultaneously in *The Serials Librarian* (The Haworth Information Press, an imprint of The Haworth Press, Inc.) Vol. 44, No. 3/4, 2003, pp. 279-284; and: *Transforming Serials: The Revolution Continues* (ed: Susan L. Scheiberg, and Shelley Neville) The Haworth Information Press, an imprint of The Haworth Press, Inc., 2003, pp. 279-284. Single or multiple copies of this article are available for a fee from The Haworth Document Delivery Service [1-800-HAWORTH, 9:00 a.m. - 5:00 p.m. (EST). E-mail address: docdelivery@haworthpress.com].

Slagell's first anecdote gave us a peek at the humor and real-life experience that was to be a part of his presentation. He spoke of the very first time he supervised a student. As a Circulation staff member, he couldn't find the student who was supposed to be emptying the book drop. Concerned that he might have "lost" a student employee, he finally opened the book drop and was relieved and amazed to find the student inside, reading a book with a flashlight!

While Slagell stated that much of the information presented would seem to be commonsense, he wanted to pull together a wide range of resources on student employees for the audience's benefit. Most of the published articles on supervising student employees looked at their use in public services; very little has been published about their use in technical services. Yet, many of the ideas are transferable to technical services.

As student employees constantly test boundaries, supervisors need to state expectations clearly. In Constantinon's article, the "Pygmalion effect" was discussed.[1] He suggests that individuals will perform to the level that is expected of them. At the first sign of a problem, bring it to the student's attention. Plan to provide a lot of direct supervision because student employees frequently have little or no job experience.

Understanding the student's perspective is important. Keep in mind that the students' main priority is their education. Their job is only one of several important activities in their life. They may still be learning how to balance a class schedule and work. Work with your students so they will work with you. Oltmanns suggests communicating to the student employee that their work is valuable and how they fit into the overall scheme of work in the library.[2]

There are distinctions between student and staff jobs, so clearly articulate the job requirements so there are no surprises. This can be done effectively by using written job descriptions. Because student workers typically require more supervision and instruction than regular staff, high turnover can be frustrating for a department and create an "assembly line" mentality. Communication is especially important with students having disparate work schedules. The first weeks on the job are crucial: Work closely with your students and help them out. Keep in mind the diversity of students you hire, as this can influence the way you train, reward, and discipline individual student employees. Also, across the years, students have been asked to take on jobs with greater responsibility, as staff have taken on work that professionals formerly did.

Remember that a good work environment builds a positive reputation that will make it easier to recruit and hire students in the future. Word gets out and students will come looking for you! If students with Federal Work Study are hired, they can be a big benefit to the library, as the library pays only a percentage of their hourly wage. While first or second year students may require more training and supervision initially than upper class students, they offer the possibility of a longer-term commitment. Graduate students may bring greater maturity with them to the work, but they may see the work as beneath them. Occasionally graduate students can get assistantships in a library, although these are not offered at all institutions. While many supervisors must "take what we can get," Slagell states that, " experience has shown me that [having] NO student is better than [having] a problem student."

Scheduling student work hours requires the supervisor to be flexible as students' class schedules and other commitments must be balanced against the needs of the department. Make sure students know how to sign in and out so that you can keep track of the hours they have worked. Keep them informed of their wages, payroll time periods, procedures, and how they get their paycheck.

Department policies and procedures must be written and kept up-to-date to use in training and for the student to refer to later. In addition, use a training checklist as a means to orient your new employees and keep track of the tasks they learn. Include the specifics of performing tasks, such as the greeting to be used for answering the telephone. The training checklist can be tailor-made for student employees, and may prove useful for staff use, too.

Evaluation of student employees is necessary to document performance. Evaluation should be done informally everyday, not just during a formal performance appraisal at the end of semester or once a year. Regularly provide students with feedback about their performance, allowing students to participate in and respond to your evaluation of their work. Use the evaluation as a basis for rehiring, raises, recommendations, and disciplinary action. Evaluations also prepare students for their work life after graduation. Keep the paperwork, as one never knows when a student might request a reference.

Slagell named his approach for working with student employees the "Trident Approach." It consists of training, supervision and motivation. He quoted Theodore Roosevelt, humorously saying, "Speak softly and carry a big stick . . ." In addition, consistently applying your management behaviors will make it easier on your students and bring great results.

In training, include a general library orientation, so the student employee gets a sense of the "big picture"–the physical library, the work of the library, and who the major players are (dean, associate dean, department head, etc.) Utilize your policies and procedures as the foundation for teaching the job and be explicit about the work the student employee is to perform.

Create and use a training checklist to train new student employees. As skills are mastered they can be checked off. When the student has completed training, consider having the student sign his or her checklist as a way of documenting their understanding of departmental policies and the student employee's responsibilities. Also, use the training checklist with continuing student employees as a means to update and test their knowledge and skills. Training is a constant process as work changes; student workers need regular reminders and testing to insure that their information and skills are satisfactory since they work relatively few hours per week.

As a supervisor, be consistent. Establish clear expectations and stick to them, especially at first. It's easier to let up a bit than to do the reverse! Follow up on the tasks assigned after students have completed their work, especially in the beginning. Students are more likely to understand that mistakes have ramifications and they will know that you, as the supervisor, value and are concerned about their performance. One way to emphasize the importance of good performance is to develop and use a student contract that includes your core principles and performance expectations, and then have the students sign it. The contract symbolizes the student workers' ownership of their performance, and if signed, could be used as documentation for disciplinary action.

Motivation is a key element in getting and keeping good student workers. If you can give raises, be even-handed and fair. Take your student budget allocation seriously and base raises on objective performance measures and evaluations. Let students know that you write enthusiastic recommendations when they have performed well. Be sure your evaluations support the recommendations you write, and that you follow the recommendations of your human resources unit and state law. In short, show your student employees that you appreciate them. Tell them "thank you!" Write notes and letters of commendation for their good performance on special projects, or send e-cards to express your thoughts. Give them tokens of your appreciation by occasionally providing them with snacks (e.g., sodas, candy bars, cookies, etc.). Consider celebrating the end of a semester with a department or library-wide student employee appreciation party. Keeping in mind cultural differences that might color how recognition is perceived, give awards of money, gift certificates to the bookstore, a copy card with value, or donate a book with their name on the bookplate. If your student employees receive fringe benefits from working in the library, name those benefits (e.g., using the staff lounge, one-on-one research assistance, faculty/staff due dates, etc.).

No discussion of student employees can avoid the "problem child." One poorly performing student employee can detrimentally impact all the others, just as a good student employee can motivate everyone else. If you must discipline a student employee, first use verbal warnings that focus on *performance behaviors* and not personal characteristics. After issuing the verbal warning, establish a plan for corrective action. Discuss ways the student can improve and set a future date to review progress. List the steps decided upon, establish a time frame, and have both people sign and date the document. Keep good records: take notes, including dates and witnesses, to establish a history of actions taken. If you must issue a written warning because the work performance has not improved, be sure to state the behavior problems and the proper procedure they are to follow. The written warning lets the student know that you are keeping a record of their poor performance. If termination of employment is necessary, put in writing the reasons and statement of termination, date and sign it and have your dean or director sign, too. Then, be prepared for any response from no reaction to a blow-up.

Encourage your student employees, reward them, and make the workplace fun. Be positive in your interactions with your student employees, as a positive attitude is contagious. When there are problems, be fair. Stand up for your students when necessary and treat them as you treat your staff. Your consistency will be rewarded!

Throughout the presentation, audience members actively participated by asking questions and sharing their experiences working with student employees. The presenter packed a hefty amount of material into his presentation, yet still had time for questions and answers at the end. Participants were given copies of the outline of his presentation, his training checklist and a bibliography of selected resources (see list below).

NOTES

1. Constatinon, Constantia. "Recruiting, Training and Motivating Student Assistants in Academic Libraries," *Catholic Library World* 69 no. 1 (December 1998): 20-23.

2. Oltmanns, Gail V. "The Student Perspective." *Journal of Library Administration* 21 no. 3/4 (1995): 63-76.

SELECTED RESOURCES

Borin, Jacqueline. "Training, Supervising and Evaluating Student Information Assistants." *The Reference Librarian* 72 (2001): 195-206.

Clark, Charlene K. "Motivating and Rewarding Student Workers." *Journal of Library Administration* 21, no. 3/4 (1995): 87-93.

Constatinon, Constantia. "Recruiting, Training and Motivating Student Assistants in Academic Libraries." *Catholic Library World* 69 no. 1 (December 1998): 20-23.

Fuller, F. Jay. "Evaluating Student Assistants as Library Employees." *College & Research Libraries News* 51 no. 1 (January 1990): 11-13.

Kathman, Jane McGurn; Kathman, Michael D. "What Difference Does Diversity Make in Managing Student Employees?" *College & Research Libraries* 59 no. 4 (July 1998): 378-389.

_____. "Training Student Employees for Quality Service." *The Journal of Academic Librarianship* 26 no. 3 (May 2000): 176-182.

Marks, Susan; Gregory, David. "Student Employment in Academic Libraries: Recommended Readings and Resources." *Journal of Library Administration* 21 no. 3/4 (1995): 161-176.

Oltmanns, Gail V. "The Student Perspective." *Journal of Library Administration* 21 no. 3/4 (1995): 63-76.

White, Emilie C. "Student Assistance in Academic Libraries: From Reluctance to Reliance." *The Journal of Academic Librarianship* 11 no. 2 (May 1995): 93-97.

CONTRIBUTORS' NOTES

Jeff Slagell is Head, Serials and Interlibrary Loan at Delta State University. Jeanne M. Langendorfer is Coordinator of Serials for Bowling Green State University.

Report of the Death of the Catalog Is Greatly Exaggerated: The E-Journal Access Journey at the University of Tennessee

Kay Johnson
Maribeth Manoff

Workshop Leaders

Rebecca Sheffield

Recorder

SUMMARY. Kay Johnson and Maribeth Manoff described the various ways in which the University of Tennessee Libraries provide e-journal access to its patrons. The early history of e-journal cataloging at UTL was given followed by the methods currently used. Notes, fields, and subfields used in the bibliographic records, and the E-Journal Wizard, which was developed by UTL personnel, were explained in detail. Johnson and Manoff gave an excellent description of how article aggregated and title aggregated databases are handled via Hooks-to-Holdings. *[Article copies available for a fee from The Haworth Document Delivery Service: 1-800-HAWORTH. E-mail address: <docdelivery@haworthpress.com> Website: <http://www.HaworthPress.com>]*

[Haworth co-indexing entry note]: "Report of the Death of the Catalog Is Greatly Exaggerated: The E-Journal Access Journey at the University of Tennessee." Sheffield, Rebecca. Co-published simultaneously in *The Serials Librarian* (The Haworth Information Press, an imprint of The Haworth Press, Inc.) Vol. 44, No. 3/4, 2003, pp. 285-292; and: *Transforming Serials: The Revolution Continues* (ed: Susan L. Scheiberg, and Shelley Neville) The Haworth Information Press, an imprint of The Haworth Press, Inc., 2003, pp. 285-292. Single or multiple copies of this article are available for a fee from The Haworth Document Delivery Service [1-800-HAWORTH, 9:00 a.m. - 5:00 p.m. (EST). E-mail address: docdelivery@haworthpress.com].

http://www.haworthpress.com/store/product.asp?sku=J123
10.1300/J123v44n34_37

INTRODUCTION

How best to provide patrons access to e-journals is one of the most discussed issues among librarians. As personnel at the University of Tennessee Libraries (UTL) examined this issue, they kept returning to the idea that providing access through the online public access catalog was desirable. This workshop described the University of Tennessee Libraries' evolving effort to provide better access to e-journals.

E-JOURNALS INTO THE CATALOG

Mid-1990 projects at UTL involved Lynx, FTP and Gopher journals and OCLC's Internet Cataloging (InterCat) Project. Two of the practices established during this time period were eventually abandoned: adding "Ask at Reference Desk" notes to e-journal records, and using "Computer network resources" as a defacto form subdivision. Two established practices were continued: adding generic notes to e-journal records, and not assigning call numbers for e-resources.

A standing committee of librarians and staff representing a cross-section of library functions was established. The Catalog Advisory Group (CAG) makes decisions affecting catalog display, indexing and content. CAG decisions affecting individual catalog records are:

- Continue the process UTL uses with microforms of having a single record approach.
- Add an access restrictions note of "Access restrictions may apply."
- Provide an online ISSN in addition to the print ISSN for each title.
- Provide a pseudo-GMD, which overrides the provided GMD and can be turned on or off, on each catalog record.
- Provide a pseudo-barcode, which is a generic code to display holdings and an easy way to get holdings statements into records.

Following these procedures, a record for a title for which both e-journal and print or microform holdings would result in adding:

- The online ISSN if available: XXX-XXXX (Online).
- A 506 note: "Access restrictions may apply."
- A 530 note: "Also available online via the Internet."
- An 856 for print or microform and establish E-Journal Wizard URL for paid subscriptions.
- A 945 $h: "[print and electronic]."

A record for which there are only e-journal holdings would result in:

- Adding a 506 note "Access restrictions may apply."
- Adding a 538 note: "Mode of access: Internet."
- Changing 245 $h to read: "[electronic journal]" (only added to the local catalog record and not to the OCLC record).
- Adding a pseudo-barcode to display "holdings" note.

URLS FOR E-JOURNAL ACCESS (AKA, THE E-JOURNAL WIZARD)

Since URLs are apt to change, UTL developed a method to ensure the new URL is recorded in all the necessary places. A combination of the E-Journal Wizard and connect.cgi scripts provides persistent URLs for electronic resources. This is accomplished by entering URLs into a MySQL database via the Wizard. The connect.cgi URL can then be used in the catalog and elsewhere. When URLs change, the change is entered in the Wizard and records are automatically updated. The Wizard allows for entering data such as the username and password or more than one URL per title, which will be displayed on an interim screen.

Previous to the E-Journal Wizard, patron access was restricted to the utk.edu domain. Now, the connect.cgi script checks the IP address and if off-campus, asks for NetID and password. It then checks these against the UTL LDAP database and prepends the EZProxy logon to the URL if authenticated.

TITLES FROM FULL-TEXT AGGREGATORS (HOOKS-TO-HOLDINGS, AKA H2H)

By the late 1990s, UTL had access to more than 10,000 electronic journal titles through full-text aggregator databases. Making those resources more accessible by providing information about these titles through UTL's catalog became an important goal. It was not desirable to have the catalogers forced to deal with the aggregator databases, so a Hooks-to-Holdings (H2H) subgroup of CAG was formed. Some of the considerations of the H2H subgroup were that each aggregator service included thousands of records, that cancellation of a service would render thousands of catalog records out-of-date, and that vendors often add or drop titles from their full-text services or modify their range of coverage.

Two types of aggregators were chosen for H2H treatment: article aggregators of Dow Jones, Proquest, and Ethnic NewsWatch; and title aggregators of JSTOR, Project Muse, and ScienceDirect. Information supplied by an aggregator service was used to prepare a file of records that could be loaded into the catalog in batch mode. For each record set, an identifier would be provided that would allow these records to be selected for removal en masse. Catalog updates would be done by periodically deleting all the records for a given aggregator and reloading a fresh set. An additional consideration was that for many titles, UTL might own a print subscription as well as have access through more than one aggregator. These would be represented in the catalog by multiple entries. The obvious problem is that this contradicts the idea of using a single record. Therefore, local modifications to standard MARC would provide additional data elements for distinguishing among these similar catalog entries and highlighting electronic resources.

Two modifications were made to MARC standards. First, a locally defined $9 would be added to the 022. This is searchable in the online catalog, but is excluded from retrieval in the serials control module. This prevents potential check-ins on incorrect records by UTL personnel. Secondly, a 945 with separate subfields is locally defined for each non-standard data element:

- $a–service/vendor information
- $d–dates of coverage
- $e–lag time between print publication and appearance in the aggregated service
- $h–pseudo-GMD
- $n–access notes
- $p–control number (the "hook" from which the records could be pulled, e.g., all ProQuest records would have the same number)
- $z–internal notes

The first step to get from a vendor list to a MARC record is to compile a list of titles, coverage dates, ISSN, etc., offered by each vendor. This was often done using information from the vendor's Web site. Then a PERL script, unique to each vendor, transformed the data elements into a uniform format, supplemented each record with the data elements common to all records for a particular vendor (e.g., access restrictions, the URL of the subscription service, control number, etc.), and provided a default MARC leader with coding needed for the MARCMakr utility. The MARCMakr utility converts the information into MARC format by supplying the complete record leader and record directory structure and replacing special characters (e.g., "\," "$," "hard return") with the correct ASCII value. Files of the MARC records are then added to the catalog using the normal import utility in the cataloging module. One of the recognized drawbacks to this method is when the patron clicks on the catalog link, he is taken to the main page of the aggregator database and the search has to be re-typed.

In order to remove records from the catalog, methods for the title aggregator services and the article aggregator services have to be devised. Records for the title aggregator services are removed when the cataloger deletes the H2H record after providing a full cataloging record. Records for the article aggregator services are removed with an SQL script that directly updates the database in three steps: identify a given aggregator's record using the control number in the 945 $p, delete the record, and delete references to the record in the indexes.

TITLE AGGREGATORS
THROUGH CONSORTIAL AGREEMENT

University of Tennessee joined a consortia including Vanderbilt University and East Tennessee State University College of Medicine Library in late 2000. What is considered a "best case" scenario of a consortial arrangement that provides access to titles which otherwise would not be available translates to a "worst case" of how to handle the cataloging and how to provide the access. Elsevier's ScienceDirect is an example of how this was handled at UTL.

There were three types of aggregator titles:

1. "Ours"–406 titles
   - UTL held a current print subscription with a record already in the catalog;
   - A link may already exist to a URL from Elsevier Web Editions, and;
   - Partner(s) may also have a current print subscription(s).
2. "Partner"–238 titles
   - Partner(s) have a current print subscription, and;
   - No current print subscription at UTL.

3. "None"–652 titles
- No current print subscription held by any member of the consortia, and;
- Access is provided via token and/or pay-per-article.

The first step in cataloging these aggregator titles is to load Hooks-to-Holdings (H2H) records for all ScienceDirect titles, thereby providing brief records in the catalog. For the "Ours" category titles, procedures are followed for print and electronic holdings (i.e., a 530 is added with the note, "Also available online via ScienceDirect" and the H2H record is deleted). For the "Partners" category titles, procedures are followed for print and electronic holdings if print holdings exist and procedures are followed for electronic-only holdings if no print holdings exist, (i.e., a 538 is added with the note "Mode of access: Internet via ScienceDirect" and the H2H record is deleted). For the "None" category titles, the H2H brief record remains in the catalog.

Each partner gathered data by title regarding presence of a print subscription and the total use for 2001 (the number of views of full-text articles). Impressively, but not surprisingly, it was found that use of subscribed and non-subscribed titles doubled when catalog records were added.

E-JOURNALS OUTSIDE THE CATALOG

Because patrons want immediate desktop access to electronic journals and there is no way to limit a search in the catalog to electronic journals, a tool to identify electronically accessed titles was needed. A separate online list had been created in 1998, but maintenance of the static HTML page was becoming unwieldy. In April 2001, CAG endorsed the idea of using the catalog to generate this list.

A script was designed to extract serial records for periodicals and newspapers (serial type "p" or "n" in 008) and having at least one 856 with indicators "4" or "40" or "41" or records having a 945 $j = t (e.g., would add "annual review" titles to the list since a local subfield is added for titles selector has requested to be added). The following fields are extracted and stored in a MySQL database:

- ISSNs (022s)
- Call number (050, 090 or 099)
- SuDoc number (086)
- Title (245)
- URLs (856s)

In addition, subject searching is made available by inserting subject codes into database records. A subject list was created that roughly matched the subject list already in place for databases. LC call numbers are mapped to this subject list; when the database is created, subject codes are added using this map. PHP programming language is used to create the interface and lists are created dynamically by pulling records from the database:

- by the first letter of the title;
- that match a search string within the title;
- by subject code.

CONCLUSION AND DISCUSSION

So far, the journey at the University of Tennessee Libraries has led to the online public access catalog as the central repository for e-journal information. Not abandoning the catalog was a desire of the majority of individuals attending this workshop. However, the ever-changing nature of e-journals calls for creative alternatives to traditional cataloging. For example, UTL has decided to continue providing an e-journal database in addition to catalog access. This is primarily due to the fear that discontinuing the database would be unpopular with UTL patrons. However, several in the audience were concerned that patrons would use only the database and would never check the catalog for accessible electronic titles. New tools, such as link servers like SFX, are also becoming available. These new tools will have pros and cons and individual institutions will need to assess their situation to decide the best way to provide access to their patrons.

ADDITIONAL INFORMATION SOURCES

For more information about Hooks-to-Holdings (H2H):

Britten, William A. et al. "Access to Periodicals Holdings Information: Creating Links Between Databases and the Library Catalog." *Library Collections, Acquisitions & Technical Services* 24 (2000): 7-20.

For more information about MARCMakr:

http://lcweb.loc.gov/marc/marctools.html

University of Tennessee Libraries catalog:

http://pac.lib.utk.edu:8000/

CONTRIBUTORS' NOTES

Kay Johnson is Serials Coordinator, and Maribeth Manoff is Coordinator for Network Services Integration, both at the University of Tennessee. Rebecca Sheffield is Head of Acquisitions Services at Ball State University.

Web-Based Tracking Systems
for Electronic Resources Management

Thinking.Robert Alan
Lai-Ying Hsiung

Workshop Leaders

Sharon McCaslin

Recorder

SUMMARY. Robert Alan reported on the development of ERLIC^2, Penn State's tracking system, which will include optical imaging of critical documentation such as licenses, access and authentication information, financial information, and statistics for library staff, as well as information on access problems and new products. Lai-Ying Hsiung reported on how UCSC is using the Web-based program Request Tracker to receive queries from their users, share responsibility for responding to these communications, and archive the resolved transactions. Both projects satisfy specific local needs in responding to the problem of managing electronic resources. *[Article copies available for a fee from The Haworth Document Delivery Service: 1-800-HAWORTH. E-mail address: <docdelivery@haworthpress.com> Website: <http://www.HaworthPress.com>]*

[Haworth co-indexing entry note]: "Web-Based Tracking Systems for Electronic Resources Management." McCaslin, Sharon. Co-published simultaneously in *The Serials Librarian* (The Haworth Information Press, an imprint of The Haworth Press, Inc.) Vol. 44, No. 3/4, 2003, pp. 293-297; and: *Transforming Serials: The Revolution Continues* (ed: Susan L. Scheiberg, and Shelley Neville) The Haworth Information Press, an imprint of The Haworth Press, Inc., 2003, pp. 293-297. Single or multiple copies of this article are available for a fee from The Haworth Document Delivery Service [1-800-HAWORTH, 9:00 a.m. - 5:00 p.m. (EST). E-mail address: docdelivery@haworthpress.com].

INTRODUCTION

Keeping records and statistics on traditional printed resources is a well-established process in most libraries. However, electronic resources have complicated the process, requiring additional access to proposed and finalized licenses, renewal dates, content and coverage, access procedures, usage statistics, and reporting and resolution of access problems. As electronic resources of various types provide an ever-increasing part of library resources, more library staff members need to use this information. Both of the presenters in this workshop are working on different aspects of this complex problem.

KEEPING TRACK OF ELECTRONIC RESOURCES TO KEEP THEM ON TRACK

Robert Alan reported on Penn State's Electronic Resources Licensing and Information Center (ERLIC), which attempts to provide information within the 23 campus university system. The ERLIC system was developed on Microsoft Access in 1999 as a relational database, primarily used for acquisitions and renewals. ERLIC quickly evolved into a centralized source for ordering, access, authentication, and licensing information. With increasing demand for access to this data in all of the university branches, Cold Fusion Web pages were developed in 2001 to enhance access to a subset of ERLIC data. However the Cold ERLIC pages are not as comprehensive and up-to-date as ERLIC itself.

Before making major changes to ERLIC this year, stakeholders' information needs were assessed. Technical services personnel need to manage and update critical data and documents, to generate reports and extract data, to follow progress on access problem resolution, and to view potential new products. Collection development, interlibrary loan, and systems personnel need access to the licenses and other documents, the ability to generate reports and statistics, the capability of observing and managing access problem resolution, and access to new products and trials. Public services personnel need access to selected information about access, restrictions, and privileges, as well as the ability to view problem resolution and new products. Library patrons need access to the full text e-journal list, as well as the ability to view selected information on access problems and new products.

ERLIC^2 is being developed to enhance access to the current data as well as provide timely information on access problems and resolution, new trials, etc. ERLIC itself was transferred to the Cold Fusion server and will eventually be moved into Oracle. An optical imaging database has been installed on Oracle to provide system-wide access to licenses and other critical documents. The optical imaging database will be linked to the ERLIC[2] database and both will be available to the appropriate library personnel in technical services, collection development, fiscal management, systems, etc. In addition, a Billboard is being developed as a Cold Fusion Webpage. This will be an interface for public services to provide current information on access problems and resolution, announcements of trials and new resources, and a record of reliability and performance, with the ability to control or restrict access to sensitive data. Finally, the Cold Fusion Web pages are being expanded and refined to update and coordinate the information in ERLIC and the Billboard. Pieces of ERLIC[2] are in development and should be implemented over the 2002 fall semester for review by subject selectors. Access to selected data and Billboard information will eventually be available through the Library's new SIRSI Unicorn library system, which is intended to be the access point for patrons.

Several future challenges and issues were identified, including the creation of standards for electronic resources management, integrating digital rights management into the system, the comparison and coordination with other electronic resource management systems (the University of Georgia, MIT, and UCLA being mentioned specifically), the potential for ILS vendor support (Innovative having already developed a module with some similar features), and the role of commercial e-journal management services, publishers, and vendors (Serials Solutions, TDNet, etc.).

WEB-BASED TRACKING SYSTEM
FOR ELECTRONIC RESOURCE MANAGEMENT

Lai-Ying Hsiung reported on the Web-based interactive tracking system being used at the University of California, Santa Cruz (UCSC). While not a comprehensive solution for the management of electronic resources, the project is a fully operational Web-based module, focusing on the reporting and resolution of access problems. UCSC is a part of the California Digital Library (CDL) and has access to consortial acquisitions and licensing as well as a shared cataloging program, although each campus has its own automation system and handles the acquisition and management of its resources individually. The UCSC

Library relies heavily on electronic resources, which account for 45% of the collection budget. The importance of these resources, as well as the desire to maximize the effectiveness of CDL resources, led to the development of an electronic resource management system. Problems caused by the loss of a key staff person led to the decision that the system must be a team approach with a Web interface, to ensure reliable and timely communication among all interested parties.

The software used in this tracking system is Request Tracker (RT), an open source software program which creates e-mail tickets for incident reporting, which are then tracked through to the resolution of the problem and ultimately archived for later reference. This program is widely used by IT and computing units. For UCSC the system solves many of the communications problems concerning access to electronic resources. As an e-mail question or complaint is received, a ticket is created on the RT system. All team members can review the incoming tickets and take action, respond, or otherwise enrich the data. These responses are clearly visible to other members of the team and when final resolution of the problem is achieved, the ticket can be archived. Tickets on the same subject can be linked together to provide efficient responses. The RT system can be either searched or sorted by embedded metadata, assigned subject, chronology, user, or staff member. Not only have communications been enhanced, but management statistics are available to support evaluation of electronic resources.

The staff at UCSC is enthusiastic about the benefits of such tracking systems. For the future, this kind of software would work well for tracking access problems, and it would make an effective building block in a more comprehensive electronic resources management system. Standards will have to be developed to integrate the e-mail message tracking process with other types of resource tracking.

DISCUSSION

Audience members were interested in the flexibility of the systems, learning that the RT system can be designed for shifts or assigning specific subjects to specific staff members, in addition to the looser team approach now used by UCSC. In the UCSC system a user can initiate a ticket, while both systems permit library staff to record and track user problems, with or without initial e-mail contact. The RT system can produce e-mails to alert the vendor, using the "comment" feature, but neither system generates alerts automatically.

A question from the audience concerned the number of staff members involved in designing each institution's project. In the larger and more formalized project, Penn State had five people on their design team. UCSC's experiment with an existing system used by the library's computing unit lays the groundwork for more formal planning and upgrading.

Discussion from the audience also brought up the need for renewal alerts, which would allow time to evaluate the resource in a selection process. Penn State has their tracking system set to allow 90 days between notification and the renewal deadline. The RT system permits UCSC to sort by "due" date to produce renewal alerts. Their relationship with CDL has made this a much easier task, because the consortium already manages many UCSC titles. UCSC only needs to use the tracking system for reporting consortium title access problems to CDL, which is responsible for resolving those problems with the vendor.

CONCLUSION

Both presentations demonstrated important steps being taken toward a comprehensive solution to electronic resources management. While Alan continues to develop a larger and more complex project, Hsiung demonstrated a much smaller, completed module, usable for reporting and tracking access problems. Both Alan and Hsiung supported the need for further standardization and support from others working with and providing electronic resources.

CONTRIBUTORS' NOTES

Robert Alan is Head, Serials Department at Pennsylvania State University. Lai-Ying Hsiung is E-Resources/Serials Librarian at University of California, Santa Cruz. Sharon McCaslin is Serials Librarian for the Longwood University Libraries.

A Is for Acronym:
Library and Internet Standards for Serialists

Shelley Neville
Howard Rosenbaum

Workshop Leaders

Sarah E. George

Recorder

SUMMARY. The rise of the Internet has caused acronyms and standards to proliferate. Shelley Neville took "the snooze out of the standards" by explaining how serials standards are created and why we should care about standards and the development process. Howard Rosenbaum then led the participants through a web of Internet acronyms most used in libraries and industry. *[Article copies available for a fee from The Haworth Document Delivery Service: 1-800-HAWORTH. E-mail address: <docdelivery@haworthpress.com> Website: <http://www.HaworthPress.com>]*

Most serials-related standards are created under the jurisdiction of the National Information Standards Organization (NISO) and fall into four main groups: identifiers (e.g., ISSN), electronic data exchange (e.g., Edifact), bibliographic data exchange (e.g., MARC), and search

[Haworth co-indexing entry note]: "A Is for Acronym: Library and Internet Standards for Serialists." George, Sarah E. Co-published simultaneously in *The Serials Librarian* (The Haworth Information Press, an imprint of The Haworth Press, Inc.) Vol. 44, No. 3/4, 2003, pp. 299-301; and: *Transforming Serials: The Revolution Continues* (ed: Susan L. Scheiberg, and Shelley Neville) The Haworth Information Press, an imprint of The Haworth Press, Inc., 2003, pp. 299-301. Single or multiple copies of this article are available for a fee from The Haworth Document Delivery Service [1-800-HAWORTH, 9:00 a.m. - 5:00 p.m. (EST). E-mail address: docdelivery@haworthpress.com].

and retrieval (e.g., Z39.50). These standards facilitate communication between publishers and suppliers, arrange data for citations, link information sources, identify a specific item or title, and simplify interlibrary loan (ILL) procedures. A few de facto standards are not covered by NISO; examples include 3M circulation protocol (CIP) standard for self-checkout, extensible markup language (XML) for electronic data exchange (EDI) transactions, online information exchange (ONIX) for transmission of bibliographic metadata, and open archival information services (OAIS) for long term preservation of digital information.

The process of developing a new standard is typically slow and arduous. Volunteers serve on NISO committees; feedback is sought on every proposal, and draft statements must be tested in the field, which requires two parties willing to work within similar implementations schedules. After final approval, implementation of new standards in integrated library systems (ILS) may seem random, but often differing development timelines and priorities significantly influence which standards are implemented and how quickly.

Internet standards develop through formal, noncommercial structures and less controlled commercial initiatives. The Internet Committee for Assigned Names and Numbers (ICANN), the Internet Society (ISOC), and the World Wide Web Consortium (W3C) are key organizations using formal procedures to create and approve Internet standards. Their areas of influence include coordinating domain names (ICANN), facilitating the development of technical standards (ISOC), and developing common Web protocols (W3C). Industry also influences standards in an ad hoc fashion; for example, Netscape and Microsoft influenced the development of HTML in the early 1990s by creating specialized tags only used by their own browsers.

A variety of technical and metadata standards exist for Internet communication and architecture. Communication standards include transmission control protocol/Internet protocol (TCP/IP), hypertext transfer protocol (HTTP), Internet Protocol Version 6 (Ipv6, which theoretically would provide enough IP addressees for everyone in the world), Institute of Electrical and Electronics Engineers 801.11b (IEEE801.11b, which involves wireless networks), and top level domains (TLD). Architectural standards include document object model (DOM) and Simple Object Access Protocol (SOAP). Metadata standards include the W3C's resource description format (RDF) and OCLC's persistent URL (PURL).

Applications standards include the basic markup languages (e.g., SGML, HTML) and basic programming languages (e.g., CGI, Perl,

JavaScript, Java). Rosenbaum concluded his presentation with an overview of extensible markup language (XML), which he says is the application standard that is "most likely to show up on your desktop someday soon." A copy of his presentation is available at *http://www.slis.indiana.edu/rosenbaum/www/Pres/nasig_02/index.htm*.

CONTRIBUTORS' NOTES

Shelley Neville is Library Systems Analyst at epixtech, inc. Howard Rosenbaum is Assistant Professor of Library and Information Science, Indiana University. Sarah E. George is Serials Librarian at Illinois Wesleyan University.

Does a Core Exist?
Electronic Journals Available
in Selected Fields

Ellen Safley
Carolyn Henebry

Workshop Leaders

Elizabeth Parang

Recorder

SUMMARY. A collection of core titles relevant to University of Texas, Dallas (UTD) was assembled from *Magazines for Libraries.* The presenters determined whether the titles were available online, for free or by subscription, and whether an online archive was available. They looked first at publishers' Web sites and then at aggregators. Their presentation slides are available at http://www.utdallas.edu/~safley. *[Article copies available for a fee from The Haworth Document Delivery Service: 1-800-HAWORTH. E-mail address: <docdelivery@haworthpress.com> Website: <http://www.HaworthPress.com>]*

WHAT WE WANTED TO KNOW

NASIG's 2002 theme, Revolution, prompted Safler and Henebry to ask, "Are we the ones deciding what we get? Who's driving this ship?"

[Haworth co-indexing entry note]: "Does a Core Exist? Electronic Journals Available in Selected Fields." Parang, Elizabeth. Co-published simultaneously in *The Serials Librarian* (The Haworth Information Press, an imprint of The Haworth Press, Inc.) Vol. 44, No. 3/4, 2003, pp. 303-309; and: *Transforming Serials: The Revolution Continues* (ed: Susan L. Scheiberg, and Shelley Neville) The Haworth Information Press, an imprint of The Haworth Press, Inc., 2003, pp. 303-309. Single or multiple copies of this article are available for a fee from The Haworth Document Delivery Service [1-800-HAWORTH, 9:00 a.m. - 5:00 p.m. (EST). E-mail address: docdelivery@haworthpress.com].

http://www.haworthpress.com/store/product.asp?sku=J123
10.1300/J123v44n34_40

As part of the University of Texas system, McDermott Library participates in a group purchase of 1900 paper titles and over 15,000 electronic titles received both directly and through aggregators. The librarians wondered if these titles were the ones most relevant to UTD, a relatively young university established in 1969. They further refined their questions to the following: Is our library subscribing to core titles and are they available electronically? Are we subscribing to core titles through aggregators or directly from the publisher?

DEFINITIONS

Their first dilemma was to identify what should be defined as core. Candidates for such a definition included what the library subscribed to, what the library subscribed to and was deemed necessary, which titles were most cited in a discipline, which were indexed in a particular index/database, and the inclusion in reliable sources such as *Magazines for Libraries* bibliographic review articles.

Safley and Henebry wanted a complete look at journals, not just academic journals. In examining standard sources, they felt that *Journal Citation Reports* from ISI was too academic, and noted that *Magazines for Libraries* included titles for both academic and public libraries. They also looked at standard indexes such as *Social Sciences Index, Business Periodicals Index, General Science Index* and *Applied Science and Technology Index.*

METHODOLOGY

Safley and Henebry created a list of core titles for social science, science, and business subjects in the curriculum at University of Texas, Dallas. The list consisted of those titles from the 10th ed. (2000) of *Magazines for Libraries* that were also included in H. W. Wilson Indexes. Next they examined hundreds of publishers' Web sites to answer the following questions:

- Were titles for academic readers more available online than popular titles?
- Was there an archive/back file online?
- Could you buy the article online without a subscription?
- Was any content free?

The presenters checked the following aggregators to see if the core titles were included:

- EBSCO–Academic Search Premier, Business Source Premier
- Gale Group/InfoTrac–Expanded Academic ASAP, Business Index ASAP
- Dow Jones
- OCLC ECO
- Academic Universe (Lexis-Nexis)
- EMERALD
- ProQuest–ABI/INFORM, Periodical Abstracts

SUBJECT DISTRIBUTION

Of the titles examined for this study, 39% were business, 34% were social science, and 27% were science. Safley and Henebry had determined that *Magazines for Libraries* would be a source for core titles because the publication included a mix of titles; some general, nonspecialist periodicals of interest to the layperson, the main English-language research journals sponsored by distinguished societies in the United States, Canada, and Great Britain, and high-quality commercial publications commonly found in academic/special libraries

Business subjects relevant to the UTD curriculum, ranked by percentage distribution, included finance 30%, accounting/tax 14%, trade and industry 14%, marketing 10%, labor 9%, administration 9%, insurance 7%, small business 4%, and multinational 3%.

Relevant science areas included biology 29%, computer science 18%, physics 13%, earth science 12%, science/technology 9%, chemistry 8%, mathematics 4%, atmospheric sciences 4%, astronomy 2%, and statistics 1%.

Social sciences disciplines selected as relevant to UTD included political science 26%, sociology 26%, economics 20%, criminology 9%, geography 6%, cultural-social studies 6%, urban studies 5% and population studies 2%.

ONLINE AVAILABILITY

Online availability and online archives were the next issues considered. Titles were categorized as current online (comes with a print subscription or can be purchased as an electronic subscription), free (complete issues online for at least one year), selected free (some issues or articles are available for free), and not online (they could not locate an electronic version or publisher stated it was available in print only).

The results showed 39% of the core business titles were not online, 32% were current online, 22% were free, and 7% were selected free. The social sciences had 34% that were not online, 56% were current online, 3% were free, and 6% were selected free. Sciences revealed 71% were current online, 5% were free, 9% were selected free, and only 15% were not online.

However, a look at the subgroups revealed that generalizations do not apply. Examining the three areas of business comprising a large percentage of the material available, they found that while trade/industry had no titles available by online paid subscription, 45% were free online, 30% had selected articles free online, and only 25% of the titles were not available online. Finance had 22% available by paid subscription, 27% were free online, 5% were selected free, and 46% were not online. The percentage of management titles not online was even higher, 48%; 36% were available by paid subscription, 12% were free online and 5% had selected free articles.

In the science subgroups, physics was chosen because Henebry had heard that this discipline took rapidly to online materials. In fact, all the material was available online: 94% by paid subscription and 6% were selected free. Biology had 77% available by paid subscription, 3% were free, and 21% were not online. Computer science had 84% by paid subscription, 8% were selected free, and 8% were not online.

In the social sciences, criminology was selected as being both research- and practitioner-oriented. Forty percent were available by paid subscription and 20% were available for free, but an additional 40% of the titles were not online. In the area of sociology, 65% were available by subscription while the remaining 45% were not available online. The third subgroup selected, political science, had 57% available by subscription, 5% were free, and 38% were not online. Some of the publishers' Web sites were good and some were bad; the free sites tended to be of lower quality. An audience member indicated librarians at her institution wanted to purchase 300 titles owned by libraries in their consortium but could not find them all online.

ARCHIVAL ISSUES

Availability of online archives is important. Safley and Henebry found 48% of their core titles were not archived. The publishers archived 43% of the titles, 7% were archived by the publisher and JSTOR, and 2% were archived by JSTOR alone. Most of the materials archived by the publisher were available for purchase. For the titles in their study, the presence and depth of archives varied significantly by discipline: sciences provided archives 3/4 of the time, social science about 2/3 of the time, but business only 1/3 of the time. For example, the trade and industry titles have no back files; all are published currently and for free. Finance had 21% archived by the publisher, 2% by JSTOR and 76% not archived. Management rose to 34% publisher archived, 7% in JSTOR, and the remaining 59% not archived. The sciences tend to have back files available for a fee from the publisher: 77% in biology, 84% in computer science, and 94% in physics. JSTOR contained 5% of the core biology titles while 18% had no archive. No online archive was available for 6% of the physics and 16% of the computer science titles. The presenters concluded that pragmatic disciplines such as criminology and trade/industry are less likely to be archived than titles from scholarly disciplines. They found that science titles have the greatest depth and breadth of archives: 12 years on the average. Surprisingly, they found less depth and breadth for social sciences than for business.

The 255 selected core titles with archives on the publishers' sites had a total of 1,806 years of text an average 7.1 years per title. This could be refined to an average of 5 years per business title, 12 years per science title, and 3.7 years per social science title.

AGGREGATED DATABASES AND CORE TITLES

Safley and Henebry identified several aggravations in dealing with aggregators. First, content is not stable–titles are added and removed monthly. Adding information, including holdings, into OPACs is frustrating. Furthermore, one cannot rely on the content being available in perpetuity, and quality varies–digitized versions of articles are not equal. However, undergraduates like the aggregators and tend to go there first when writing a paper.

The presenters found a large number of business titles in aggregators. Almost 80% of their core business titles were available in Dow Jones, nearly 70% in the EBSCO databases, over 60% in InfoTrac and between 50% and 60% in ProQuest. When asked by an audience member whether they had determined if titles in Dow Jones were full text or only selected full text, Safley and Henebry indicated that they had not; nor had they done so for Lexis-Nexis Academic Universe.

Not as many core social sciences titles appeared in aggregators: 50% were in EBSCO, between 40% and 50% were in OCLC ECO and InfoTrac, between 30% and 40% were in ProQuest, and close to 20% were in JSTOR. Science titles appeared even less frequently: between 20% and 30% in InfoTrac, just over 20% in EBSCO and OCLC ECO, and just under 10% in JSTOR. Very little physics material is found in aggregators because it is available from the publishers. A large number of political science titles are found in aggregators. Slides portraying the various percentages were displayed utilizing various scales; they are available on Safley's Web site. In choosing among the databases available at UTD, InfoTrac or ProQuest appeared to be good databases for general full-text articles and EBSCO or Dow Jones seemed a good choice for business articles. However, for the social sciences and sciences, aggregators do not provide the depth of coverage needed by many libraries; purchasing directly from the publisher would be the better option

When asked why Wilson Online indexes were not included, they replied that they did not have access to them. However, the Wilson print indexes were used in selecting the core titles. An audience member asked if they had considered dropping one of their current aggregated databases in favor of the Wilson online indexes; they indicated that this was being considered.

Safley and Henebry felt that before selecting an aggregator, librarians should answer three key questions concerning what their library needs in a database: a source of indexing with some content, a source of content for a range of subjects, or quick resource to provide general coverage across disciplines, or some combination thereof?

Safley and Henebry were asked if they felt that aggregated databases include a lot of non-useful material. They replied that poor quality articles appeared more often in the humanities. Audience members wanted to know if they felt aggregators could be pressured to include what librarians want. Safley and Henebry felt that librarians are often too busy trying to determine what they have access to already. Usage statistics indicate that the titles being used are often ones that would not have been selected as core but that people are using; this is often a surprise to the librarians. This use could be driven by convenience or cost, i.e., free printing. The audience responded that there is no way to tell how such printed articles are actually used. The presenters noted that the top twelve titles used in their databases were never available in their library nor were they at the top of their interlibrary loan list. They noted that linking lead patrons to titles not previously utilized.

PURCHASING ARTICLES

Suppliers have created a number ways of buying individual articles: by the download, by time period (e.g., the hour, day, week, or month), a subscription to a set for a period, online or mailed, and/or rushed or normal delivery. Some examples of current article suppliers include Ingenta/Catchword, Infotrieve, High Wire Press, INFOSOURCE database, and individual publishers such as ACS.

Within their core titles, the presenters found only 26% had articles available for purchase. Examining the three chosen disciplines revealed only 10% of the business titles were available for purchase by the article while 30% of the science and 33% of the social sciences titles had articles available for purchase. The average cost of a business article was $17.07, social sciences articles averaged $17.74, and science averaged $22.02. Document providers will continue to exist as long as people are willing to buy articles. Faculty can often pay for article purchases with grant money.

CONCLUSIONS

Safley and Henebry summarized by reminding participants that however you define core, some of the desired content will not be available electronically. Forty-one (8%) of their core titles were not available online. Furthermore, to get core titles, you need to subscribe to a combination of direct subscriptions and aggregated databases. They cautioned that back files are growing but without depth, that availability varies by discipline, and that libraries will have lots of duplication in aggregated databases. Finally, they warned "buyer beware"–aggregators are both saviors and demons or both at the same time

CONTRIBUTORS' NOTES

Ellen Safley is Associate Library Director for Public Services and Collection Development, University of Texas at Dallas Library. Carolyn Henebry is Associate Library Director for Administration, University of Texas at Dallas Library. Elizabeth Parang is Serials/Electronic Resources Librarian, Pepperdine University.

We Have Met the Enemy, and, Sometimes, He Is Us!

Nancy Chaffin

Workshop Leader

Kate Manuel

Recorder

SUMMARY. In dealing with the "serials crisis" over the years, librarians have often called upon faculty authors and editors in other disciplines to be more "responsible" in their publishing behaviors by, for example, not working with journals that routinely engage in sizable increases in subscription prices. The issuance of *Declaring Independence: A Guide to Creating Community Controlled Science Journals* by the Scholarly Publishing and Academic Resources Coalition (SPARC) and the Triangle Research Libraries Network (TRLN) in 2001 provided Chaffin with a framework for comparison of journals in library and information science with those in other disciplines more commonly cited as culprits in producing the "serials crisis." Comparisons of three years of data on annual subscription prices in journals, copyright policies, and use of alternate publishing models for library and information science, physics, and sociology revealed no significant differences in journals by

[Haworth co-indexing entry note]: "We Have Met the Enemy, and, Sometimes, He Is Us!" Manuel, Kate. Co-published simultaneously in *The Serials Librarian* (The Haworth Information Press, an imprint of The Haworth Press, Inc.) Vol. 44, No. 3/4, 2003, pp. 311-316; and: *Transforming Serials: The Revolution Continues* (ed: Susan L. Scheiberg, and Shelley Neville) The Haworth Information Press, an imprint of The Haworth Press, Inc., 2003, pp. 311-316. Single or multiple copies of this article are available for a fee from The Haworth Document Delivery Service [1-800-HAWORTH, 9:00 a.m. - 5:00 p.m. (EST). E-mail address: docdelivery@haworthpress.com].

http://www.haworthpress.com/store/product.asp?sku=J123
10.1300/J123v44n34_41

disciplinary fields. The finding that librarians and information scientists behaved no better than those in field commonly cited for behaving "irresponsibly" prompted both the title of this workshop–inspired by Walt Kelley's Pogo comic strip–and much stimulating discussion within it. *[Article copies available for a fee from The Haworth Document Delivery Service: 1-800-HAWORTH. E-mail address: <docdelivery@haworthpress.com> Website: <http://www.HaworthPress.com>]*

In "We Have Met the Enemy, and Sometimes, He Is Us!" Nancy Chaffin, Metadata Librarian at Colorado State University, discussed the findings of a study on the degree to which journals in library and information science, physics, and sociology comply with the guidelines for price increases, copyright assignment, and exploration of alternative publication options formulated by the Scholarly Publishing & Academic Resources Coalition (SPARC) and the Triangle Research Libraries Network (TRLN) in *Declaring Independence: A Guide to Creating Community Controlled Science Journals.*[1]

Declaring Independence attempts to address problems regarding journal publications, especially the hefty increases in annual subscription prices that in the early 1990s came to be known as the "serials crisis." These problems antedate the 1990s, though; as Chaffin noted, "For years, for my entire career, libraries have been discussing the problems surrounding serials." They include more than increases in annual subscription costs, which have been hovering at around 10 percent per year for journals in all subject areas. Copyright assignment has also been a problem: "University professors have regularly been giving away copyrights to publishers for materials that publishers add value to and then sell back to the university," said Chaffin. Production time has been another problem area; "traditional publication times," with six months or more between acceptance of an article and its appearance in print, "are no longer acceptable," as researchers in many fields "need to read and access information sooner," Chaffin suggested.

Libraries have attempted to deal with these problems by subscription cancellations, as well as by reliance upon e-journals and upon consortial purchase agreements. Subscription cancellations "have worked in terms of keeping the library within its budget, but they erode the income stream for publishers, causing further price increases–a vicious cycle," Chaffin said. E-journals are often purchased under consortial agreements, which themselves impact publishers' revenue streams, are subject to various pricing models, and tend to come bundled with print.

Chaffin noted that this bundling of print with electronic access results in "two formats for the price of two formats" and questioned "how often do we need to buy the same content?" All of these solutions, moreover, are "still resulting in user dissatisfaction," with faculty in particular being vocally resistant to changes and fiercely loyal to specific journal titles.

It is within this context of problems and attempted solutions that SPARC and TRLN produced *Declaring Independence*, a publication specifically addressed to the editors of science, technology, and medicine (STM) journals with the goal of "making journals 'behave better.'" *Declaring Independence* asks editors of STM journals to think in three "stages" about their journals. Stage one is diagnostic, with editors looking at the pricing of their journals (is the journal fairly priced? Is the pricing consistent with the journal's use and impact?), the circulation and renewal statistics for the journal (has circulation been rising or falling? Does the price reflect a marked decrease in renewals?), the production process (how long does it take to publish an article, and at how much cost? Could the publication process be made more efficient with the savings passed on to subscribers?), and the publisher's performance (are the editors satisfied with what the publishers are doing with the journal?). In stage two, the editors are encouraged to explore alternative options to their current publishing arrangements, such as moving their journal to a university press instead of a commercial publisher, publishing in conjunction with scientific societies, utilizing academic digital initiatives, partnering with government projects, or using departmental hosting of e-journals or other electronic content. Editors can look to the work of MIT Press, Project Muse, University of Chicago Press Online, the International Consortium for Alternative Academic Publishers, Project Euclid, Columbia Earthscape, the National Research Council, CISTI, and ArXiv for models. In stage three, editors are to evaluate their options realistically. As Chaffin noted, "Sometimes editors really don't have a lot of options; some editors have nothing to say about the business side of the journal." Before making changes in a journal's publication arrangement, editors should consider the following questions:

- Are all the basic components of the journal in place?
- Is there a loyal subscriber base?
- Can alternative business models (author fees for putting content on the Web, dispensing with an annual subscription) work for the journal?
- Is the journal being marketed and sold to consortia?
- Where, and how, is the journal being indexed?

Chaffin's study was inspired by *Declaring Independence*, for "after looking at the document, [she] wondered how our own literature stacked up" to the criteria for "responsible" journal publishing. "All I ever see is the nasty stuff, and my perception was that the library science stuff was pretty nasty," said Chaffin. Using the annual U.S. Periodical Price Index,[2] Chaffin identified between 128-130 library and information science journals, 91-94 physics journals, and 33 sociology journals whose pricing history over the past three years and whose generic copyright agreements were explored along with the existence of alternative models for journal publication in these fields. The U.S. Periodical Price Index was used to identify the titles studied because U.S. imprints were desired and because the U.S. Periodical Price Index provides consistent title information and other data. Over the three years of the U.S. Periodical Price Index consulted, the number of journal titles listed for two of these disciplines changed, prompting the range of titles mentioned above.

Library and information science journals went from an average cost of $119.69 in 2000 to an average cost of $143.00 in 2002. Physics journals went from $1,507.00 to $1,770.00 in the same time period, while sociology journals went from $246.00 to $297.00. Overall, Chaffin reported, "there was not one decrease in average price of journals for these disciplines." As to the percent of price increase from 2000 to 2001 and from 2001 to 2002, library and information science journals increased by 6% and 9%, respectively, while physics journals increased by 9% both years and sociology journals by 10% both years. For 2001-2002, library and information science journals subscription prices increased at the same rate as physics and sociology journals.

Standard copyright agreement forms for these journals either were obtained from the journal or publisher's Web site or were requested from the publisher. An important caveat, though, is that many authors will negotiate their copyright agreements with the publisher. Chaffin made any necessary interpretations of the generic copyright agreement's terms. These agreements were examined to see whether they assigned all rights to the publisher, split rights between the publisher and the author, or assigned all rights to the author. Fifty-eight percent of library and information science journals, 60 percent of physics journals, and 62 percent of sociology journals assigned all rights to the publisher. Thirty-eight percent of library and information science journals, 40 percent of physics journals, and 36 percent of sociology journals distributed some rights to both publishers and authors. Two percent of library and information science journals, 0 percent of physics journals, and 2 percent of sociology journals assigned all rights to the author. Chaffin emphasized that the sample included far fewer publishers than there were journal titles, as one publisher may have been responsible for many individual journal titles, and thus its copyright agreement conditions would be over-represented in these findings.

The presence of alternatives to "traditional" journal publications proved "very hard to assess," Chaffin said. Free, peer-reviewed Web journals existed in all disciplines, as did low cost subscriptions. Pre-print services, though, only existed in physics, but they may be the only discipline in need of such services. While alternatives were "not as prevalent in all kinds across the disciplines, it does look like scholars are looking for alternatives" to "traditional" journal publications in all areas. Alternative publications are not without their own costs, though, which are variously met by subscriptions, author-subsidized publication, institutions, governments, or societies.

Overall, while Chaffin had "expected us to be terrible about living in a glass house and throwing stones," she "basically found no significant differences" in journal publication patterns among these three disciplines. Library and information science journals are "behaving no better and no worse than those in other disciplines," she concluded.

Throughout her presentation, Chaffin emphasized that hers was not a "fully fleshed out study" and that part of her purpose in presenting it was to get advice on how to make the study more useful to librarians and information scientists. The discussion portions of the workshop thus centered on future directions in which this line of research could be taken. Exploration of price per page, price per article, or price per issue instead of simply subscription price was one suggestion, as journals that are adding thousands of pages to their annual publication output could be expected to have higher increases in annual subscription prices than journals publishing the same number of pages. Another similar suggestion was looking at price per impact using the Institute for Scientific Information (ISI) *Journal Citation Reports*. As the U.S. Periodical Price Index lists peer-reviewed journals along with newsletters, it was suggested that the sample be limited to only peer-reviewed publications. One audience member wondered how the data thus gathered could be used strategically to identify high price journals for subscription cuts. The need to deal with e-journal pricing in some way in the future was also mentioned: Pricing information on e-journals is currently hard to include in such studies because it is so license-driven, and yet electronic formats are becoming predominant. Some method of studying e-journals' pricing needs to be identified. Judging by the audience's comments, they found this a productive line of research, and one that can be profitably continued into the future.

NOTES

1. Scholarly Publishing and Academic Resources Consortium. (2001). *Declaring independence: A guide to creating community controlled science journals.* Available at http://www.arl.org/sparc/DI/Declaring_Independence.pdf.

2. Data from these annual U.S. Periodical Price Indices can be found each April in *American Libraries.* The data were gathered by a survey conducted by the ALA/ ALCTS Library Materials Price Index Committee working in conjunction with divine/ Faxon Library Services.

CONTRIBUTORS' NOTES

Nancy Chaffin is Metadata Librarian at Colorado State University. Kate Manuel is Instruction Coordinator at New Mexico State University.

Electronic Journals
and Aggregated Databases:
New Roles for Public Service Librarians

Jeanie M. Welch
Melissa Holmberg

Workshop Leaders

Pamela Cipkowski

Recorder

SUMMARY. Electronic journals and aggregated databases affect the roles and tasks of public service librarians in several ways. Jeanie Welch and Melissa Holmberg discuss significantly different roles they have acquired as a result of their libraries' electronic journals and aggregated databases. Welch elaborates on her changing roles in collection development as she evaluates serial collections in a mixed print and electronic environment, decides which print serials titles to cancel when duplicated by full-text electronic access, and negotiates new print serials when electronic access is not available. Holmberg describes her new role of partnering with Instructional Technology to educate teaching faculty about full-text

[Haworth co-indexing entry note]: "Electronic Journals and Aggregated Databases: New Roles for Public Service Librarians." Cipkowski, Pamela. Co-published simultaneously in *The Serials Librarian* (The Haworth Information Press, an imprint of The Haworth Press, Inc.) Vol. 44, No. 3/4, 2003, pp. 317-323; and: *Transforming Serials: The Revolution Continues* (ed: Susan L. Scheiberg, and Shelley Neville) The Haworth Information Press, an imprint of The Haworth Press, Inc., 2003, pp. 317-323. Single or multiple copies of this article are available for a fee from The Haworth Document Delivery Service [1-800-HAWORTH, 9:00 a.m. - 5:00 p.m. (EST). E-mail address: docdelivery@haworthpress.com].

http://www.haworthpress.com/store/product.asp?sku=J123
10.1300/J123v44n34_42

electronic resources that legally and technologically can be incorporated into online course materials. *[Article copies available for a fee from The Haworth Document Delivery Service: 1-800-HAWORTH. E-mail address: <docdelivery@haworthpress.com> Website: <http://www.HaworthPress.com>]*

HEY! WHAT ABOUT US?
TRANSFORMED ROLES OF SUBJECT SPECIALISTS
AND REFERENCE LIBRARIANS
IN THE AGE OF ELECTRONIC RESOURCES

Jeanie Welch began her part of the presentation by explaining that the topic germinated from a discussion group at ALA in which reference librarians expressed a concern that they were feeling left behind in the process of serials management. The selector role of subject specialists and reference librarians in terms of the acquisition of serials and indexes essentially has been transformed by electronic access. Despite the changes electronic access has brought, these librarians can still make important collection management decisions and can still be part of the decision-making process.

The traditional role of subject specialists has included the recommendation of new print serial titles, indexes, and abstracts based on traditional criteria. This includes relevance of the subject material, quality of the material and of the respective publishers, the relationship of a new title to the existing collection and whether it possibly fills a hole or need in the collection, use of the title, and projected costs. Recently, this process has also come to include the recommendation of new electronic resources. Reference and public service librarians evaluate an electronic resource's ease of use as well as the resource's compatibility with the library's electronic environment, determining whether the resource will load easily, and whether it will have any potential networking problems or issues.

The advent of electronic serials has brought about several changes and challenges for reference librarians in evaluating these materials. Traditional methods of serial collection evaluation have included usage studies, such as reshelving counts, examining interlibrary loan requests to determine if an inordinate number of requests means acquiring the title for the library's own collection, and citation analysis, including monitoring *Journal Citation Reports* and coverage in indexes and abstracts.

Because of these changes in collection development due to electronic resources, it can be argued that the subject specialist's role has been diminished, with collection management now out of the subject specialist's hands. Factors that have contributed to this include demands of technology, including networking considerations; licensing negotiations, where the number of simultaneous users is one of many points to consider; aggregator databases, with decisions on full access to titles made by the publishers and vendors; and by consortia agreements where decisions on databases are made outside individual libraries. These days, the subject specialist may be far removed from all this.

The subject specialist's responsibilities, however, can be seen as evolving rather than diminishing. The subject specialist's role is still very much needed, as they need to balance declining budgets with the evaluation of materials under a set of criteria that grows increasingly complex as electronic resources are thrown into the mix. Nowadays, subject specialists' responsibilities include evaluating serials collections to determine strengths and weaknesses in a mixed print and electronic environment, making cancellation decisions for print serials (based on full-text electronic access as one of the criteria), and adding new print subscriptions for titles not available in full-text electronic format.

Because of the addition of electronic resources to the mix, serials collection management in a mixed print/electronic environment requires a different approach. Welch offered a list of suggested steps to follow in this mixed environment: Use a standard list of core titles, develop a spreadsheet or database with access to these titles (stating whether the title is available in print, electronic, or both), develop a list of print titles (duplicated by electronic access) for consideration for cancellation, consult with faculty and other librarians (since some journals are interdisciplinary) on possible cancellations, cancel titles and determine savings, develop a wish list of new print titles to add, and finally, add and recommend new print titles.

CASE STUDY: REVIEWING A PERIODICAL COLLECTION

Welch followed with a case study following the collection development process and decisions made at her workplace, the University of North Carolina-Charlotte, first providing some background information on the institution. UNC Charlotte is a Doctoral II institution of 18,000 students that became a university in 1965. The university includes the Belk College of Business Administration, which offers both undergraduate and MBA degrees and is accredited by the AACSB-I (Association to Advance Collegiate Schools of Business-International). UNC Charlotte has a centralized library, with all electronic journals fully cataloged in the OPAC. Electronic databases at the library include NC LIVE, EbscoHOST, Infotrac, ABI/INFORM, and Academic Universe.

A review of the print periodicals collection was conducted. The College of Business was coming up for reaccreditation, and a review of the library's business periodicals would be done for the AACSB-I self-study. Welch began her review by checking the business monograph holdings against the Harvard University Baker Library list of core titles and by the *Business Periodicals Index* title list for business periodical holdings. She then created a spreadsheet of electronic holdings that included elements such as whether there was a print subscription to the title as well, the aggregator or vendor providing the electronic full-text access, the years for which full-text electronic access was available, and the cost. A list of print titles for possible cancellation was then created. So-called "browsing" titles were eliminated, and titles that appeared in at least two full-text databases were on the cancellation list as well. The list was circulated to business faculty and other librarians for review and feedback. Duplicated titles were eventually cancelled, and new titles from the faculty "wish list" were considered–a process sometimes difficult to negotiate and rationalize.

The "wish list" of titles proved to be a challenging step. Advice Welch offered included sticking to a set dollar amount, checking faculty wish list titles for electronic full-text access, weighing faculty and students' needs (e.g., faculty research vs. student research), and trying to reach compromises.

While the system proved effective for Welch's situation, she warned of potential pitfalls, including the limitations of using core lists which include local considerations and interests; time constraints in creating lengthy, involved spreadsheets, with some databases easier to check than others; vendors and publishers "pulling the plug" on electronic access and/or restricting access to archives; "time-delayed" access, including embargoes and moving walls; and conflicting interests, such as faculty vs. student research and needs.

Welch stated, however, that the lengthy, involved process was necessary, as economic realities have forced them to take this route. These economic realities, coupled with the growing number of electronic resources used in libraries, reaffirm that the role of the reference librarian and subject specialist is rapidly changing.

EFFECT OF E-RESOURCES
ON PUBLIC SERVICE LIBRARIANS' ROLES

Melissa Holmberg continued the workshop, detailing the new roles she has taken on in the public services area. Holmberg began with a background on her institution of Minnesota State University, Mankato, which offers more than 120 undergraduate degrees and more than 70 graduate degrees. The university has almost 800 teaching faculty. Eighteen librarians are employed, and the library's holdings consist of 1.2 million volumes, 3,200 print subscriptions, and 14,000+ electronic serials (according to information obtained from SerialsSolutions) in more than 100 electronic resources.

Holmberg's main role as electronic resources librarian, according to her position description, is to "provide leadership in developing and integrating electronic resources into the library's reference and instruction programs." This involves taking on several multi-faceted roles that are fairly new to public services librarianship. Her responsibilities include monitoring multiple electronic lists for new developments and current issues, sharing information with librarians about content and interface changes of electronic resources through e-mails and semi-monthly informational sessions, and serving as the primary contact person with vendors. Holmberg also promotes new resources and trials on the library's Web site and through campus and departmental announcements.

In addition, her position involves collecting and utilizing usage statistics. This is especially important, Holmberg explained, as the campus and state face budget cuts in the next year. Use statistics also help highlight and substantiate points of discussion in meetings. For example, when usage statistics showed that per-search use of FirstSearch resources skyrocketed at Mankato, staff had to discuss if access should be removed for some resources and where funding would come from to continue access.

Holmberg also tracks license agreements as part of her position. This was originally not part of her job, but as responsibilities associated with electronic resources evolved, it soon became one of her duties. Most licenses at Mankato do not need to be negotiated, although Holmberg does go through the licensing agreements to check parameters and determine what the limitations are. She also informs interlibrary loan, instruction, and reference what effect licensing restrictions will have in their departments.

PARTNERSHIP WITH INSTRUCTIONAL TECHNOLOGY

One of Holmberg's major initiatives has been to partner with Instructional Technology on campus to provide a series of faculty workshops highlighting the library's resources. The initial partnership involved distributing paper and electronic campus announcements, resulting in six workshops–two in the spring, one in summer, and three in the fall– which 39 participants attended.

Holmberg distributed a handout, *Bringing Online Journal Resources into the Classroom,* used at the workshop sessions. The workshop/ handout discusses legal and technological issues and options for authenticating users and linking to sources. It also demonstrates some of the differences among electronic resources, describing which resources have stable content, indicating which resources allow faculty to link to search results, and explaining that content can change anytime. The workshop also offers the opportunity to practice searching for articles and linking to articles from course Web sites and online course software.

Benefits of these workshops, explained Holmberg, have been great, giving librarians the opportunity to educate faculty about the library's resources. Faculty have gained knowledge about copyright, license agreements, and leased content. There has been better utilization of library resources for curricula, classroom exercises, and assignments. The workshops have generated a good deal of interaction and questions between faculty and librarians.

Overall, better relationships have been fostered between the library, instructional technology, and teaching faculty as a result of the workshops. The library hasn't formally asked for feedback or evaluations, but a good deal of individual feedback has been given. More instruction requests for classes have also resulted from faculty members attending the workshops. Faculty attending the workshops have frequently contacted Holmberg with other questions about the library. Through this new role in the public services sphere, Holmberg has succeeded in increasing usage of the library's electronic resources by getting the word out about the new technology and educating faculty about it.

WORKSHOP QUESTIONS

Several questions from workshop attendees following Welch and Holmberg's presentations focused on the changing roles and extra duties taken on by both librarians. Welch was asked if her institution was going to expand on her periodicals study, and if she would recommend to others to look at cancellations in a similar process. Welch admitted that the project was quite tedious, and if others were to undertake something similar, she stressed that they must understand that they would be the ones accountable for the integrity of the information. You have to rely on yourself, Welch said, especially in UNC-Charlotte's case, where they needed to put themselves in the best possible light in regards to their reaccreditation process. You can't always accept the vendor's word as to whether the material they include is truly full-text; it is important that you check for yourself for any errors or discrepancies.

Holmberg was asked if she envisioned her "split job" eventually leaning more toward working full-time in electronic resources, rather than being combined with instructional and other duties. Holmberg would welcome that opportunity, but felt it would be unlikely. She also mentioned that because of her expanded duties, she has been working with others, including a student and a graduate assistant, to help with various projects such as creating and maintaining a database of use statistics and compiling a chart of steps and rules to follow when examining licensing agreements.

From both librarians' experiences, it is clear that the role of reference and public services librarians and subject specialists is changing and will constantly be evolving as electronic resources become a greater part of libraries' collections.

CONTRIBUTORS' NOTES

Jeanie M. Welch is Professor and Reference Librarian at the University of North Carolina, Charlotte. Melissa Holmberg is Electronic Resources/Science Librarian at Minnesota State University, Mankato. Pamela Cipkowski is Serials Cataloger at University of Wisconsin, Milwaukee.

The Battle of the Dumpster
and Other Stories:
Processing the Censorship

Stephanie Schmitt

Workshop Leader

Lee Krieger

Recorder

SUMMARY. This workshop offered a chance to discuss a subject not often addressed in the library community–incidents of censorship by library employees. Personal experiences of incidents were discussed and shared by the presenter, Stephanie Schmitt of Yale Law Library, and by the audience. Ms. Schmitt recommended methods to avoid problems that result from staff objections to library material's content. She suggested ways to develop policies that support intellectual freedom and also serve to educate staff and administration as well. *[Article copies available for a fee from The Haworth Document Delivery Service: 1-800-HAWORTH. E-mail address: <docdelivery@haworthpress.com> Website: <http://www.HaworthPress.com>]*

[Haworth co-indexing entry note]: "The Battle of the Dumpster and Other Stories: Processing the Censorship." Krieger, Lee. Co-published simultaneously in *The Serials Librarian* (The Haworth Information Press, an imprint of The Haworth Press, Inc.) Vol. 44, No. 3/4, 2003, pp. 325-329; and: *Transforming Serials: The Revolution Continues* (ed: Susan L. Scheiberg, and Shelley Neville) The Haworth Information Press, an imprint of The Haworth Press, Inc., 2003, pp. 325-329. Single or multiple copies of this article are available for a fee from The Haworth Document Delivery Service [1-800-HAWORTH, 9:00 a.m. - 5:00 p.m. (EST). E-mail address: docdelivery@haworthpress.com].

http://www.haworthpress.com/store/product.asp?sku=J123
10.1300/J123v44n34_43

BACKGROUND FOR THE DISCUSSION

The genesis for this discussion was rooted in the personal experiences of the presenter and the behaviors of staff and colleagues in dealing with library materials that are morally, religiously, or politically controversial. Slides of examples which have raised censorship issues were displayed: *Turner Diaries* by Andrew Macdonald, Ku Klux Klan pamphlets, *Anarchist Cookbook, Playboy*, photography books by Robert Mapplethorpe, *Sex* by Madonna, videocassettes of *Tin Drum* and *Taxi zum Klo*. Ms. Schmitt stated that censorship exists in libraries, that it is present in all areas of a library, and it may be carried out by anyone. However, for the purpose of this discussion, the scope and focus is on technical services staff and management behavior. Censorship may occur at any stage of acquisitions, from materials selection to materials processing.

CENSORSHIP IN LIBRARIES

Ms. Schmitt proceeded to give examples of methods and types of censorship in the acquiring and processing of library materials. In Acquisitions, censorship can occur when an order is neglected by staff and not sent, or when processing notes are added that restrict or specify special handling, location or security. In the receipt of materials, processing can be neglected, material discarded or stolen, or in the case of approval books, returned to the vendor without consulting the selector, or simply be refused processing. In Cataloging, Serials Processing, and Serials Binding, the same actions and conditions can be observed to occur, effectively denying access to materials. Sometimes, the backlog of unprocessed materials is given as the excuse for not processing controversial materials. These behaviors all amount to unofficial censorship of library materials.

Some scenarios from the workplace were described to illustrate how library staff and administration carried out these censorship activities. An acquisitions example concerned a faculty member who placed a request for a magazine subscription. Staff considered this magazine difficult to add to the library collection due to the content, and they decided to acquire the magazine in the microfilm format instead of paper. Their decision rendered the material unusable by the faculty member who, in turn, ordered a personal subscription, thus bypassing the services of the library.

A cataloging example was concerned with controversial books covering anarchist and militia interests. These materials were ordered and received by an ARL library acquisitions department. The materials were sent to the cataloging department where they were deemed inappropriate materials for the library. This assessment was shared with higher library administration and the materials were sent to the dumpster.

Finally, an example for serials processing was given which concerned a particular issue received by the library every year as part of a weekly subscription. The clerk was told to do her best to preserve the issue, as it was routinely lost or mutilated. She attempted to "clothe" a few of the main photos with strategically placed security stickers. As censorship and security attempts, this strategy fails and the issue was "lost" after two days.

Not only are technical services departments guilty of this behavior, special collections and archives also indulge in censorship. At another university library, Ku Klux Klan pamphlets, recruitment flyers and other materials received and collected over decades have been left unprocessed because of their content, staff repulsion over their existence, opinion urging that they should be destroyed, and emotional distress complaints. After these examples given by the presenter, a number of audience participants volunteered examples for discussion of similar behavior from their libraries' staff and colleagues.

ROLE OF MANAGEMENT

Library management make certain assumptions about problems resulting from censorship issues raised by library staff. One such assumption is that personal viewpoints affect workplace productivity. Another is that individual opinions may impede the decisions of others. Lastly, they harbor the assumption that some staff members believe it is ethical to censor based on belief or moral viewpoints. However, one of the basic tenets of professional librarians as expressed in the Library Bill of Rights is that a balanced presentation of all viewpoints should be available and that diversity of belief and opinion should be supported by library collections. On the other hand, library management also has a responsibility to provide a work atmosphere that is non-threatening and respects the beliefs of workers and to see that the work continues despite disagreements over the appropriateness of materials.

SOLUTIONS TO THE PROBLEM

The solution is to develop a policy on intellectual freedom and censorship, and then make sure that the policy is consistently applied and enforced library-wide. An understanding of the library management's expectations must be understood library-wide as well. To ensure that the policy is supported, it should be formulated after open discussion and collaborative input from staff, and formal consultation with the institution's Legal Services and Human Resources Departments. Once the policy has been approved, everyone must be notified and policy application and expectations must be clearly communicated.

Management has the obligation to insist on consistent application all across the organization. Supervisors must be accountable for enforcing the policy. However, there should also be time for a period of adjustment while the policy is tested and questions are raised about interpretation of the policy; additionally, a method of contesting or protesting the policy should be developed. Good management practice should encourage the promotion of a non-confrontational work environment and the possibility of using workaround and collaborative solutions to deal with feelings of discomfort staff may have with certain materials. Management should also allow open debate about the suitability of materials and be able to defend and justify selections.

Although librarians have the responsibility to promote intellectual freedom and diversity, management also has legal responsibilities to prevent and punish harassment and to protect workers from harm. Library management must also be aware that some workers are legally minors and must be protected according to laws governing what is acceptable for minors. These factors must be included in formulating policy and solutions to conflict about library materials' content.

It is up to those with administrative responsibility to establish a policy, implement methods for discussion and encourage debate. This issue is an opportunity to educate and be educated about intellectual freedom. It should also be part of the hiring and orientation process for new employees.

Once policy has been established, and channels for staff to voice their objections have been provided and alternative workflows for processing have been implemented, the task is not finished. Management must remember to keep the appropriate groups and personnel at the institution aware of all situations as they occur. Library management needs to maintain connections and awareness of related issues in the legal and human resources departments. As situations and legal opinions change, the library must be prepared to update policy as needed.

CONCLUSION

The workshop was concluded with a question and answer session, although the audience offered questions and observations during the course of the presentation as well. One of the more important points of contention discussed was how much effort management needs to put into providing a work-around solution for staff. The disciplinary action that should be taken against staff that prevent access to materials through neglect, theft or deliberate destruction was discussed, as well as whether management has the right to demand performance of processing duties despite objections. Should new hires on probation be provided the same right to object to handling materials as long-term employees?

Discussion was quite lively at times and several people commented on how disappointing it was that there was such a small turnout for a topic that obviously was of concern. There was some discussion about why turn out was low (approximately 15). Was it because technical services librarians feel that there is no widespread problem of staff sabotaging access to materials, or was it perhaps because the program description seemed incomplete or misleading? The workshop may have lost attendees because of its location in a small room next to the facilities' offices in the entry hallway. In conclusion, however, the topic generated lively discussion, indicating there was possibly a need for a more thorough exploration of the topic.

CONTRIBUTORS' NOTES

Stephanie Schmitt is Manager, Serials Services, Yale University Law School. Mr. Lee A. Krieger is Head of Acquisitions, Otto G. Richter Library, University of Miami.

Poster Sessions

Accessible and Meaningful Serials Reports for Bibliographers

E. Gaele Gillespie

University of Kansas

The current role of the bibliographer as defined at KU Libraries includes a complex decision-making process for acquisition and retention of serials, including the identification of prospective cancellations. Therefore, it is increasingly important to provide serials data in more meaningful and easily accessible ways. By extracting bibliographic and financial information from Voyager and employing MS Access, we have developed online subject fund reports that provide three fiscal years of subscription price information and calculate the percent spent from the serials allocation. Using macros, these reports can be updated frequently and are available via hot link from the Libraries' Intranet site. We are now adding *current* publisher information to the report design. This will help bibliographers more easily identify titles that are available as individual e-journals or as part of an aggregator database. The reports are arranged behind tabs by subject name for quick identification and access. There are also tabs for broad disciplines, so a report may appear behind several tabs. This provides an easy way for bibliographers to see titles and financials on other subject funds and more easily identify interdisciplinary titles that they need to discuss together. If utilized regularly, creatively, and in the spirit of the current role of bibliographers, these reports can supply valuable information about serials for ongoing evaluation, planning, and collaboration.

[Haworth co-indexing entry note]: "Poster Sessions." Susan L. Scheiberg and Shelley Neville, eds. Co-published simultaneously in *The Serials Librarian* (The Haworth Information Press, an imprint of The Haworth Press, Inc.) Vol. 44, No. 3/4, 2003, pp. 331-338; and: *Transforming Serials: The Revolution Continues* (ed: Susan L. Scheiberg, and Shelley Neville) The Haworth Information Press, an imprint of The Haworth Press, Inc., 2003, pp. 331-338. Single or multiple copies of this article are available for a fee from The Haworth Document Delivery Service [1-800-HAWORTH, 9:00 a.m. - 5:00 p.m. (EST). E-mail address: docdelivery@haworthpress.com].

http://www.haworthpress.com/store/product.asp?sku=J123
10.1300/J123v44n34_44

Are Microfilm Serial Backfiles
Still the Most Cost Effective Alternative?

Kitti Canepi

Florida Gulf Coast University

For the past thirty years, libraries have made serials backfile decisions based on an understanding that microfilm is a more cost effective format than bound print. Yet with the rising cost of microfilm, is this still the case? Space constraints generally force a decision in favor of microfilm, or a combination of microfilm and electronic formats, for serial backfiles. In the wake of issues arising from electronic journals, a re-examination of microfilm costs tends to get put aside. As part of efforts to formulate a serials backfile policy at Florida Gulf Coast University, the Collection Development Team Leader attempted to identify the relative cost effectiveness of microfilm, bound print, and stable electronic formats. The results of that research project are presented in this poster.

Electronic Integrating Resources and Authority Control

Althea Aschmann

Virginia Polytechnic Institute and State University

From selecting a bibliographic record on OCLC or RLIN to selection of access points for one's local catalog, questions arise about what cataloging rules to apply and how much authority control needs to be done. Add vendor-supplied authority control and batch tape-loads to the puzzle, and the picture is further complicated. In addition to discussing these issues, this presentation also addresses the related topics of uniform title usage and choosing appropriate added entries.

Electronic Resource Librarian Web Based Administration Tool

Thomas McLaughlin

Drexel University

Development of a Web Based Electronic Resource Administration Tool (WBERAT) for the Electronic Resource Librarian (ERL) at Hagerty Library is currently being completed. When completed, WBERAT will allow the ERL to administrate the Web content and applications associated with her job description dynamically through the tool. The features of WBERAT include:

- The ability to automatically build pages (Database by Title, Database by Subject, Electronic Journals by Title, Electronic Journals by Subject, Newspapers, and Encyclopedias) after making changes to the content through an interface to the database. Our current *Electronic Resource home page* is available.
- The ability to rebuild the data for our "Combined Print and Electronic Journals Title Search" after making changes to content. The tool is currently available at: http://www.library.drexel.edu/er/searchform.html
- The ability to administer the configuration of our proxy server (EZProxy) remotely and restart the server after configuration changes are finished. This feature is currently in testing and is nearly finished.
- The ability to access Web based reports tracking a record of hits to electronic resources for comparison with vendor statistics. A sample Vendor Count by Month report is available at: http://www.library.drexel.edu/cgi-bin/vreport/vreport1.cgi.
- A Web based parser to load data from vendors into the database model.
- A database for electronic resources in 3rd Normal Form (3NF).

WBERAT's benefits including allowing the ERL to independently administrate dynamic content and resources on Web with little or no programming knowledge; allowing the ERL to resolve Web content issues immediately; allowing the ERL to make required proxy adjustments immediately; and enabling easier replacement of the ERL in case of turnover.

Getting a Handle and Maintaining a Grip: Managing E-Resources at Indiana University, Bloomington

Jo McClamroch and Pam Owens

Indiana University

Out of an $8 million materials budget, $1.2 million (15%) is devoted to electronic resources. Our acquisitions range from inexpensive, single-title electronic journals in the humanities to high-priced, multi-title e-journal aggregators in the sciences. Over the past year, we have developed a framework for managing the complexities and intricacies of e-resource acquisitions. The framework is depicted as a really big Venn diagram of a dozen or so interconnected elements. The data in each of the Venn circles is drawn from a number of sources: our SIRSI/Unicorn system, item information from work forms, and a variety of information collected from EXCEL and ACCESS spreadsheets. This data collection and aggregation has allowed us to get a handle on the numerous elements that need to be tracked. We will eventually be able to maintain a grip on expiry/renewal dates, license particulars, consortia relationships, and much more. Our poster session features an array of the printed data we produce to manage our virtual holdings: samples of forms, standardized letters, and spreadsheets; task flowcharts; and more.

Implementing a Reference Linking Solution

Kevin Petsche

Indiana University Purdue University, Indianapolis

Indiana University Purdue University Indianapolis' (IUPUI) University Library was one of the original beta test sites for Ex Libris' SFX reference linking software as well as one of the first libraries in the nation to go live with its SFX implementation for users. This poster describes the work necessary to bring this powerful linking software into production. The poster illustrates three parts of the process:

- The work involved in configuring the local database, including description of manpower needed and the intimate working relationships between the library and vendors.
- Some of the past and current limitations of the software, such as bibliographic services' being offered when they do not exist.
- Some possible future uses, including collaboration with CrossRef and its DOI application.

Improving User Access to E-Journals at the University of Kansas

Judith Emde and Margaret Wilson

University of Kansas

The University of Kansas Libraries has developed a strategy for improving user access to electronic journals and reducing overall staff effort in the maintenance of the total system. The strategy that the Libraries uses is based on:

- Primary access to e-journals through Voyager database(s) rather than through an in-house database.
- A separate Voyager database of e-journal MARC records which includes licensed e-journals, government document serials, titles in aggregator databases, and holdings information for each provider source of a given e-journal.
- Aggregator data supplied by Serials Solution.
- Inclusion in the main OPAC of all resources in the e-journal catalog, including holdings.
- The serials cataloging single record model.
- The provision of subject access.

The poster session addresses the advantages and disadvantages to the recommended strategy and the other strategies that were considered; describes the creation of the e-journal catalog, which was put into operation in December; and illustrates features of the e-journal catalog.

Journal Finder: Simplifying Access to E-Journals, Print and Document Delivery Options

Beth Bernhardt

University of North Carolina at Greensboro

With the growth of electronic journals over the past few years, libraries have been struggling to provide easy access to journal articles. UNC Greensboro's new journal searching service, *Journal Finder*, provides unmediated access to full-text print and electronic journals and document delivery options. Whether they start in the library catalog or in our Journal Finder interface, or even from a citation in a commercial database (InfoTrac, ProQuest, etc.), patrons can easily see ALL of their options for obtaining the full text of any given article. Journal Finder has a number of advanced features including:

- a sophisticated https database administration module, for use in maintaining data and generating reports

- integration with our OPAC, allowing the library catalog to be used to find all electronic and print journal titles while eliminating the need to populate or maintain the MARC 856 fields for serials in the catalog
- direct links to the journal title level for over 90% of our approximately 12,000 e-titles, including most major aggregators' titles
- the ability to link from a citation in one commercial database to the library catalog or directly to the full text article in another database (just as SFX does, but using locally written scripts).

Plug-Ins and E-Journals:
How Browser Extensions Transform
Electronic Journal Content and Access

Diana Kichuk

University of Saskatchewan

In March 2001, 64 members of the Canadian National Site Licensing Project (CNSLP) added seven primarily STM electronic resources to their Library collections, including five electronic journal collections. The CNSLP package added over 700 electronic titles to the University of Saskatchewan Library collection. The Library went from having one electronic journal collection (Project MUSE) to six licenses. This sudden large acquisition had a significant impact on the Library's technical infrastructure: access, cataloguing, and systems. Public services are overwhelmed by the changes to patron expectations, patterns of library use, instruction, and research. The CNSLP collection introduced a new breed of electronic journal and a complex and intriguing range of content and viewing experiences for Library patrons. Until then, Library patrons were accustomed to a narrow range of formats: ASCII, HTML, image files, a growing number of Acrobat pdf files, and the occasional audio file. The new CNSLP resources introduced a new slate of plug-ins. Pre-CNSLP, scientific content of the journals accessed in the Library included text, tables, and images. CNSLP electronic journals could include a wide range of content that radically transformed the range of opportunity for authors to present their research and for readers to read or interact with that research. The expanded list of plug-ins enable: viewing word-processing files, 3-D images, animations, video clips, virtual reality, and chemical-structure data; listening to audio files; and launching interactive applications. This poster describes the plug-ins associated with the CNSLP journals and details some of the implications for authors and readers.

Reinventing the Wheel:
The Microsoft Access Alternative

Paolina Taglienti and Sandhya Srivastava

Long Island University, Brooklyn Campus

This poster documents our experimentation, from September 1999 through August 2001, with designing and modifying various databases using Microsoft Access 97 and 2000. The Acquisitions staff is responsible not only for ordering, receiving, and invoicing of monographic and audiovisual materials, but also for maintaining all periodicals and standing-order functions including check-in, claiming, renewals and invoicing. Prior to exploration of the possible use of Access in meeting these duties, a manual Kardex file was used for check-in; Microsoft Excel spreadsheets for accounting and statistics; a paper on-order card file for avoiding duplicates and processing notifications; and a paper purchase-order file for invoicing and auditing. The Acquisitions Department began to look at options for automating its functions and eliminating the cumbersome manual system in 1999. We theorized that migrating to a homegrown Acquisitions Module would be preferable to forcing ourselves into an ILS module that could not meet local reporting needs. We also believed that the labor involved in constructing and modifying local databases would be a worthwhile investment and would improve efficiency in the long run.

S-Link S-Holdings:
An XML Format for Distribution of Serials Holdings Information

Eric Hellman

Openly Informatics, Inc.

To the outsider, it seems odd that libraries should be paying people to supply lists of the full-text sources that they pay other people to provide. In a better world, well-conceived standards would allow automatic compilation and re-distribution of such lists from multiple sources and would involve publishers, aggregators, subscription agents, OPAC software and linking engines. This poster proposes a free, open XML format designed for this purpose and describes its use in the serials information architecture of the future. The design of the format recognizes the importance of article linking methods and OpenURL metadata and uses a simple yet flexible approach to the description of availability ranges.

Utilizing Inmagic Software to Enhance Marcive Records Processing

Jian Wang

Portland State University

Inmagic is a database management system designed to organize textual information so that it is easy to search and retrieve. This poster session illustrates the successful adoption of Inmagic software in the Portland State University (PSU) Library as a complementary library system to enhance the processing of Marcive records. PSU Library began to integrate Government Printing Office cataloging records purchased from Marcive, Inc. into the local online catalog in 1997. After the initial retrospective load of 248,323 bibliographic records to the database, the Library has been receiving regularly scheduled loads of new GPO cataloging records, including the weekly shipping lists and monthly full cataloging records via ftp from Marcive. Because of the constraints of the local library system, Inmagic was used to help with processing statistical information and data quality control for Marcive records. The database allows the creation of customized reports and the generation of statistics with ease. It also offers flexibility in processing data. Search commands include basic GET, as well as Boolean and relational searching; search results can be used in conjunction with Word for editing or other types of data manipulation. The choice of Inmagic was based on such factors as cost-effectiveness (free DOS version), unique features of the software, and in-house expertise. PSU Library's experience in using Inmagic to enhance the processing of Marcive records has been successful.

17th Annual NASIG Conference Registrants

Conference Registrants	Organization/Institution
Abbott, John	Appalachian State Univ.
Acosta, Adriana	Elsevier Science
Acreman, Beverley	Taylor & Francis
Acton, Deena	National Library of Medicine
Aiello, Helen	Wesleyan University
Aitchison, Jada	ULAR/Pulaski County Law Library
Alan, Robert	Pennsylvania State University
Albano, Christine	Cleveland Public Library
Alexander, Whitney	Santa Clara University
Allen, Lenny	Nature Publishing
Allman, Miriam	Tufts University
Alvarez, Josefa (Josie)	UTEP Library
Amos, Alcione M.	World Bank
Anderson, Gail	Medical College of Georgia
Anderson, Rick	University of Nevada
Andrews, Susan	Texas A&M University-Commerce
Andrews, Susan	University of B.C. Library
Aschmann, Althea	Virginia Tech University Libraries
Ashman, Allen	University of Louisville
Ashton-Pritting, Randi	University of Hartford
Astle, Deana	East Carolina University
Aufdemberge, Karen	University of Toledo
Austin, Gary	Morehead State University
Ayala, Yesenia	Elsevier Science
Baden, Marla	Indiana University Purdue University Fort Wayne
Badertscher, David	Washington and Lee University
Badics, Joe	Eastern Michigan University
Baia, Wendy	University of Colorado
Bailey, Mary	Kansas State University Libraries
Baker, Carol	University of Calgary
Baker, Gayle	University of Tennessee Library

http://www.haworthpress.com/store/product.asp?sku=J123
10.1300/J123v44n34_45

Baker, Jeanne	University of Maryland
Baker, Mary Ellen	California Polytechnic State University
Baker, Ruth	Community College of Philadelphia
Bakke, Celia	San Jose State University
Ballard, Rochelle	Princeton University
Barnes, Suzanne	EBSCO
Barnett, Molly	Wake Forest University School of Medicine
Barrow, Charlotte	Boeing
Barstow, Sandra	University of Wyoming
Basar, Ivan	National Library of Canada
Basch, Buzzy	Basch Subscriptions, Inc.
Bass, Wilma	University of Maryland, Health Sci. & Human Sci. Library
Bauer, Erin	Creighton University
Bauer, Kathleen	Yale University
Baumeister, Michael	University of Karlsruhe
Bazin, Paul	Providence College
Beckett, Chris	Ingenta
Beehler, Sandra	Lewis & Clark College
Bell, Carole	Temple University
Bellinger, Christina	University of New Hampshire
Belskis, Sandy	Absolute Backorder Service Inc.
Bennett, Marsha	Boston Public Library
Bernards, Dennis	Brigham Young University
Bishop, Christine	Swets Blackwell
Black, Steve	College of Saint Rose
Blackman, Christine	Williams College Libraries
Blackwell, Lisa	Children's Hospital
Blatchley, Jeremy	Bryn Mawr College
Bloss, Alex	University of Illinois, Chicago
Blosser, John	Northwestern University
Bohen, Mary Lou	Parklawn Health Library
Bonner, D. Ellen	Rensselaer Polytechnic Institute
Boone, Cecelia	MINITEX Library Information Network
Bordner, Georgi	Regent University
Born, Kathleen	EBSCO Information Services
Boucher, Amy	Harvard University
Bowersox, Kathlyn	Southern University
Boyd, Morag	Illinois State University
Bracken, Lee	Northeastern University
Brady, Katie	Drexel University

Branch, Denise	Virginia Commonwealth University
Branham, Janie	Sims Memorial Library
Brannon, Kathy	Swets Blackwell
Brass, Evelyn	University of Houston
Breen, Barbara	UTHSC/School of Public Health Library
Brewer, Kevin	Utah State University
Bright, Nancy	University of Tennessee Library
Broadwater, Deborah	Vanderbilt University
Broadway, Rita	University of Memphis
Bross, Valerie	UCLA
Brower, Stewart	Univ. at Buffalo Health Sciences Lib.
Brown, Ladd	Virginia Tech
Brown, Liz	Johns Hopkins University
Brown, Michael	University of Chicago Law Library
Brown, Micheline	Coastal Carolina University
Brubaker, Jana	Northern Illinois University
Buelow, John	Virginia Tech
Bull, Greg	University of St. Thomas
Bullington, Jeff	University of Houston
Burke, David	Villanova University
Burnette, Jane	Carilion Health System
Buttner, Mary	Lane Library, Stanford University
Bynog, David	Rice University
Byrd, Jo	Library of Virginia
Caelleigh, Addeane	Science Publishing Services
Callahan, Patricia	Massachusetts General Hospital
Canepi, Kitti	Florida Gulf Coast University
Caraway, Bea	Trinity University
Carey, Roni	St. Cloud State University
Carter, Kathy	University of Alberta
Casey, Carol	Washington State Univ.
Castle, Mary	University of Texas-Arlington
Castrataro, James	Indiana University
Caudill, Kim	Middletown Public Library
Chaffin, Nancy	Colorado State University
Chamberlain, Clint	Trinity University
Chambers, Paul	Kluwer
Champagne, Thomas	University of Michigan
Chan, Karen	California University of Pennsylvania
Chappell, Mary Ann	James Madison University
Chen, Cecilia	CSU Dominguez Hills

Cheng, Daisy	University of Mississippi
Chesler, Adam	Kluwer Academic Publishers
Cheung, Ada	Hong Kong University of Science & Technology
Chiao, Tsung-Nien Julia	Texas Tech University Libraries
Childs, Miriam	University of New Orleans
Chinoransky, Susan	George Washington University Law Library
Chisholm, Lorrie	University of Virginia
Christensen, John	Brigham Young University
Cipkowski, Pam	University of Wisconsin-Milwaukee
Clark, Bridget	Longwood Library
Clark, Stephen	College of William and Mary
Coates, Carolyn	American Theological Library Association
Cochenour, Donnice	Colorado State University
Coffman, Ila	University of Oklahoma Libraries
Collins, Jill	Boise State University
Collins, Maria	Mississippi State University Libraries
Conger, Joan	University of Georgia
Conger, Mary Jane	University of North Carolina at Greensboro
Congleton, Robert	Rider University
Contreras, Julie	Joint Bank-Fund Library-IMF
Cook, Eleanor	Appalachian State University
Corbett, Lauren	Emory University
Costakos, Chuck	OCLC
Council, Evelyn	Fayetteville State University
Courtney, Keith	Taylor and Francis Ltd.
Cox, Fannie	University of Louisville
Creamer, Marilyn	Haverford College
Creech, Anna	Eastern Kentucky University
Crews, Lucy	Mary Baldwin College
Cross, Neil	Swets Blackwell
Culbertson, Becky	University of California, San Diego
Culota, Wendy	Cal State Univ.
Cunningham, Nancy	Roswell Park Cancer Institute
Danks, Theresa	Elsevier Science
Darling, Karen	University of Missouri-Columbia
Dauria, Erin	Saint Joseph's University
Davis, Eve	EBSCO Information Services

Davis, Renette	University of Chicago
Davis, Susan	University at Buffalo
Day, Nancy	Linda Hall Library
de la Mora Lugo, Paula	
DeBlois, Lillian	Arizona Health Sciences Library
Deeken, JoAnne	University of Tennessee, Knoxville
Degener, Christie	UNC-Chapel Hill Health Sciences
Del Baglivo, Megan	University of Maryland, Baltimore-HS/HSL
DePaul, Tom	
DeVeer, Joseph	MBL/WHOI Library
Diez, George	National Library of Education
Diodato, Louise	Cardinal Stritch University
Diven, Yvette	R. R. Bowker
Dorn, Knut	Harrassowitz
Douglass, Janet	Texas Christian University
Downey, Kay	Cleveland Museum of Art Library
Doyle, Ann	University of Kentucky
Dray, Heather	Solinet
Duhon, Lucy	University of Toledo Libraries
Dumais, Rosemary	United States Naval Academy
Dunn, Christina	U.S. Department of Education
Dygert, Claire	American University
Easton, Christa	Stanford University
Edwards, Jennifer	Massachusetts Institute of Technology
Ellett, Jr., Robert	Joint Forces Staff College
Elliott, Lirlyn	University of the West Indies
Elswick, Rebecca	Mary Washington College
Elwell, Sandy Jelar	Cleveland Public Library
Emery, Jill	University of Houston Libraries
Emser, Ellen	Old Dominion University
England, Deberah	Wright State University
Ericson, L. Christine	University of Alaska-Consortium Library
Erlandson, Rene	University of Illinois Urbana-Champaign
Essency, Janet	Minot State University
Farley, Karen	EBSCO
Farwell, Anne	EBSCO Canada Ltd.
Feick, Tina	Swets Blackwell, Inc.
Feis, Nathaniel	Art Institute
Fenwick, Roni	Arcadia University

Goetz, Steven	Swets Blackwell
Goldberg, Sylvia	University of California, Irvine
Gomes, Debra	Elms College, Alumnae Library
Goodman, David	Princeton University
Gordon, Martin	Franklin and Marshall College
Gormley, Alice	Marquette University Library
Grande, Dolores	John Jay College
Graves, Tonia	Old Dominion University
Green, Carol	University of Southern Mississippi
Greiner, Charles	University of Toronto
Griffin, Linda Smith	Louisiana State University Libraries
Griffin, Lynne	University of Michigan Law Library
Groeschen, Margaret	Xavier University Libraries
Guajardo, Richard	University of Houston
Gurevich, Konstantin	University of Rochester
Gurshman, Sandra	Divine Information Services
Guzi, Gloria	Cleveland Public Library
Haas, Ruth	Harvard University
Hagan, Timothy	Northwestern University
Hahn, Karla	University of Maryland
Haimovsky, Kira	Fordham University Libraries
Halford, Gwendolyn	National Institute of Standards and Technology
Hamilton, Arlene	USAF Academy Library
Hamilton, Fred	Louisiana Tech University
Hamilton, Gloria	University of Chicago
Hanrahan, Kathleen	Cuyahoga County Public Library
Hardy, Ronald Kane	Central College
Harmon, Joseph	IUPUI University Library
Harpster, John	Annual Reviews
Harris, Jay	Lister Hill Library-UAB
Harrison, Dorothy	Library of Virginia
Hart, Eileen	Berea College
Hartz, Viviane	Public Library of Cincinnati & Hamilton County
Harvey, Phyllis	Palmer College
Haug, Mary	USAF Academy Library
Havert, Mandy	University Libraries of Notre Dame
Hawkins, Les	Library of Congress
Hellman, Eric	Openly Informatics
Heminger, Sharon	JSTOR/University of Michigan

Hendren, Carol — CCLA
Henebry, Carolyn — Univ. of Texas at Dallas
Henry, Elizabeth — Mansfield University
Hepfer, Cindy — University at Buffalo
Hess, Alan
Hiatt, Derrik — Brigham Young University
Hickey, Lady Jane — Sam Houston State University
Hill, Thomas — Self Regional Healthcare
Hillery, Leanne — Florida International University Law Library

Hillman, Diane
Hinger, Joseph — St. John's Univ. Law Library
Hirons, Jean — Library of Congress
Holley, Beth — University of Alabama, Tuscaloosa
Hollis, Rachel — Robert Crown Law Library
Hollyfield, Diane — Virginia Commonwealth University
Holmberg, Melissa — Minnesota State Univ., Mankato
Hood, Kate — Guilford College
Hoover, Lona — Mississippi State University
Hopkins, Sandra — Harvard Law School Library
Horn, Maggie — SUNY/OLIS
Houle, Louis — McGill University
Hoyer, Craig — Swets Blackwell, Inc.
Hsiung, Lai-Ying — University of California, Santa Cruz
Hudgins, Donna — Mary Washington College
Hughes, John — Georgia State University
Hughes-Oldenburg Donna K. — Old Dominion University
Hulm, Janet — University of Iowa Libraries
Hutchinson, Robin — St. Lawrence University
Iber, Mary — Cornell College
Innes, Julia — Brookfield Zoo
Irvin, Judy — Louisiana Tech University
Isaacs, Kathryn (Kate) — Library of Virginia
Ives, Gary — Texas A&M University Libraries
Ivins, October — Information Industry Consulting
Jacobs, Mark — Washington State University
Jaeger, Don — Alfred Jaeger Inc.
Jaeger, Glenn — Absolute Backorder Service, Inc.
Jander, Karen — University of Wisconsin-Milwaukee
Jank, David — Dowling College
Janosko, Joann — Indiana University of Pennsylvania

Jascur, Andrea	Univ. of Wis, Milwaukee & Cardinal Stritch Univ.
Jayes, Linda	University of New Hampshire Library
Jiang, Yumin	Health Sciences Library System, University of Pitt
Johnson, Kay	University of Tennessee
Johnston, Judith	University of North Texas Libraries
Jones, Cathy	Sirsi
Jones, Danny	Harrassowitz
Joshipura, Smita	ASU(W)
Julian, Gail	University of South Carolina
Julian, Suzanne	Southern Utah University
Kabelac, Julie	Cornell University
Kaplan, Michael	Ex Libris USA, Inc.
Kawecki, Barbara	EBSCO
Kebede, Yodit	Teachers College, Columbia University
Kebert, Joyce	Grove City College
Kelley, Steve	Ball State University
Kellogg, Betty	National University
Kennedy, Kit	Swets Blackwell
Keogh, Trish	St. Mary's University
Kern, Kristen	Portland State University
Kerr, Susan	Davidson College Library
Keys, JoAnn	George Mason University
Khosh-khui, Sam	Southwest Texas State University
Kichuk, Diana	University of Saskatchewan Library
Kimball, Merle	College of William and Mary
King, Shawn	Maryland General Assembly
Klaessig, Janet	Delaware Valley College
Knapp, Leslie	EBSCO
Knight, Sharon	University of Wisconsin Whitewater
Koehler, Regina	Dumbarton Oaks Research Library
Koller, Rita	Lake Forest College
Kortesoja, Sandra	University of Michigan
Koveleskie, Judith	Seton Hill College
Koveleskie, Robert	
Kraemer, Alfred	Medical College of Wisconsin
Krieger, Lee	University of Miami
Kropf, Blythe	New York Public Library
Krueger, Janice M.	University of the Pacific Library
Kulp, William	Johns Hopkins University

La Rooy, Pauline	Victoria University of Wellington
Laherty, Jennifer	California State University
Lai, Janet	Loyola Marymount University
Lamborn, Joan	University of Northern Colorado
Lamoureux, Selden	University of North Carolina at Chapel Hill
Landesman, Betty	Infocurrent/CRS
Lang, Jennifer	University of Cincinnati
Lang, Mary	Augustana College
Lange, Holley	Colorado State University
Langendorfer, Jeanne	Bowling Green State University
Latyszewskyj, Maria	Environment Canada Library, Downsview
Lauer, Anita	Teachers College, Columbia University
LaVecchia, Kelli	Johnson & Wales University
Lawlor, Rod	Dumbarton Oaks Research Library
Layton, Lisa	Elsevier Science
Leadem, Ellen	National Inst. of Environmental Health Sciences
Legace, Nettie	
Legg, Ardelle	Boston University
Lehman, Lisa	Rasmuson Library University of Alaska Fairbanks
Lehman, Mary	University of Notre Dame
Leiding, Reba	James Madison University
Leister, Elizabeth	Rutgers University
Lenville, Jean	Harvard University
Lesher, Marcella	St. Mary's University
Leshinsky, Anastasia	Harvard University
Lessard, Sophie	CISTI
Li, Xin	Cornell Univ. Library
Libby, Katy	Sherrid Library East Tennessee State University
Liebowitz, Faye	University of Pittsburgh
Lindquist, Janice	Rice University
Loescher, Nancy	Bristol-Myers Squibb
Loffredo, Robert	
Loghry, Pat	University of Notre Dame
Lord, Jonathan	University of Virginia
Lu, Wen-ying	Michigan State University
Lucas, John	University of Mississippi Medical Ctr.

Lyandres, Natasha	Notre Dame University
MacAdam, Carol	JSTOR
MacArthur, Susan	Bates College
Macklin, Lisa	Georgia Tech
MacLennan, Birdie	University of Vermont
Magenau, Carol	Dartmouth College Library
Maguire, Jean	New England Historic Genealogical Society
Malar, Gregory	Rockefeller University Press
Malinowski, Teresa	California State University
Malone, Debbie	University of San Francisco
Malta, Mavis	Utah State University
Manahan, Meghan	American Museum of Natural History
Mann, Marjorie	OCLC Western
Manoff, Maribeth	Univ. of Tennessee at Knoxville
Manuel, Kate	New Mexico State University
Markley, Susan	Villanova University
Markwith, Michael	TDNet, Inc
Martin, Charity	University of Nebraska, Lincoln
Martin, Sylvia	Retired (Vanderbilt)
Martonik, Renee	University of Chicago
Matthews, Karen	Dana Medical Library
Matuz, Roger	ProQuest Information and Learning
Maxwell, Kim	MIT Libraries
Mayo, Doug	Colonial Williamsburg Foundation
Mays, Allison	Millsaps College
McAdam, Tim	University of California, Irvine
McAphee, Sylvia	Lister Hill Library/UAB
McCaslin, Sharon	Longwood College Library
McCawley, Christina	West Chester University
McClamroch, Jo	Indiana University Libraries
McClary, Maryon	University of Alberta
McCracken, Peter	Serials Solutions
McCutcheon, Dianne	Library of Congress
McDougald, Barbara	U.S. Patent Office
McGuire, Connie	University of Michigan
McKee, Anne	Greater Western Library Alliance
McKee, Eileen	Brooklyn Public Library
McKiernan, Gerry	Iowa State University
McLaughlin, Tom	Drexel University-Hagerty Library
McNaughton, Liz	Liz McNaughton

McSweeney, Marilyn	MIT Libraries
Meddings, Kirsty	Ingenta
Meinert, Elizabeth	Ingenta, Inc.
Meneely, Kathleen	Cleveland Health Sciences Library
Menefee, Daviess	Elsevier Science
Mering, Meg	University of Nebraska
Merriman, Faith	Central Connecticut State University
Meyer, Pat	National University
Meyers, Barbara	Meyers Consulting Services
Milam, Barbara	Kennesaw State University
Milano, Annette	Swets Blackwell
Miller, Heather	SUNY
Miller, Judy	Valparaiso University
Mitchell, Vanessa	Library of Congress
Mitchell, Anne	University of Houston
Mobley, Emily	Purdue University
Moeller, Paul	University of Colorado
Moeller, Ulrike	Otto Harrassowitz
Moles, Jean	University of Arkansas for Medical Sciences Library
Moran, Sheila	Massachusetts General Hospital
Morrison, Laura	Clemson University
Mudrak, Angela	Youngstown State University
Murden, Steven	
Murphy, Amy	Mississippi State University Libraries
Murphy, Pency	Alcon Research, Ltd
Murphy, Sandra	Harvard University
Myers, Myrtle	OCLC, Inc.
Nadeski, Karen	Connecticut State Library
Nauta, Laura	Nimitz Library-USNA
Neilson, Susan	American University
Nelson, Carol	Ball State University
Nelson, Catherine	University of California, Santa Barbara
Nelson, Stephanie	University of Hawaii at Manoa
Neuville, Amy	JSTOR/University of Michigan
Neville, Shelley	epixtech, inc.
Nguyen, Hien	National Library of Medicine
Nicholas, Pamela	University of Notre Dame
Norton, Nancy	Innovative Interfaces, Inc.
Novak, Denise	Carnegie Mellon University

Nye, Julie	Fretwell-Downing
Oberg, Judy	National Renewable Energy Lab.
O'Connell, Jennifer	EBSCO Information Services
Okuhara, Keiko	University of Pittsburgh
O'Leary, Susan	EBSCO Subscription Svcs.
Oliver, Marina	Texas Tech University Libraries
O'Malley, Terrence	Case Western Reserve University
Ono, Shigeharu	Kinokuniya
Orcutt, Darby	NCSU Libraries
Owen, Noella	Elsevier Science
Owens, Pamela	Indiana University Library
Packer, Donna	Western Washington University Libraries
Page, Mary	Rutgers University Libraries
Paldan, Diane	Wayne State University
Palmer, Janet	Univ. of Michigan
Paradis, Olga	Baylor University
Parang, Elizabeth	Pepperdine University
Parker, Susan	California State University Northridge
Parks, Bonnie	Oregon State University
Parker, Kimberly	Yale Univ. Library
Patterson, Sandra	Library of Congress
Pawson, Roger	Canadian Agriculture Library
Peckover, Rachel	Ingenta
Persing, Bob	University of Pennsylvania
Peters, Victoria	Swets Blackwell
Petsche, Kevin	IUPUI University Library
Phillips, Patricia	UTEP Library
Picerno, Peter	Nova Southeastern University
Pierce, Louise	York College of Pennsylvania
Pingitore, Janet	EBSCO Subscription Services
Plymale, Lisa	NE Ohio Universities College of Medicine
Pohler, Janice	Swets Blackwell
Poorman, Kathryn	University of Texas at El Paso
Pope, Michele	Loyola University Law Library
Powers, Susanna	Tulane University
Prager, George	New York University Law School Library
Pugh, Penny	Penny Pugh
Rabner, Lanell	Brigham Young University

Radcliff, Joyce	Tennessee State University
Radencich, John	Florida International University
Rafter, William	West Virginia University
Rais, Shirley	Loma Linda University
Randall, Kevin	Northwestern University Library
Randall, Michael	UCLA
Rathbone, Marjorie	Saint Joseph's University
Rausch, Mary	West Texas A&M University
Reynolds, Regina Romano	Library of Congress
Rhoades, Alice	Rice University
Richards, Wendy	Washington & Lee University
Riggio, Angela	UCLA
Riley, Cheryl	Central Missouri State University
Rinderknecht, Deborah	University of Pittsburgh at Johnstown
Rioux, Margaret	MBL/WHOI Library
Ripley, Erika	Southern Methodist University
River, Sandra	Texas Tech University Library
Roach, Dani	Macalester College-DeWitt Wallace Library
Roberson, Marla	Oklahoma State University-Oklahoma City
Roberts, Constance	Hamilton College
Robischon, Rose	USMA Library
Ronn, Christina	Swets Blackwell
Rosati, Karen	USC School of Medicine
Rose, Kathryn	
Rosenbaum, Howard	Indiana Univ.
Rosenberg, Frieda	University of North Carolina at Chapel Hill
Ross, Keith	Faxon Library Services
Rossignol, Lu	Smithsonian Institution Libraries
Ruelle, Barbara	Emory University
Rumph, Virginia	Butler University
Rupp, Nathan	Cornell University
Sadowski, Frank	University of Rochester
Safley, Ellen	Univ. of Texas at Dallas
Sandercock, Pat	Divine Information Services
Sannon, Kurtie	Fordham University Law Library
Satterwhite, Robin	Colorado College
Saunders, Sharon	Bates College
Savage, Steve	University of Michigan

Saxe, Minna
Saxton, Elna — University of Cincinnati
Scales, Ruth Richardson — Guilford College
Scanlon, Lucinda — Middle Tennessee State University
Schatz, Bob — Everetts
Scheier, Bob — New York Institute of Technology
Schein, Anna — West Virginia University
Schmitt, Stephanie — Yale Law Library
Schnell, Tammy — Lincoln Land Community College
Schoen, Dena — Harrassowitz
Schwartz, Marla — American University
Scott, Sharon — Texas Tech University School of Law
Seaman, David — University of Virginia
Seamans, Marsha — University of Kentucky
Seitter, Keith — American Meteorological Society
Seminaro, David — Swets Blackwell, Inc.
Sercan, Cecilia — Cornell University
Sharp, Allison — Lee University
Shea, Marsha — San Diego State University
Sheffield, Becky — Ball State University
Shelton, Yolande — University of Maryland
Shuttleworth, Jeanne
Siar, Janet — University of Maryland
Silva, Judy — Slippery Rock University
Silvera, Paula — AstraZeneca Pharmaceuticals
Silverman, Judy — Centre Canadien d'Architecture
Simmons, Ellen — University of Dallas
Simpson, Esther — NSDP Library of Congress
Simser, Char — Kansas State University
Singh, Frances — Hamline University Law Library
Skinner, Debra — Georgia Southern University
Slagell, Jeff — Delta State University
Slaughter, Gloria — Hope College
Slaughter, Philenese — Austin Peay State University
Sleeman, Allison — University of Virginia
Smith, Kerry — Mississippi State University Libraries
Smith, Merrill — EBSCO Information Services
Smulewitz, Gracemary — Rutgers University
Snead, Barbara — Goucher College
Snider, Elizabeth — Chemical Abstract Service
Somers, Mike — Indiana State University

Tenney, Joyce	University of Maryland, Baltimore County
Thomas, Molly	Temple University
Thomas, Suzanne	University of Pittsburgh
Thompson, Jane	University of Cincinnati Health Science Library
Thompson, Lyn	University of Alberta Library
Thompson, Sandra	Wellesley College
Thornberry, Pat	University of South Florida
Thorne, Patti	University of Alaska, Anchorage
Thornton, Christopher	Case Western Reserve University
Throumoulos, Mary	Rollins College
Thunell, Allen	Michigan State University
Tong, Dieu	UAB, Stern Library
Tonkery, Dan	EBSCO
Trish, Margaret	University of Missouri-Rolla
Tucker, Alice	U.S. Geological Survey Library
Tumlin, Markel	San Diego State University-Love Library
Tusa, Sarah	Lamar University
Tuttle, Marcia	
Urka, Mary Ann	Johns Hopkins University
Van Auken, Gayle	Linda Hall Library
Van Griensven, Gina	
Van Meter, Dana	Historical Studies-Social Science Library
van Sickle, Jennifer	Trinity College
VanderVeen, Fina	CISTI
Velilla, Kerry	Allen Press, Inc.
Velterop, Jan	BioMed Central
Vent, Marilyn	University of Nevada
Villalba Roldan, Angel	
Vukas, Rachel	EBSCO Information Services
Wadeborn, Germaine	UCLA
Waite, Carolyn	MIT Lincoln Laboratory
Wakimoto, Jina Choi	California State University
Walker, Dana	University of Georgia Libraries
Walker, Veronica	University of Kentucky
Wallas, Philip	EBSCO Information Services
Walravens, Hartmut	Staatsbibliothek
Walsh, Terry	

Walters, Laura — Tufts University
Wang, Jane — University of Scranton
Wang, Jian — Portland State University
Washburn, Judy — Lane Medical Library
Washkevich, Peter

Waters, Daisy — State University of New York at Buffalo
Watson, Virginia — Brigham Young University
Weiss, Amy — Appalachian State University
Weiss, Paul — UC San Diego
Weisser, Teresa — Millersville University of PA
Weklar, Patrick — Rensselaer Polytechnic Institute
Welch, Jeanie — UNC Charlotte
Wells, Steven — ICI Binding Corp
Weng, Cathy — Temple University
Wesley, Kathryn — Clemson University Libraries
Westman, Janice — AstraZeneca Pharmaceuticals
Weston, Beth — National Library of Medicine
Whiting, Peter — University of Southern Indiana
Whitney, Marla

Wiggins, John — Drexel University
Wiles-Young, Sharon — Lehigh University
Wilhelme, Judy — University of Michigan
Wilkinson, Fran — University of New Mexico
Williams, Gerry — Northern Kentucky University
Williams, Mary — Tarleton State University
Williams, Sheryl — University of Nebraska Medical Center
Willingham, Margaret — EBSCO Information Svcs.
Willman, Diane — State University of New York, Oswego
Wilson, Margaret — University of Kansas Libraries
Winchester, David — Washburn University
Wishnetsky, Susan — Galter Health Science Library
Wittenbach, Stefanie — UC Riverside (Univ. of California)
Wong, Ellen — University of Texas Medical Branch
Wood, Kelly — Davidson College
Wood, Ross — Wellesley College
Worthing, Rick — California State Library
Worthington, Michele — National Library of Education
Wright, Phyllis — Brock University
Yaples, Jill D. — Binghamton University Library
Young, Jennifer — Pius XII Memorial Library
Yu, Ying — Gallaudet University

Yue, Paoshan	Brigham Young University
Zeter, Mary Jo	Michigan State University
Zhang, Yvonne	California Polytechnic State University, Pomona
Zink, Steven	University of Nevada, Reno
Zupko, Laura	Chicago Public Library

Index